George Peck

**Wyoming**

Its History, Stirring Incidents and Romantic Adventures. Third Edition

George Peck

**Wyoming**
*Its History, Stirring Incidents and Romantic Adventures. Third Edition*

ISBN/EAN: 9783744776127

Printed in Europe, USA, Canada, Australia, Japan

Cover: Foto ©ninafisch / pixelio.de

More available books at **www.hansebooks.com**

# WYOMING;

ITS

HISTORY, STIRRING INCIDENTS, AND

ROMANTIC ADVENTURES.

By GEORGE PECK, D.D.

WITH ILLUSTRATIONS.

THIRD EDITION.

NEW YORK:
HARPER & BROTHERS, PUBLISHERS,
FRANKLIN SQUARE.
1868.

# PREFACE.

THE present work is composed of a brief history of Wyoming, followed by a series of historic scenes, which constitute natural amplifications of the general outline. Each story is a complete picture in itself, and yet is a necessary part of the whole. The plan has the advantage of presenting independent views of the historic drama from many different stand-points. Our heroes not only reflect the lights and shades of their own character and actions, but give us their separate versions of the eventful scenes through which they passed.

Forty years since we first visited Wyoming, and from that period we have enjoyed rare advantages for the study of its history. How we have improved our opportunities will appear in the work which we now present to the public. Our object has been strict conformity to historic truth, and we have spared no pains in the collection of facts, and in their study and exposition.

The events herein recorded constitute a part of the wonderful history of the early development and fearful struggles of America, and we believe they will not fall behind any portion of that story in exciting interest.

With the diffidence which a profound sense of the difficulties to be overcome in the execution of such a work naturally inspires, we publish the result of our labors, hoping that it may both interest and instruct the reading community. The work, so far as we are concerned, has been a "labor of love," and our desire is that it may inspire in the reader a spirit of enlarged patriotism, noble heroism, patient endurance under severe trials, trust in Providence, and gratitude to God.

We have the pleasure to acknowledge the kindness of several who have afforded us valuable assistance in our labors. In addition to the acknowledgments of favors which will be found in the body of the work, we would return thanks to the Hon. George Bancroft for the use of an important document, and for various suggestions; to Benson J. Lossing, Esq., for several important authorities, and much valuable aid in the illustrations; to the Hon. George W. Woodward, and to the Hon. George M. Dallas, our minister to the court of St. James, for the use of an important paper from the archives of the British government; also to several ladies for fine artistic sketches of objects and scenes which are used as illustrations. We owe to Mrs. Rev. Selah Stocking, of Pittston, thanks for original sketches of Campbell's Ledge and Falling Spring; to Mrs. Dr. Crane, of Pennington, N. J., for a sketch of the old Myers House; and to Miss Miranda Myers for sketches of Toby's Cave and the Umbrella-tree.

To all who in any way have given us facilities, we return many thanks, and it is to be hoped that they will find their reward in a conviction that they have contributed something to the object of giving permanency to the facts of history which will be valuable to posterity, but which might otherwise have passed into oblivion.

GEORGE PECK.

SCRANTON, 18th April, 1858.

# CONTENTS.

| Chapter | Page |
|---|---|
| I. WYOMING—ITS HISTORY | 9 |
| II. BRANT AND HIS TORY ASSOCIATES | 71 |
| III. COLONEL MATTHIAS HOLLENBACK | 99 |
| IV. INCIDENTS AND ADVENTURES RELATED BY MRS. MARTHA MYERS | 133 |
| V. SKETCHES AND INCIDENTS COMMUNICATED BY MRS. DEBORAH BEDFORD | 200 |
| VI. INCIDENTS OF THE WARS IN THE LACKAWANNA PORTION OF THE SETTLEMENT, RELATED BY MRS. MARTHA MARCY | 220 |
| VII. MRS. SYLVIA SEYBOLT'S ACCOUNT OF THE BATTLE AND FLIGHT | 231 |
| VIII. THE CAPTIVE GIRL, FRANCES SLOCUM | 234 |
| IX. QUEEN ESTHER'S ROCK | 284 |
| X. CAPTIVITY AND ESCAPE OF THOMAS AND ANDREW BENNET AND LEBBEUS HAMMOND | 291 |
| XI. THE CAPTURE AND ESCAPE OF JONAH ROGERS, MOSES VAN CAMPEN, PETER PENCE, AND ABRAM PIKE | 304 |
| XII. THE CAPTIVITY AND ESCAPE OF GEORGE P. RANSOM AND OTHERS | 315 |
| XIII. BENJAMIN BIDLACK—CAPTURE BY THE PENNAMITES AND SINGULAR ESCAPE | 330 |
| XIV. A VIEW FROM CAMPBELL'S LEDGE, CONTRIBUTED BY REV. L. W. PECK | 344 |
| XV. AN INTERVIEW WITH RICHARD GARDNER | 351 |
| XVI. PROVIDENTIAL DELIVERANCE OF RUFUS BENNET ON THE FATAL 3D OF JULY | 362 |
| XVII. NOAH HOPKINS—HIS LIFE SAVED BY A SPIDER | 369 |
| XVIII. THE FRATRICIDE | 371 |
| XIX. THE MONUMENT | 376 |
| XX. COLONEL JOHN JENKINS | 388 |
| XXI. ORIGINAL JOURNAL OF CHRISTOPHER HURLBUT | 405 |
| XXII. MISCELLANEOUS ARTICLES | 417 |
|     The Umbrella-Tree—Prospect Rock—Harvey's Lake—Toby's Eddy—Toby's Cave—Seminaries. | |
| INDEX | 431 |

# WYOMING.

## I.

#### ITS HISTORY.

AMONG the mountains which lift up their heads, in countless numbers and in all shapes, between the Blue Ridge and the Alleghanies, on the banks of the winding Susquehanna, lies the classic vale of Wyoming. It is not so much distinguished for its magnitude as for its beauty, its mineral wealth, and its historical incidents.

WYOMING is a corruption of the name given to the locality by the Indians. They called it Maughwauwame. The word is compounded of *maughwau*, large, and *wame*, plains. The name, then, signifies THE LARGE PLAINS. The Delawares pronounced the first syllable short, and the German missionaries, in order to come as near as possible to the Indian pronunciation, wrote the name M'chweuwami. The early settlers, finding it difficult to pronounce the word correctly, spoke it Wauwaumie, then Wiawumie, then Wiomic, and, finally, Wyoming.

The valley of Wyoming lies northeast and southwest, is twenty-one miles in length, and an average of three miles in breadth. The face of the country is considerably diversified. The bottom-lands along the river overflow at high water. The plains are in some places perfectly level, and in others rolling. The soil is exceedingly productive, being suited to all sorts of grain and grass.

Two ranges of mountains hem in the valley, the eastern range being of an average height of one thousand feet, and the western about eight hundred. The eastern range is precipitous and generally barren, but is strikingly diversified with clefts, ravines, and forests, and presents a most picturesque view. The western range is rapidly yielding to the process of cultivation.

There are several charming points of view which invite the attention of the lovers of the beautiful and the grand in nature: Prospect Rock, east of the old town of Wilkesbarre, being the easiest of access from the town, and the most frequently visited, is the most celebrated in the annals of travel. From this point the valley, with the slope of the west mountain, presents the appearance of a beautiful ascending plain, with the remotest border merged in the clouds, or bounded by the blue sky. A more charming landscape can not be imagined. The view from the mountain side west of Forty Fort gives you a more extensive prospect of the northern and southern extremities of the valley. From this point you have a fair view of the northern gap through which the Susquehanna forces its way—of the Lackawanna Valley, Pittston, Wyoming, Wilkesbarre, Kingston, Newport, and Jacob's Plains. Campbell's Ledge is becoming a favorite point of view for the romantic and athletic. This high peak is situated at the head of the valley. The ascent is laborious, but the sublimity of the scene amply rewards the toil of the traveler.

Torrents gush through deep gorges in the mountains on either side, slackening their speed as they enter the valley, and sluggishly meander through the level plains and flats until they find their way to the river. These creeks are each dignified by the name of some Indian chief who dwelt on its banks, and figure considerably in the history of the country.

From whatever point the valley is surveyed, the noble Susquehanna is one of the many beautiful objects which present themselves to the gaze. Such are its windings, and such the variety which characterizes its banks, that you have no extended view of it. It is only seen in sections, varied in size and form by the position occupied. Now it hides itself among the bowers of willow, sycamore, and maple which fringe and beautify its borders, and now it throws open its mirror bosom to the kisses of the sunlight, and reflects the forms of beauty and grandeur of the surrounding scenery.

"The Large Plains," when first visited by the whites for purposes of settlement, were in the possession of the Delaware Indians. The Delawares had once been a powerful tribe, but had been subjected by the Iroquois, or the six confederated nations, and by them were ordered to leave the country on the Delaware, east of the Blue Ridge, and occupy Wyoming. The Nanticokes had settled on the lower extremity of the valley, on the east side of the river, and the Shawanese were located on the flats immediately over against them on the west side. But these tribes finally removed—the Nanticokes up the river, and the Shawanese to Ohio. How the Delawares became sole masters of the valley may be learned from the following interesting relation:

"While the warriors of the Delawares were engaged upon the mountains in a hunting expedition, a number of squaws, or female Indians, from Maughwauwame, were gathering wild fruits along the margin of the river, below the town, where they found a number of Shawanese squaws and their children, who had crossed the river in their canoes upon the same business. A child belonging to the Shawanese having taken a large grasshopper, a quarrel arose among the children for the possession of it, in which their mothers soon took a part, and, as the Delaware squaws contended that the Shawanese had no privileges upon that side of the river, the quarrel soon became general; but the Delawares, being the most numerous, soon drove the Shawanese to their canoes and to their own bank, a few having been killed on both sides. Upon the return of the warriors, both tribes prepared for battle, to revenge the wrongs which they considered their wives had sustained.

"The Shawanese, upon crossing the river, found the Delawares ready to receive them and oppose their landing. A dreadful conflict took place between the Shawanese in their canoes and the Delawares on the bank. At length, after great numbers had been killed, the Shawanese effected a landing, and a battle took place about a mile below Maughwauwame, in which many hundred warriors are said to have been killed on both sides; but the Shawanese were so much weakened in landing that they were not able to sustain the conflict, and, after the loss of about half their tribe, the remainder were forced to flee to their own side of the river, shortly after which they abandoned their town and removed to the Ohio."—*Chapman's History of Wyoming.*

The ancient fortifications which are found scattered over the country, and prove that it was once peopled by warlike tribes or nations which had made considerable advances in civilization, were found in Wyoming. One of these was situated on the eastern branch of Toby's Creek, below the old Esquire Pierce place, or the place occupied by the late Pierce Butler, Esq. There are persons still living who recollect this ancient monument of an extinguished race, but every trace of it is now obliterated. Another of these ancient relics was situated on the east side of the Susquehanna, opposite Forty Fort. We explored this ground some twenty years since, in company with the venerable historian of Wyoming, Hon. Charles Miner. At that time, a lane running along the side of one of the embankments had protected it from being leveled by the plow. It was then in a good state of preservation, several feet in height, with a corresponding ditch. When the whites first visited the valley, there were large pine and oak trees growing on the embankments of these ancient forts, and the oldest Indians could give no account of their origin, or the purposes which they were designed to serve.

It was missionary zeal that first penetrated this secluded region.

Count Zinzendorf is believed to be the first white man who set his foot upon *The Great Plains*. In 1742 he came with an interpreter, and erected his tent near the Indian village, and proposed a talk. He was a messenger from the Great Spirit, sent to teach the red man the true worship. He had crossed the seas upon this benevolent errand, without the hope of earthly gain. The savages could not comprehend the fact that he had taken so much pains to visit them with no selfish motive. Concluding that it was the object of the pale faces to take their lands from them, they resolved to terminate the enterprise by their immediate

COUNT ZINZENDORF.

destruction. A few warriors selected for the purpose stealthily approached the tent of the unsuspecting stranger by night to accomplish their designs, when a strange providence interfered. Peeping through an opening of the tent, they saw a huge rattlesnake crawl over the feet of the strange visitor without interrupting his composure, as he sat upon a bundle of weeds engaged in writing. Considering that he was protected by the Great Spirit, they departed without offering him the least molestation. To this circumstance has been attributed the success of the Moravian missionaries among the Delawares, or at least their first favorable reception among that savage people.

As early as 1750, a few daring adventurers from New England had crossed the mountains, and pushed their way toward the setting sun, until from the heights of the Susquehanna range they gazed upon the most lovely natural landscape which the eye ever beheld. The primeval forests covered the slopes of the mountains, while the plains and river-bottom were here and there imperfectly cultivated by the Indians, who as yet held undisputed possession of the country west of the Delaware. Wild fruits and flowers garnished the hill sides, the deep ravines, and the river banks. The wild grape hung in clusters upon the vines, which clung to the branches of the trees and waved in the breeze. Vegetation of all kinds flourished in wonderful luxuriance.

> "So on he fares, and to the border comes
> Of Eden, where delicious Paradise,
> Now nearer, crowns with her inclosure green,
> As with a rural mound, the champaign head
> Of a steep wilderness, whose hairy sides
> With thicket overgrown, grotesque and wild:
> \* \* \* and overhead up grew,
> Insuperable height of loftiest shade,
> Cedar, and pine, and fir, and branching palm,
> A sylvan scene; and as the ranks ascend
> Shade above shade, a woody theatre
> Of stateliest mien.
> \* \* \* \* \* \* \*
> Another side, umbrageous grots and caves
> Of cool recess, o'er which the mantling vine
> Lays forth her purple grape, and gently creeps
> Luxuriant: meanwhile murmuring waters fall
> Down the slope hills, dispersed, or in a lake,
> That to the fringed bank with myrtle crowned
> Her crystal mirror holds, unite their streams."
> 
> MILTON.

The mountains and the vales were thickly inhabited by an endless variety of wild game, which had not yet learned to fear the white man and to elude his arts; the waters were stored with an abundance of fish; and

the air was made vocal with the songs of the feathered tribes that discoursed the sweet music of nature.

> "Then, when of Indian hills the daylight takes
>   His leave, how might you the flamingo see
> Disporting like a meteor on the lakes—
>   And playful squirrel on his nut-grown tree:
> And every sound of life was full of glee,
>   From merry mock-bird's song or hum of men;
> While hearkening, fearing naught their revelry,
>   The wild deer arched his neck from glades, and then,
> Unhunted, sought his woods and wilderness again."
>
> <div align="right">CAMPBELL'S <i>Gertrude of Wyoming</i>.</div>

These adventurers returned to the rocky hills of Connecticut and Massachusetts with the most wonderful tales of a sort of "Paradise" which lay away among the western mountains. To the visitors themselves, the imagery which lingered in their memory seemed like a vision of celestial scenery; and to those who listened to their vivid descriptions, the whole seemed a mere romance. New parties followed " to spy out the land," and they returned with something more than a mere confirmation of the reports of their predecessors. The whole country was filled with wonder, and a desire naturally sprung up in many minds to see the glories of the goodly land for themselves. Plans were formed for early emigration to "Wyoming on the Susquehanna," and many hearts beat high, and many strong arms were ready for the hazards of the enterprise.

The mountains and rivers could be crossed, the wilderness could be threaded, the wild beasts could be driven from their lairs; but there was still a difficulty which seemed insuperable—it was the ownership and occupancy of the soil by the Indians. This obstacle must be overcome by negotiation, by purchase, by kind treatment, if possible; but if not, by the appliances of war. The settlement of Wyoming by the whites was a foregone conclusion, and the only question about it was that of time. The country was visited every season by small parties, whose object was to test the state of the savage mind, and to determine the question of the safety of white settlers in the neighborhood of the Indians.*

* In 1754, Conrad Weiser, a famous Indian interpreter, and agent for the proprietary government of Pennsylvania, on a visit to the Indians at Shemokin, reports: "The Indians in Susquehanna and about Shemokin saw some of the New England men that came as spies to Woyomock last fall; and they saw them making drafts of the land and rivers, and are much offended about it. They asked me about them. I told them we had heard so much as that, and that we had intelligence from New England that they came against

The conflicts which occurred between the people of Connecticut and Pennsylvania in relation to the right of settlement and jurisdiction constitute so prominent a part of the early history of Wyoming, that it will be proper here to notice the grounds of their respective claims. "King Charles II., by letters patent, under the great seal of England, granted a tract of land in America to William Penn, Esq., his heirs and assigns, and made him and them the true and absolute proprietors thereof, saving always to the crown the faith and allegiance of the said William Penn, his heirs and assigns, and of the tenants and inhabitants of the premises, and saving also unto the crown the *sovereignty* of the said country."

The country was "thereby erected into a province and sovereignty, and called Pennsylvania."

"And thereby granted free, full, and absolute power unto the said William Penn and his heirs, and to his and their deputies and lieutenants, for the good and happy government of the country, to ordain, make, enact, and, under his and their seals, to publish any laws whatsoever."—See *Pennsylvania Archives*, vol. ii., p. 100, 101.

Under this charter a government was instituted, consisting of a governor and council, but the Penns

---

the advice of their superiors as a parcel of headstrong men, and disturbers of the peace. They, the Indians, said they were glad to hear that neither their brother Onos nor their own chief men had sent them, and they hoped they would not be supported by any English government in their so doing."—*Letter to the Governor: Colonial Records*, vol. vi., p. 35.

This was the first attempt which was made to sketch a rude map of the country preparatory to the formation of a settlement. It is believed by their descendants that the elder John Jenkins and Thomas Bennet were in this company.

owned the soil in fee. Their policy was to lay out all the best lands into manors, and settle them by tenants under leases. Thus some of the most objectionable features of the old feudal system were established in Pennsylvania. The proprietaries, of course, were opposed to emigrations from other states to their lands, except to such of them as were worthless. Settlers were, consequently, often driven off by force, and their houses burned.

In 1754, Governor Hamilton, of Pennsylvania, wrote to Governor Wolcott, of Connecticut, remonstrating against the scheme of some of the Connecticut people to settle Wyoming. At the same time, he offered them lands "in the western parts of this province," or to use his good offices to procure them the privilege of settling in "Virginia."

Governor Wolcott made a very cautious but pertinent answer, taking special pains to urge that wherever settlers were permitted to take possession of lands in Pennsylvania, they should be made "freeholders." He suggested that, in the event of war with the French, "the resolution of the soldier will be very much, in fighting for his country, according to his interest in it." "If I must go out," says he, "let me have an army of freeholders or freeholders' sons." He then proceeds to give the result of his experience in the case of "the siege of Louisburg," and then continues:

"Whenever the war commences with you, I think a small army of such men, well appointed and disciplined, will soon convince the French of their error in provoking and insulting of you; I think a few of them will be more than a match for a multitude of their plebs, brought up in slavery, and who have nothing to fight for of their own.

"This brings to mind a story a gentleman told me, that he went in to see his negro man, then dying, and seeing him just gone, said to him, 'Cuffy, you are just going; are you not sorry?' 'No,' says the fellow; 'master, the loss won't be mine.'"

The Pennamite and Yankee wars were not merely a conflict between the proprietaries of Pennsylvania and the Susquehanna Company for the jurisdiction of the country—it was not a mere question of boundary, but a question between landlord and tenantry. The question was one in which the tenantry of Pennsylvania generally were interested, and, consequently, the cause of the proprietaries was never popular with that class. Wyoming was the battle-field where the question was to be settled whether the people who cultivated the soil should be serfs or freeholders. We do not pretend that this was the open ostensible issue made, but it is beyond a doubt that this question lay at the bottom of the controversy, and had much to do with its progress and termination. If the laborers and producers were to be made freeholders, it could make but little difference whence they came; but if they were to be mere tenants, it would be somewhat important that they should not have been educated in the spirit of freedom and independence, but should have the views and feelings of servants rather than those of citizens. The New England people might be allowed to settle in the Alleghanies, to constitute a sort of breakwater against the overflowing of the French arms, but it would never do to give them possession of the fertile plains and valleys along the Delaware and Susquehanna. The Yankees were not likely to be the pliant tools suited to the objects and policy of the aristocratic proprietaries. They had trouble enough with those whom they had trained to their hand, and the tide of Yankee emigration which was setting in from the east bid fair to result in more general discontent, if not in revolution. Hence the diplomacy of the proprietaries had for its object, not the settlement of the northern boundary of the province, but preventing emigration from the east; and, as will be seen as we proceed, the *quasi* civil, but really *military* proceedings with the settlers was not designed to secure their recognition of the civil jurisdiction of the proprietaries, but *nolens volens* to expel the intruders from the country.

The charter granted to "The Plymouth Company" by James I. covered the territory " from the fortieth to the forty-sixth degree of north latitude, extending *from the Atlantic to the Pacific Ocean.*" This charter was granted under the great seal of England, on November 3, 1620, to the Duke of Lenox, the Marquis of Buckingham, the Earl of Arundel and Warwick, and their associates, "for the planting, ruling, ordering, and governing of New England, in America." The charter of Connecticut was derived from the Plymouth Company, of which the Earl of Warwick was president. This grant was made in March, 1621, to Viscount Say and Seal, Lord Brooke, and their associates. It covered the country west of Connecticut "to the extent of its breadth, being about one degree of latitude *from sea to sea.*" This grant was confirmed by the king the same year, and also in 1662. "The New Netherlands," or New York, being then a Dutch possession, was excepted in these grants under the general limitation of such portions of territory as were "then possessed or inhabited by any other Christian prince or state."—See *Col. Stone's History of Wyoming.*

By the terms of this charter, the people of Connecticut very reasonably considered themselves entitled to the territory within the latitudes above specified, west of "the New Netherlands," and began to cast a longing eye upon the fertile lands lying upon the Delaware and Susquehanna. About fifty years after the charter to Lords Say and Seal, and Brooke, the crown granted a charter to William Penn, which covered a portion of the grant to Connecticut, equal to one degree of latitude and five of longitude, which embraced the rich and inviting valley of Wyoming. This was the first ground of the feuds which arose between the Connecticut and Pennsylvania people, and which occasioned much trouble and distress to the early settlers.

In 1753 an association was formed in Connecticut, called "The Susquehanna Company," for the purpose of forming a settlement in Wyoming; but, that this company might not come into conflict with the native occupants of the soil, a commission was appointed "to explore the country and conciliate their good-will." The company now embraced about six hundred persons, many of them men of wealth and high respectability. A deputation was appointed to meet a great council of the Six Nations at Albany in 1754, and, if possible, effect a purchase of the land. As the transaction was not secret, Governor Hamilton, of Pennsylvania, sent to Albany a deputation, consisting of "*John and Richard Penn, Isaac Norris, and Benjamin Franklin,*" to prevent the purchase by the Susquehanna Company. Notwithstanding this formidable opposition, strengthened as it was by the influence of Sir William Johnson, the purchase was effected. The sum paid was "two thousand pounds, of current money of the province of New York." Colonel Stone has given us, in an Appendix to the second edition of his History, a "copy of the deed of purchase," duly executed by the "chief sachems and heads of the Five Nations of Indians, called the Iroquois, and the native proprietors," &c. Among these "chief sachems" is the famous Mohawk chief *Brant*, who subsequently figured so largely in the war of the Revolution. The names of the purchasers are also embraced, owners of full shares "five hundred and thirty-four in number," and of "half shares" "one hundred and thirty-six;" most of them from "y<sup>e</sup> colony of Connecticut, in New England," some "of the colony of Rhode Island," some "of the government of Pennsylvania," some "of the province of y<sup>e</sup> Massachusetts Bay," and some "of the province of New York." The following are the boundaries of the purchase:

"Beginning from the one and fortieth degree of north latitude at ten miles distance east of Susquehanna River, and from thence with a northwardly line ten miles east of the river, to the forty-second or beginning of the forty-third degree north latitude, and so to extend west, two degrees of longitude, one hundred and twenty miles south, to the beginning of the forty-second degree, and from thence east to the afore-mentioned bound, which is ten miles east of the Susquehanna River."—*Colonel Stone's History*, p. 389.

Having thus procured what they considered a valid title to the soil, the Susquehanna Company took preparatory steps for the planting of a settlement in Wyoming; but the agitations among the Indians, occasioned by "the French war," prevented them from accomplishing their purposes until the year 1762, when about two hundred men pushed their way into the valley, and commenced clearing farms just below Mill

Creek, and at a sufficient distance from the Indian town, which was situated on the flats below the present town of Wilkesbarre. They felled the timber, and constructed huts, and, before winter set in, had sown extensive fields of wheat. They secured their implements, and returned to Connecticut to winter. In the spring they returned with their families, cattle, furniture, &c., but little meditating the dreadful fate which awaited them.

"The season had been favorable; their various crops on those fertile plains had proved abundant, and they were looking forward with hope to scenes of prosperity and happiness; but suddenly, without the least warning, on the 15th of October, a large party of savages raised the war-whoop, and attacked them with fury. Unprepared for resistance, about twenty men fell and were scalped; the residue, men, women, and children, fled, in wild disorder, to the mountains. Language can not describe the sufferings of the fugitives as they traversed the wilderness, destitute of food or clothing, on their way to their former homes."—*Miner's History of Wyoming*, p. 54.

After this massacre, the Indians, anticipating a military movement against them on the part of the governor of Pennsylvania, left the valley, the Christian portion of them removing east to the Moravian town, Gnadenhutten, and the others north to Tioga. Six years now intervened before the Connecticut people made another attempt to settle Wyoming. But in the mean time "the proprietaries of Pennsylvania" availed themselves of an Indian council assembled at Fort Stanwix in 1768, and purchased the disputed territory from some of the chiefs. A deputation of four chiefs from the Six Nations had been sent to Hartford in

1763 to disclaim the sale made to the Susquehanna Company, and in the talk of the speaker, he asserted that the Six Nations knew nothing of the sale of this land, and furthermore remarked, "What little we have left we intend to keep for ourselves." This was a mere ruse, as is evident from their selling the same land five years subsequently to the proprietaries of Pennsylvania. They were, in fact, ready to sell land whenever they could find purchasers; and as to any conflict which might afterward arise among rival claimants, that was not their look out. After all, the poor Indians were not so much in fault as were the designing white men, who had interests to serve by involving them in improper and contradictory acts.

This fair valley was next to be made the scene of civil war; and in contending for the rich prize, the blood of one white man was to be spilled by the hand of another white man. The parties had exhausted their diplomatic skill; each had sent deputations to the mother country, and in turn obtained the most respectable legal decisions in their favor. Nothing seemed left to them but to maintain their claims by force.

The Susquehanna Company sent a body of forty pioneers into the valley in February, 1769, to be followed by two hundred more in the spring. But the proprietaries of Pennsylvania, anticipating the movement, had leased the valley for seven years to *Charles Stuart, Amos Ogden, and John Jennings*, on condition that they should establish a trading-house for the accommodation of the Indians, and adopt the necessary measures for defending themselves, and those who might settle under their lease. These men, with a small party, had proceeded to Wyoming, and fortified

B

themselves in a block-house, where the forty Yankees found them upon their arrival.

A series of conflicts now ensued, which we can not here detail, but which were characterized by the usual circumstances and elements of war upon the largest scale, and attended with incidents and adventures of rare interest, many of which will be found in the following sketches. Erecting fortifications, investments, escalades, capitulations, surprises, ambuscades, battles, marches, countermarches, retreats, taking prisoners, and violating pledges for the security of property, are all duly chronicled in the histories. During this period the Yankees were three times driven from the valley, and obliged to thread their way, with their wives and children, through an unbroken wilderness of two hundred miles, back to their former homes. But they as often rallied and returned to the charge with accumulated numbers, until, finally, they were able to keep possession of the prize. The proprietaries were unpopular even in Pennsylvania, and it became impossible for them, even with the aid of all the industry and skill of Captain Ogden, to raise a sufficient force finally to dispossess the Yankees, until the rupture between Great Britain and her colonies directed the attention of all parties to the common defense of the country, and, for the time being, put a period to the civil war.

The object of the Connecticut people had been the establishment of an independent colony, and they had, accordingly, petitioned the parent government to this effect. But, as this object could not be secured without much delay, and as the Legislature of Connecticut was cautious of assuming any responsibility which would involve the state in the quarrel, the Susquehanna Company met at Hartford, June 2, 1773, and adopted a provisional plan of government, on truly republican principles, and every way worthy of the heads and hearts of the best statesmen of the age.*

Under this form of government the people lived in great harmony and prosperity, and the colony rapidly increased in numbers. In the mean time, the Legislative Assembly of Connecticut made an effort to procure a settlement of the difficulty, but Governor Penn closed his ears to all propositions, and even refused to recognize the deputation sent from Connecticut. Upon this the assembly made up a case, and transmitted it to England for the legal opinions of the ablest counsel.

"This case was submitted to Edward, afterward Lord Thurlow, Alexander Wedderburn, Richard Jackson, and J. Dunning, all famous for their learning in the law, who gave a united opinion in favor of the company. Thus fortified, the General Assembly of Connecticut took higher ground, and, perceiving how greatly the colony was flourishing, in October, 1773, they passed a resolution asserting their claim to the jurisdiction of the territory, and their determination, in some proper way, to support the claim."—*Col. Stone.*

The following year Wyoming was constituted a town, by the name of *Westmoreland*, and connected with *Litchfield* county, and a census taken at the close of the year showed that the town numbered one thousand nine hundred and twenty-two inhabitants.

The great events of 1775 seriously affected the inhabitants of Westmoreland. The Indians committed some outrages within the limits of the town, and, though they made hollow professions of a pacific disposition, were evidently preparing for war. Several families from the north, who were hostile to the American

* For which, see Mr. Miner's History, p. 146-149.

cause, came into the settlement, who, with good reason, were considered bad neighbors. The following notes of the town meetings will show the spirit of the people in taking incipient steps for the common defense:

"At a town meeting, held March 10, Voted, that the first man that shall make fifty weight of good saltpetre in this town, shall be entitled to a bounty of ten pounds, lawful money, to be paid out of the town treasury.

"Voted, that the selectmen be directed to dispose of the grain now in the hands of the treasurer, or collector, in such way as to obtain powder and lead to the value of forty pounds, lawful money, if they can do the same."

"At a town meeting legally warned and held, in Westmoreland, Wilkesbarre District, August 24, 1776,

"Colonel Butler was chosen moderator for the work of the day.

"Voted, as the opinion of this meeting, that it now becomes necessary for the inhabitants of this town to erect suitable forts, as a defense against our common enemy."

A regiment of militia having been established, the meeting voted that "the three field officers should be a committee to fix on the sites of the forts, lay them out, and give directions how they should be built." Then was adopted what Mr. Miner calls "the following beautiful vote, which," says he, "we leave, in its simplicity, to speak its own eulogium."

"That the above said committee do recommend it to the people to proceed forthwith in building said forts, without either fee or reward from yᵉ town."

In November of this memorable year (1776), Westmoreland was, by the Legislative Council of Connecticut, erected into a county, with a complete civil and military organization. Congress also ordered that "two companies, on the Continental establishment, be raised in the town of Westmoreland, *and stationed in proper places for the defense of the inhabitants of said town, and posts adjacent*, till farther orders from Congress." The companies, consisting of eighty-two men each, were organized, and officers appointed. But when the British took possession of New York, Washington crossed the Delaware, and Congress were taking measures to retire from Philadelphia to Baltimore, the two companies were ordered to join General Washington "with all possible expedition." This order was promptly obeyed, which took nearly all the able-bodied men and arms from the settlement.

In the summer of 1777 the Six Nations were brought into the field as auxiliaries of the British forces, and commenced their operations in their own peculiar mode of warfare all along the frontier. Wyoming was peculiarly exposed, being situated at the distance of sixty miles from the white settlements, east and south, and their strength having been drawn away by the emergencies of the war; for, in addition to the two companies above referred to, further enlistments were made, in all amounting to some three hundred. Application was made to Congress for aid, but without effect. The helpless females sent to the army the most pressing calls to their sons, husbands, fathers, and brothers, who constituted the Westmoreland companies, to hasten to their relief, and the men begged for the privilege of fulfilling the purposes of their enlistment—"the defense of the inhabitants of said town." But Congress and Connecticut were both deaf to every entreaty. All that was done was an order passed by Congress that "one full company of foot be raised *in the town of West-moreland*, for the defense of the said town," and "that the said company *find their own arms, ammunition, and blankets!*" This amounted to nothing, as it did not increase the force of the settlement. The commissioned officers resigned, and, together with twenty or thirty men who obtained leave, or went without leave, returned to the settlement to share the common peril. The Indians made a great show of peace; but a drunken Indian in a revel—one of a company of spies who came upon a pretense of negotiation—let out the secret of a meditated onslaught upon the settlement. This, together with the suspicious movements of the Tory settlers, several families of whom were situated at the head of the valley, and seemed to be acting the part of spies, created no inconsiderable alarm. The settlers had erected, on each side of the river, several *forts*, some of them consisting of logs planted in the ground, and standing about fourteen feet high, and others mere log pens, or block-houses, with loop-holes. The former were provided with log huts, in which the women and children might find shelter in cases of danger from the enemy. The principal fort on the west side of the river was called *Forty Fort*, constructed by the *forty* pioneers who came into the valley in the winter of 1769, and enlarged and strengthened in 1776, situated two miles above Wilkesbarre. In the arrangements for the defense of the settlement, as will be seen by the following, the women acted a conspicuous part:

"Justice and gratitude demand a tribute to the praiseworthy spirit of the wives and daughters of Wyoming. While their husbands and fathers were on public duty, they cheerfully assumed a large portion of the labor which females could do. They assisted to plant, made hay, husked and garnered the corn. As the settlement was mainly dependent on its own resources for powder, Mr. Hollenback caused to be brought up the river a pounder; and the women took up their floors, dug out the earth, put it in casks, and run water through it (as ashes are leached); then took ashes in another cask, and made ley; mixed the water from the earth with weak ley, boiled it, set it to cool, and the saltpetre rose to the top. Charcoal and sulphur were then used, and powder produced for the public defense."—*Miner's History*, p. 212.

We need add nothing by way of completing the picture. While fathers and sons, *grandfathers* and grandsons, were scouring up their old muskets, mothers, daughters, and *grandmothers* were busily employed in *manufacturing powder!*

### NORTHERN BORDER WARS.

In order to a more perfect understanding of the origin and character of the disastrous war waged upon the settlers in Wyoming, we will direct the attention of the reader to the course of events upon the northern border.

Sir William Johnson came into the valley of the Mohawk when he was a young man, about forty years previous to the Revolutionary war. The emergencies of the times gave him an opportunity for the development of his talents. He entered the provincial army, and gained a victory over the French at Lake George in 1755, and this event made his fortune. He was made a baronet, and appointed Superintendent of Indian Affairs for the northern provinces. He resided at Fort Johnson, near the village of Amsterdam, for nearly twenty years, after which he removed to Johnson Hall, near Johnstown, where he died in 1774. He left one son—Sir John Johnson—and two daughters. One of his daughters was married to Colonel Daniel Claus, and the other to Colonel Guy Johnson, a distant relative.

After the death of Sir William, Guy Johnson was appointed his successor as Superintendent of Indian Affairs. There were under his superintendency at this time 130,000 Indians, of whom 50,420 were warriors. The Six Nations numbered about 10,000, about 4600 of whom were trained to the business of war.

In 1772, the county of Tryon—named after the then governor of the province of New York—was organized, and it embraced the section of the state west of a line running north and south through the centre of the present county of Schoharie. It contained a population of about 10,000, and Johnstown was the seat of justice.

The Johnson family exerted a great influence over the people in Tryon County, and had acquired almost unbounded control of the Indian mind of the Six Nations. When the troubles broke out between the mother country and her colonies, the Johnsons espoused the royal cause. Their influence over the Iroquois, or Six Nations, was used to attach them to the same cause, and they often led them on in their incursions upon the settlements in the valley of the Mohawk. Guy Johnson left Johnson Hall in 1775, passing through the country of the Six Nations, finally making his head-quarters at Montreal. Brant and his Mohawks, together with the Butlers, followed Colonel Johnson. Sir John Johnson was made a prisoner, by order of General Schuyler, in January, 1776, and taken to Fishkill, where he was released on parole. In the May following he broke his parole, and subsequently commanded a regiment of refugees, known in border warfare as "Johnson's Greens."

The last of April, 1777, Colonel Gansevoort, with the third regiment of the New York line of state troops, was ordered to Fort Schuyler.* Before the fortification was completed, it was invested by Colonel St. Leger. This division of the British forces was collected at Oswego, brought their munitions of war and stores up Wood Creek, and crossed the portage to the Mohawk. General Herkimer, with a regiment of militia, in attempting to relieve Fort Schuyler, was met by a considerable force of Indians and Tories, under the command of Brant and Butler, at Oriskany, where he was repulsed, and received a wound which occasioned his death. The patriots retreated down the river, and St. Leger pressed the siege. He raised batteries, and made many efforts to reduce the fortress by cannon shot, but failed to effect a breach. He then resorted to threats of savage barbarity, should the Indians be provoked by obstinate resistance. In such case, he said, it would not be possible for him to restrain them from their accustomed modes of redress. All this failed to move the brave men in the fort, who were then nearly out of provisions.

Colonel Willett and Lieutenant Stockwell left the fort by night, and, eluding the vigilance of the enemy,

---

* This fort was situated where the village of Rome now stands. The French had built a fort here called Fort Stanwix, which was now reconstructed. The name of the new fortification was given it in honor of General Schuyler. This fort must be distinguished from the old fort by the same name, built, during the French war, on the point of high ground now in the northeastern portion of the city of Utica, and called by the same name, after an uncle of General Schuyler.

passed down the Mohawk for the purpose of reassembling the militia and returning for the relief of the fort. This was a daring undertaking, but was so wonderfully successful that the Indians, believing Colonel Willett to have been assisted by some superhuman power, called him "the devil." The distressing events of the encounter at Oriskany had created a great sensation in the country, and called for decisive measures. General Schuyler dispatched Generals Larned and Arnold to attack St. Leger and raise the siege of Fort Schuyler.

Colonels Johnson, Claus, and Butler had issued a proclamation designed to intimidate the people of Tryon County into submission, and to procure enlistments into the king's army, and Walter N. Butler, son of Colonel John Butler, had been sent on the delicate business of circulating this proclamation, and using his personal influence with those whom he might find undecided. He visited the German Flats, in the neighborhood of Fort Dayton, and collected a company of Tories at the house of one Shoemaker, who had been a civil officer under the king. Colonel Weston, at Fort Dayton, learning of the gathering, dispatched a detachment of troops, who came upon them by surprise just as Butler was in the midst of a harangue, and made them all prisoners. Butler was tried by a court-martial for a spy, and condemned to be hung, but at the intercession of several officers, who had formerly been his personal friends and associates, he received a reprieve, and was sent a prisoner to Albany. After several months' confinement he pretended to be sick, and, as a mark of favor, he was quartered in the house of a Tory, with a single soldier to guard him. Butler and his host managed to make the soldier drunk, and, *sick* as he was, he escaped on a fleet horse, and reached Niagara.

Among those captured with Butler was a singular character by the name of *Honyost Schuyler*. Almost an idiot, he still had streaks of shrewdness which gave him no little distinction among the Indians and his half-civilized neighbors. His mother and brother Nicholas lived at Little Falls. Like Butler, he was condemned to death. His mother and brother hastened to Fort Dayton to implore General Arnold to spare his life. Arnold for a time would not listen to their intercession, and the miserable woman became almost frantic. At length General Arnold proposed terms upon which the life of the poor fellow should be spared. He must immediately go to the camp of St. Leger, and make such representations to him of the forces which were coming up against him as would induce him to raise the siege. The proposition was gladly accepted, and the old woman offered to be held a hostage for the faithful performance of the commission. General Arnold refused to receive the mother in that capacity, but took the other son, who was put in confinement, while Honyost took his departure. He took with him a friendly Oneida Indian, who was fully inducted into the secrets of the mission, and greatly aided him in its prosecution. Before his departure several balls were shot through his clothes, to help him make out his story, and the Indian took a different route, and fell into the camp at about the same time with the principal in the enterprise.

Honyost arrived at St. Leger's camp, and began immediately to give an account of his wonderful escape, and of Arnold's army. When asked as to the number of troops which Arnold had under his command, he shook his head mysteriously, and pointed to the leaves of the trees to intimate that the army was large—beyond his power of enumeration. The Oneida had in his way met with several others of his tribe, who offered him their co-operation. Honyost's story began to fly through the camp like wildfire, when lo! the story of the near approach of a great army was told by Indians who fell in from different directions. A panic had really commenced before St. Leger knew it. He summoned Honyost before him, who gave a most frightful account of his escape. He had been condemned to death, and, on his way to the gallows, he had availed himself of the carelessness of the guard, and fled. In the mean time, a volley of musketry was fired after him. Then, pointing to the holes in his coat, he showed the colonel and his officers how one ball had just grazed his side, another his shoulder, and another his thigh; but he had been miraculously preserved. As to the Indians, they also gave to St. Leger the most exaggerated accounts of the strength and numbers of the army of General Arnold. St. Leger called a council of war, and, while the officers were deliberating upon the course to be taken, the Indian forces under Brant commenced preparations to depart. St. Leger used every effort to retain them, but to no purpose. They had suffered severely in the battle of Oriskany, and, as yet, had been wholly disappointed in the promised plunder of the Yankee fort, and they were in the moody state of mind, when they were visited by Honyost and the Oneidas, which was entirely favorable to the success of these emissaries of the Yankee commander. Indeed, the Indians did what they could to make the retreat a flight.

An altercation taking place between Colonel St.

Leger and Sir John Johnson, each accusing the other of remissness in duty, in the midst of the feud two cunning sachems set up a shout, "*They are coming! they are coming!*" when the two colonels closed their angry dispute and took to flight. Their men were equally quick on foot; throwing away their guns and knapsacks, they ran for their lives.

Honyost Schuyler ran with the British and Indians until an opportunity occurred for him to escape, when he returned to Fort Schuyler, and gave Colonel Gansevoort his first information of General Arnold's approach, and of the flight of the besiegers. Gansevoort pursued the retreating army, and took prisoners and a large amount of spoil. Such was the panic of the royal army that they left their tents standing; their provisions, artillery, ammunition, and all their camp equipage were left to the Yankee forces. The Indians, in the mean time, enraged with disappointment, robbed the officers, plundered several boats on Wood Creek, and actually murdered stragglers belonging to the royal army for the sake of plundering their persons. A just retribution this for employing those heartless savages in a war upon the people of the frontier settlements.—See Campbell's *History of Tryon County*, and *Stone's Border Wars*.

We will here leave the history of the war upon the northern border, and return to the events of the period in Wyoming. We shall have occasion to refer to the narrative which we have here given as we proceed with the progress of events upon the Susquehanna, and as we give sketches of characters which figured in the predatory wars which were waged by the British provincial troops and her savage allies, the Six Nations, both in Tryon County, New York, and in Wyoming, upon the Susquehanna.

On the 29th or 30th of June, 1778, Colonel John Butler, with about four hundred British provincials, partly made up of Tories, together with six or seven hundred Indians, entered the head of the valley, and took possession of Fort Wintermoot without opposition. On that morning eight men and a boy, who had gone from Fort Jenkins to their work with their arms, three miles above, fell into the hands of the enemy; five of the men were killed, and three taken prisoners, the boy escaping by throwing himself into the river, and hiding in a clump of willows.

Colonel Zebulon Butler, who was a Continental officer, knowing the perilous condition of the people, and desirous to give his personal aid in any way possible, had obtained leave to visit the valley, and now, by common consent, assumed the command of the little army. The whole consisted of "two hundred and thirty enrolled men, and seventy old people, boys, civil magistrates, and other volunteers," the whole embracing six companies, which were mustered at Forty Fort, where the families of the settlers on the east side of the river had taken refuge. "Indian Butler," as he was called, summoned the Connecticut people to surrender Forty Fort and the valley. A council of war was called on the 3d of July, and though it was the opinion of Colonel Butler, Colonel Denison, and Lieutenant Colonel Dorrance, and others, that "a little delay would be best," in hopes of the arrival of re-enforcements, which it was thought might be on their way, yet a large majority were for marching at once upon the enemy and giving them battle. Colonel Butler mounted his horse, saying, "I tell you we go into great danger, but I can go as far as any of you," and "the column, consisting of about three hundred men, old men, and boys, marched from the fort," at about three o'clock in the afternoon, with drums beating and colors flying. The devoted little band marched up the plain, with the river on the right and a marsh upon the left, until they reached Fort Wintermoot, which was on fire —fired to make the impression upon the minds of the patriots that the enemy was retiring from the valley.

"Colonel Z. Butler, on approaching the enemy, sent forward Captains Ransom and Durkee, Lieutenants Ross and Wells, as officers whose skill he most relied on, to select the spot, and mark off the ground on which to form the order of battle. On coming up, the column displayed to the left, and under those officers every company took its station, and then advanced in line to the proper position, where it halted, the right resting on the steep bank noted, the left extending across the gravel flat to a morass, thick with timber and brush, that separated the bottom-land from the mountain. Yellow and pitch-pine trees, with oak shrubs, were scattered all over the plain. On the American right was Captain Bidlack's company. Next was Captain Hewitt's, Daniel Gore being one of his lieutenants. On the extreme left was Captain Whittlesey's. Colonel Butler, supported by Major John Garrett, commanded the right wing. Colonel Denison, supported by Lieutenant Colonel George Dorrance, commanded the left. Such was the ground, and such the order of battle. Every thing was judiciously disposed, and constructed in a strictly military and prudent manner. Captains Durkee and Ransom, as experienced officers, in whom great confidence was placed, were stationed, Durkee with Bidlack on the right wing, Ransom with Whittlesey on the left. Colonel Butler made a very brief address just before he ordered the column to display. 'Men, yonder is the enemy. The fate of the Hardings tells us what we have to expect if defeated. We come out to fight, not only for liberty, but for life itself, and, what is dearer, to preserve our homes from conflagration, our women and children from the tomahawk. Stand firm the first shock, and the Indians will give way. Every man to his duty.'

"The column had marched up the road running near the bank on which our right rested. On its display, as Denison led off his men, he repeated the expression of Colonel Butler, 'Be firm; every thing depends on resisting the first shock.'

"About four in the afternoon the battle began; Colonel Z. Butler ordered his men to fire, and at each discharge to advance a step. Along the whole line the discharges were rapid and steady. It was evident that on the more open ground the Yankees were doing most execution. As our men advanced, pouring in their platoon fires with great vivacity, the British line gave way, in spite of all their officers' efforts to prevent it. The Indian flanking party on our right kept up from their hiding-places a galling fire. Lieutenant Daniel Gore received a ball through the left arm. 'Captain Durkee,' said he, 'look sharp for the Indians in those bushes.' Captain Durkee stepped to the bank to look, preparatory to making a charge and dislodging them, when he fell. On the British Butler's right, his Indian warriors were sharply engaged. They seemed to be divided into six bands, for a yell would be raised at one end of their line, taken up, and carried through, six distinct bodies appearing at each time to repeat the cry. As the battle waxed warmer, that fearful yell was renewed again and again with more and more spirit.

It appeared to be at once their animating shout and their signal of communication. As several fell near Colonel Dorrance, one of his men gave way: 'Stand to your work, sir,' said he, firmly, but coolly, and the soldier resumed his place.

"For half an hour a hot fire had been given and sustained, when the vastly superior numbers of the enemy began to develop their power. The Indians had thrown into the swamp a large force, which now completely outflanked our left. It was impossible it should be otherwise: that wing was thrown into confusion. Colonel Denison gave orders that the company of Whittlesey should wheel back, so as to form an angle with the main line, and thus present his front, instead of flank, to the enemy. The difficulty of performing evolutions by the bravest militia on the field under a hot fire is well known. On the attempt, the savages rushed in with horrid yells. Some had mistaken the order to fall back as one to retreat, and that word, that fatal word, ran along the line. Utter confusion now prevailed on the left. Seeing the disorder, and his own men beginning to give way, Colonel Z. Butler threw himself between the fires of the opposing ranks, and rode up and down the line in the most reckless exposure. 'Don't leave me, my children, and the victory is ours.' But it was too late.

"Every captain that led a company into action was slain, and in every instance fell on or near the line. As was said of Bidlack, so of Hewitt, Whittlesey, and the others: 'they died at the head of their men.' They fought bravely; every man and officer did his duty; but they were overpowered by threefold their force. In point of numbers the enemy was overwhelmingly superior."—*Miner's History.*

It was a dreadful hour. The few old men who were left in the fort, and the women and children, lined the bank of the river with throbbing hearts, listening to the noise of the battle; and as the firing became more scattering, and advanced down the plain toward the fort, the fearful reality of a defeat was but too plainly indicated. "The boys are beat—they are retreating—they will be all cut to pieces!" exclaimed one who had been pacing the bank, and catching every indication borne upon the breeze from the scene of action.

A portion of the numerous, strange, and fearful scenes which followed are upon record, and many of them are still in the recollection of a few survivors, for which we must refer the reader to the historians. Mr. Miner says, "About one hundred and sixty of the Connecticut people were killed that day, and one hundred and forty escaped. The loss of the enemy was never known; probably from forty to eighty fell." According to the best information which we have been able to gain, more than two hundred of the patriots fell in this fearful conflict, while about sixty of the British and Indians were slain. Many were first made prisoners, and then massacred in the most cruel and barbarous manner by the savages. Colonels Butler and Denison, being mounted, first came into Forty Fort, and confirmed the apprehensions of the poor defenseless people, then waiting in a most fearful state of anxiety and suspense. They sat down by a table in Thomas Bennet's cabin, and adjusted the terms of capitulation which were to be proposed to the enemy. Colonel Butler then crossed over to Wilkesbarre, and the next day, throwing a feather-bed across his horse, and seating his wife upon the animal behind him, left the valley. He was a brave officer, and having distinguished himself in several gallant enterprises in the Revolutionary struggle, had reasons enough for not wishing to be made a prisoner of war. At nightfall the fugitives came into the fort, exhausted with the toils and terrors of the day. But oh, how many husbands and sons came not! The sadness of that night will never be adequately sketched.

The people in the fort at Wilkesbarre, on the east side of the river, early on the 4th commenced their flight, but in such haste as not to furnish themselves with provisions for a long and toilsome journey through the wilderness. A large number of women and children, with a few men, took the old war-path toward the Delaware, some perishing on the way through fatigue and hunger in a dense pine forest, which has ever since been called "The Shades of Death." The few regular soldiers who had escaped, knowing that they, if taken, would be doomed to exemplary punishment, made a hasty escape, under the orders of Colonel Butler.

On the evening of the fatal 3d, Captain John Franklin arrived at Forty Fort, with a company of militia from Huntington and Salem, which gave a little strength to the remnant which were left. On the morning of the 4th, Colonel John Butler summoned Colonel Denison to surrender Forty Fort, inviting him to his head-quarters to agree upon the terms. After some negotiation, the following articles of capitulation were duly executed:

"Westmoreland, July 4th, 1778.

"CAPITULATION AGREEMENT — Made and completed between John Butler, in behalf of his majesty King George the Third, and Colonel Nathan Denison of the United States of America:

"Art. I. It is agreed that the settlement lay down their arms, and their garrison be demolished.

"Art. II. That the inhabitants occupy their farms peaceably, and the lives of the inhabitants be preserved entire and unhurt.

"Art. III. That the Continental stores are to be given up.

"Art. IV. That Colonel Butler will use his utmost influence that the private property of the inhabitants shall be preserved entire to them.

"Art. V. That the prisoners in Forty Fort be delivered up.

"Art. VI. That the property taken from the people called Tories be made good; and that they remain in peaceable possession of their farms, and unmolested in a free trade throughout this settlement.

"Art. VII. That the inhabitants which Colonel Denison capitulates for, together with himself, do not take up arms during this contest.

  (Signed),    "John Butler,
          "Nathan Denison."

Accordingly, on the 5th of July, the gates of the fort were thrown open, and Butler, at the head of his rangers, and a Seneca chief by the name of G———n, at the head of the Indians, marched in. The arms of the men were stacked, and given as a present by Butler to the Indians, with these words: "See what a present the Yankees have made you." The Indians went about sneakingly peeping into the doors of the cabins, but for that day molested no one. On the next day, however, they began to plunder the people. Colonel Denison remained in Mr. Bennet's cabin, a place formerly occupied as a horse-shed. When Butler came into the fort, Colonel Denison sent for him, and remonstrated with him upon the conduct of the Indians, alleging that it was a breach of a most solemn engagement. Butler said, "My men shall not molest the people; I will put a stop to it." But he was no sooner gone than the plundering was resumed. Colonel Denison again sent for Butler, and again he came into the shed and gave assurances that "the plundering should cease." Toward night a company of Indians came in, some of them drunk, and commenced ransacking the houses and rifling them of their movables. Colonel Denison had another conversation with Butler, who now said, "To tell you the truth, I can do nothing with them." Colonel Denison chided him severely, but, waving his hand, he repeated the same words, and finally left the fort no more to return.

After the lapse of two weeks from the day of the battle, it was rumored that the Tories and Indians had again entered the valley, and would probably kill all that remained of the inhabitants. The people then all left the fort, some going down the river in canoes, and others taking the path "through the swamp" to Stroudsburg. Thus this beautiful valley was deserted by its inhabitants, with the exception of those who lay bleaching upon the plain, unconscious of what transpired, and beyond the reach of further wrongs.

We have not given the details of the savage cruelties which are found in other histories. But there are two well-authenticated instances of the diabolical spirit of the *Tories* which we shall recite. We do this not only to show what kind of men embraced the royal cause, but as a fearful illustration of the dreadful havoc made by the spirit of war upon all the better feelings of humanity, and all the ties of kindred.

MONOCASY ISLAND, FROM THE EAST BANK OF THE SUSQUEHANNA.

"A short distance below the battle-ground there is a large island in the river called 'Monockonock Island.' Several of the settlers, while the battle and pursuit continued, succeeded in swimming to this island, where they concealed themselves among the logs and brushwood upon it. Their arms had been thrown away in their flight previous to their entering the river, so that they were in a manner defenseless. Two of them, in particular, were concealed near and in sight of each other. While in this situation, they observed several of the enemy, who had pursued and fired at them while they were swimming the river, preparing to follow them to the island with their guns. On reaching the island, they immediately wiped their guns and loaded them. One of them, with his loaded gun, soon passed close by one of these men who lay concealed from his view, and was immediately recognized by him to be the brother of his companion who was concealed near him, but who, being a Tory, had joined the enemy. He passed slowly along, carefully examining every covert, and directly perceived his brother in his place of concealment. He suddenly stopped and said, 'So it is you, is it?' His brother, finding that he was discovered, immediately came forward a few steps, and falling on his knees, begged him to spare his life, promising to live with him and serve him, and even to be his slave as long as he lived, if he would only spare his life. '*All this is mighty good,*' replied the savage-hearted brother of the supplicating man, '*but you are a d\*\*\*\*d rebel;*' and deliberately presenting his rifle, shot him dead upon the spot. The other settler made his escape from the island, and having related this fact, the Tory brother thought it prudent to accompany the British troops on their return to Canada."—*Chapman's History*, p. 127, 128.

"This tale is too horrible for belief; but a survivor of the battle, a Mr. Baldwin, whose name will occur again, confirmed its truth to the writer with his own lips. He knew the brothers well, and in August, 1839, declared the statement to be true."—*Col. Stone's History*, p. 215.

Elijah Shoemaker was seen wading in the river, not knowing how to swim, by one Windecker, a Tory, who had been treated by Shoemaker with the kindness with which a father would treat a son. Windecker said to him, "Come out, Shoemaker." "I am afraid," said Shoemaker, "you will give me up to the Indians." "No," said Windecker, "I will save you; they sha'n't hurt you." But no sooner did Shoemaker come within his reach, than the perfidious wretch dashed his tomahawk into his head, and set his body afloat. The body was taken up at the fort, and Mrs. Shoemaker, with a child in her arms—the late Col. Elijah Shoemaker, of Kingston—came down to the water's edge to be agonized with a sight of the mangled corpse of her husband. The body was buried in the fort before the capitulation. The circumstances of Shoemaker's death were related by Esquire Carpenter and Anning Owen, who were concealed under a tree-top which lay out in the river.

These instances of horrid brutality defy all precedent. The priestess of the hellish orgies of "Bloody Rock," had she witnessed the above spectacle, would have been ashamed of the demons concerned in the transaction. She, in the true spirit of savage warfare, was taking sweet vengeance for the loss of a brother or an intimate friend. But these furies imbrued their hands in the blood of *friend* and *brother!* Alas for poor humanity, of what a height of corruption and wickedness is it capable!

"Indian Butler" soon made his exit from the valley. The following is a picture of the departure:

"With Butler a large portion of the Indians withdrew, and their march presented a picture at once melancholy and ludicrous. Squaws, to a considerable number, brought up the rear, a belt of scalps stretched on small hoops around the waist for a girdle, having on, some four, some six, and even more, dresses of chints or silk, one over the other; being mounted astride on horses (of course all stolen), and on their heads three, four, or five bonnets, one within another, worn wrong side before."—*Miner's History*, p. 237.

Mr. Miner presents two charges against Colonel John Butler, which will lie against his name to the end of time, and in mitigation of which there is not a relieving circumstance. The first is "his position—accepting command, lending his name, and associating with those bloodthirsty and unprincipled savages who were placed under his orders." His confession, after the capitulation, that he could "do nothing with them," brands him with infamy. How came he to lead on a band of murderous savages whom he knew he could not control, to an assault upon a defenseless settlement? But "the deepest stain on the character of Butler, next to his taking the command of such a horde of merciless and ungovernable wretches, arises out of the fact that but *two* prisoners were taken and saved at the time of the battle." It is altogether likely that the greatest number who fell were cruelly massacred upon the retreat; and it is certain that many of them were first made prisoners, and then tortured and butchered in cold blood. That his own men took part in the pursuit and butchery on the day of the battle is historically true, and that he tried to prevent the subsequent massacres there is no evidence.

COLONEL ZEBULON BUTLER'S REPORT OF THE BATTLE TO THE BOARD OF WAR.

"Gnadenhutten, Penn Township, July 10th, 1778.

"HONORED SIR,—On my arrival at Westmoreland, which was only four days after I left Yorktown, I found there was a large body of the enemy advancing on that settlement. On the 1st of July we mustered the militia, and marched toward them by the river above the settlement—found and killed two Indians at a place where, the day before, they had murdered nine men engaged in hoeing corn. We found some canoes, etc., but, finding no men above their main body, it was judged prudent to return; and as every man had to go to his own house for his provisions, we could not muster again till the 3d of July. In the mean time the enemy had got possession of two forts, one of which we had reason to believe was designed for them, though they burned them both. The inhabitants had some forts for the security of their women and children, extending about ten miles on the river, and too many men would stay in them to take care of them; but, after collecting about three hundred of the most spirited of them, including Captain Hewitt's company, I held a council with the officers, who all agreed that it was best to attack the enemy before they got any farther. We accordingly marched, found their situation, formed a front of the same extension of the enemy's, and attacked from right to left at the same time. Our men stood the fire well for three or four shots, till some part of the enemy gave way; but, unfortunately for us, through some mistake, the word *retreat* was understood from some officer on the left, which took so quick that it was not in the power of the officers to form them again, though I believe, if they had stood three minutes longer, the enemy would have been beaten. The utmost pains were taken by the officers, who mostly fell. A lieutenant colonel, a major, and five captains, who were in commission in the militia, all fell. Colonel Durkee, and Captains Hewitt and Ransom, were likewise killed. In the whole, about two hundred men lost their lives in the action on our side. What number of the enemy were killed is yet uncertain, though I believe a very considerable number. The loss of these men so intimidated the inhabitants that they gave up the matter of fighting. Great numbers ran off, and others would comply with the terms that I had refused. The enemy sent flags frequently; the terms you will see in the inclosed letter. They repeatedly said they had nothing to do with any but the inhabitants, and did not want to treat with me. Colonel Denison, by desire of the inhabitants, went and complied, which made it necessary for me and the little remains of Captain Hewitt's company to leave the place. Indeed, it was determined by the enemy to spare the inhabitants after the agreement, and that myself and the few Continental soldiers should be delivered up to the savages; upon which I left the place, and came away, scarcely able to move, as I have had no rest since I left Yorktown. It has not been in my power to find a horse or man to wait on the Board till now. I must submit to the Board what must be the next step. The little remains of Hewitt's company, which are about fifteen, are gone to Shamoken, and Captain Spaulding's company, I have heard, are on the Delaware. Several hundred of the inhabitants are strolling in the country destitute of provisions, who have large fields of grain and other necessaries of life at Westmoreland. In short, if the inhabitants can go back, there may yet be secured double the quantity of provisions to support themselves, otherwise they must be beggars, and a burden to the world.

"I have heard from men that came from the place since the people gave up that the Indians have killed no persons since, but have burned most of the buildings, and are collecting all the horses they can, and are moving up the river. They likewise say the enemy were eight hundred, one half white men. I should be glad that, if possible, there might be a sufficient guard sent for the defense of the place, which will be the means of saving thousands from poverty, but must submit to the wisdom of Congress. I desire further orders from the honorable Board of War with respect to myself and the soldiers under my direction.

"I have the honor to be your honor's most obedient humble servant, ZEBULON BUTLER."

## THE OTHER SIDE.—JOHN BUTLER'S REPORT OF THE BATTLE.

**MAJOR JOHN BUTLER TO LIEUTENANT COLONEL BOLTON.**

"Lacuwanack, 8th July, 1778.

"On the 30th of June I arrived with about 500 rangers and Indians* at Wyoming, and encamped on an eminence which overlooks the greatest part of the settlement, from which I sent out parties to discover the situation or strength of the enemy, who brought in eight prisoners and scalps. Two Loyalists† who came into my camp informed me that the rebels could muster about eight hundred men, who were all assembled in their forts.‡ July the 1st I marched to the distance of half a mile of Wintermoot's Fort, and sent in Lieutenant Turney with a flag to demand immediate possession of it, which was soon agreed to.§ A flag was then sent to Jenkins's Fort, which surrendered on nearly the same conditions as Wintermoot's, both of which are inclosed.‖ I next summoned Forty Fort, the commandant of which refused the conditions I sent him. July 3d, parties were sent out to collect cattle, who informed me that the rebels were preparing to attack me. This pleased the Indians highly, who observed

---

* It has always been believed in Wyoming that the numbers of Butler's army were between 700 and 1000. A scout went up to the place of debarkation the day before the battle, and from the number of their boats they estimated their force at over 1000.

† Probably the Wintermoots.

‡ Here the number is greatly exaggerated; but, as the colonel wished to magnify his exploit, he reports his own number less than it really was, and exaggerates that of the settlers.

§ "Soon agreed to!" It was arranged beforehand, for those who built and occupied it were Tories.

‖ Fort Jenkins was not entered until the day after the battle.—See the account of Richard Gardner, p. 355.

they should be on an equal footing with them in the woods. At two o'clock we observed the rebels upon their march, in number about four or five hundred.* Between four and five o'clock they were advanced within a mile of us. Finding them determined, I ordered the fort to be set on fire, which deceived the enemy into an opinion that we had retreated. We then posted ourselves in a fine open wood, and, for our greater safety, lay flat upon the ground, waiting their approach. When they were within two hundred yards of us, they began firing. We still continued upon the ground, without returning their fire, until they had fired three volleys. By this time they had advanced within one hundred yards of us, and, being quite near enough, *Gucingerachton* ordered his Indians, who were upon the right, to begin the attack upon our part, which was immediately well seconded by the Rangers on the left. Our fire was so close and well directed that the affair was soon over, not lasting half an hour from the time they gave us their first fire to their flight. In this action were taken 227 scalps and only five prisoners.† The Indians were so exasperated with their loss last year near Fort Stanwix that it was with the greatest difficulty I could save the lives of these few.‡

\* Here again is a gross exaggeration. The numbers, all told, did not exceed 320.

† Perhaps one third of the "scalps" "were taken" after the "action" was over, from the heads of prisoners who had surrendered and asked quarter.

‡ The "loss" of "the Indians" "at Fort Stanwix" was doubtless a most provoking affair; but who was to blame? Must the people of Wyoming atone for it? The Indians probably flung away a few guns and blankets at Fort Stanwix in their sudden flight, for which they doubtless fully remunerated themselves by robbing their friends. Their "great loss," however, was that of the opportunity of taking

Colonel Denniston, who came in next day with a minister and two others to treat for the remainder of the settlement of Westmoreland, assured us that they had lost one colonel, two majors, seven captains, thirteen lieutenants, eleven ensigns, two hundred and sixty-eight privates. On our side were killed one Indian, two Rangers, and eight Indians were wounded.* In this incursion we have taken eight palisades, (six) forts, and burned about one thousand dwelling-houses,† all their mills, etc. We have also killed and drove off about one thousand head of horned cattle, and sheep and swine in great numbers. But what gives me the sincerest satisfaction is that I can with great truth assure you that in the destruction of this settlement not a single person has been hurt of the inhabitants but such as were in arms; to these, indeed, the Indians gave no quarter.‡

"I have also the pleasure to inform you that the officers and Rangers behaved during this short action highly to my satisfaction, and have always supported the scalps of the garrison, and plundering it of its provisions, ammunition, and small arms.

* This story is strangely false. Three Indians were shot down in the pursuit, and probably more.—See the statement of Solomon Bennet, p. 363.

† There were not more than half so many dwelling-houses in the settlement to burn. Besides, when this dispatch was written, the settlement had not been fired at all, with the exception of here and there a cabin.—See Mrs. Myer's and Mrs. Bedford's statements.

Were the Hardings, who were killed in the field, "in arms?"—See p. 103.

‡ "Gave no quarter." None indeed. What became of those who were taken prisoners? What became of the wounded? What became of the "five prisoners" which the report says were taken? They were all massacred in cold blood, with the exception of two who lived to return. Three of the "five" which the colonel reports as saved were never heard of afterward.

themselves through hunger and fatigue with great cheerfulness.

"I have this day sent a party of men to the Delaware to destroy a small settlement there, and to bring off prisoners. In two or three days I shall send out other parties for the same purpose, if I can supply myself with provisions.* I shall harass the adjacent country, and prevent them from getting in their harvest.†

"The settlement of Scohary or the Minisinks will be my next object, both of which abound in corn and cattle, the destruction of which can not fail of greatly distressing the rebels.‡ I have not yet been able to hear any thing of the expresses I sent to the Generals Howe and Clinton; but as I sent them by ten differ-

* What! short of "provisions" only three days after taking from the settlers "one thousand head of horned cattle, and sheep, and swine in great numbers?" This is a strangely inconsistent and self-contradictory tale.

† How would he do this, as he was then on his way back to the north? He could only do it by the agency of parties of his Indians who were left behind. He, Colonel Butler, then would do more than simply to "harass the adjacent country, and prevent them from getting in their harvest." He would shoot down the settlers in the field; kill and scalp their wives and children; rob, burn, and scalp on as large a scale as possible. All this was done by the same agency as that by which the people were prevented from "getting in their harvest;" and if Colonel John Butler did the one, the same Colonel John Butler did the other.

‡ In this arrangement the brave Colonel John Butler was "behind the light-house," for this business was committed to Brant, who at that very moment was earnestly engaged in its prosecution. We do not much wonder that this famous dispatch has been so long shut up in the government archives in London. It is a perfectly bald caricature of the famous expedition of its author "down the Susquehanna to Wyoming." At the same time, we are happy to be able to give it to the public. The "journal" of which the colonel speaks must be rich. We only wish we had that.

ent routes, I am in hopes that some of them will be able to make their way to them and return.

"In a few days I do myself the honor of writing to you more fully, and send you a journal of my proceedings since I left Niagara.

"I am, sir, with respect, your most obedient and very humble servant,

(Signed), "JOHN BUTLER."

We have given, in as brief a manner as we deemed consistent with a full understanding of the subject, the

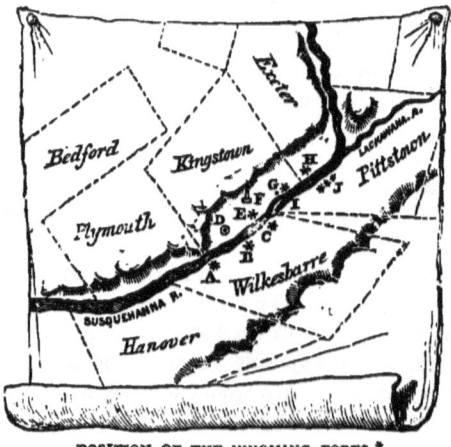

POSITION OF THE WYOMING FORTS.*

main facts of "the Wyoming massacre." It will be proper in this place to take some notice of a widely

---

\* *Explanation of the Plan.*—The several divisions, Hanover, Wilkesbarre, Kingstown, &c., mark the districts into which the town of Westmoreland was divided; in military language, the different *beats*. *A* marks the site of Fort Durkee; *B*, Wyoming or Wilkesbarre Fort; *C*, Fort Ogden; *D*, village of Kingston; *E*, Forty Fort. [This, in the early histories of the Revolution, is called Kingston Fort.] *F*, the battle-ground; *G*, Wintermoot's Fort; *H*, Fort Jenkins; *I*, Monocasy Island; *J*, the three Pittstown stockades. The dot below different report of the affair, which has gone into history and obtained a wide circulation. The account to which we refer may be found in Thatcher's Military Journal, and Gordon's History of the American Revolution. We shall simply refer to the points which are most glaringly false, and not occupy space for the whole story.

After the battle it is represented that "Fort Kingston" was "invested the next day, 4th of July, on the land side." Dr. Thatcher asserts that the fort was cannonaded the whole day, whereas there was but one cannon, a four-pounder, in the valley, and that the Yankees had in Wilkesbarre.

Again it is said, "The enemy, to sadden the drooping spirits of the weak remaining garrison, sent in for their contemplation the bloody scalps of 196 of their late friends and comrades." This is a pure fiction.

"July 5th," Colonel Denison is represented as asking "what terms" would be given on a "surrender," when "Butler answered, with more than savage phlegm, in two short words, '*the hatchet*.'" Denison, having defended the fort till most of the garrison were killed or disabled, was compelled to surrender at discretion. Some of the unhappy persons in the fort were carried away

---

the G marks the place of Queen Esther's Rock. The village of Troy is upon the battle-ground, and that of Wilkesbarre upon the site of Wilkesbarre Fort and its ravelins. The distances of the several points from the present bridge at Wilkesbarre are as follows: Fort Durkee, half a mile below, on the left bank. Fort Ogden, three and a half miles above, and the Pittstown stockades, about eight miles, on the same side. Forty Fort, three and a half miles; the Monument, on the battle-ground, five and a half; Queen Esther's Rock, six and a half; Wintermoot's Fort and Fort Jenkins, eight miles above, on the west or right bank of the river. Kingston is directly opposite Wilkesbarre, half a mile westward.

alive; but the barbarous conquerors, to save the trouble of murder in detail, shut up the rest promiscuously in the houses and barracks, which having set on fire, they enjoyed the savage pleasure of beholding the whole consumed in one general blaze."

The story proceeds: "They found about seventy Continental soldiers, who had been engaged merely for the defense of the frontiers, whom they butchered with every circumstance of horrid cruelty. The remainder of the men, with the women and children, were shut up, as before, in the houses, which being set on fire, they perished all together in the flames."

It is scarcely necessary to add here that these are not mere exaggerations, but downright *falsehoods*. That they would be extensively believed in this country, where the Tories and Indians were with no injustice regarded as a sort of demons incarnate, and that subsequent historians, living at a distance from the scene of action, should repeat them, is only what might be expected. Chief Justice Marshall, in his voluminous Life of Washington, first published in 1804, copied Gordon's tale, and others have continued to follow his example down to this date. Mr. Charles Miner wrote to the chief justice in 1806, giving him the facts as they really occurred, and informing him that the story to which he had given the sanction of his name was taken from newspaper accounts, which were published without correct information soon after the event of the massacre. *Twenty-five years* afterward, when the chief justice was contemplating a new and improved edition of the Life of Washington, he politely acknowledged the receipt of Mr. Miner's letter. Mr. Miner has published two letters from the chief justice in his History of Wyoming, p. 256-7.

In the letter of June 14, 1831, are the following short paragraphs:

"Mr. Ramsay, I presume, copied his statement from Gordon, and I relied upon both, as I know Mr. Gordon made personal inquiries into most of the events of the war, and that Mr. Ramsay was in Congress, and consequently had access to all the letters on the subject. It is surprising that they should have so readily given themselves up to the newspapers of the day.

"It was certainly our policy during the war to excite the utmost possible irritation against our enemy, and it is not surprising that we should not always have been very mindful of the verity of our publications; but when we come to the insertion of facts in serious history, truth ought never to be disregarded. Mr. Gordon and Mr. Ramsay ought to have sought for it."

All this is very sensible, but it is a curious fact that "Mr. Ramsay" never "copied" Gordon's "statements." In Ramsay's "statements," both in his "History of the United States" and his "American Revolution," nothing is said of the "*investment*," "the scalps," "the hatchet," "the burning," or "the seventy Continental soldiers;" but a simple statement of the facts connected with the capitulation of the fort, the flight of the inhabitants, and the utter desolation of the country, is given, with only slight and immaterial variations from the account as narrated by Chapman, Stone, and Miner. It is strange that so careful and conscientious a historian as Chief Justice Marshall should have committed so grave a mistake in a matter of authority. He doubtless wrote to Mr. Miner "without book," and his memory failed him. Since that time Ramsay has been associated with Gordon as authority for the fiction of "the hatchet" and the "burning of women and children." Now we hope these authors may part company, and Dr. Ramsay may no longer be held responsible for copying either Dr. Thatcher, Mr. Gordon, or "the newspapers of the day," in his account of "the Wyoming massacre." Dr. Ramsay is one of the pioneers in the work of American history. He was the first American who published a history of the American Revolution; this was in 1789. The materials for this work were collected while in Congress from 1782 to 1786. His History of the United States was published in 1808. The second volume of that work is represented by the author as "an improved new edition" of his "History of the American Revolution." His account of the Wyoming massacre is only "improved" by calling "Colonel John Butler" "a Connecticut Tory." In all other respects the account is the same in both works. But to return to the narrative.

We shall now only be able to touch a few details of the history. In the fall Colonel Butler returned with Captain Spaulding's company and some of the settlers, and buried the remains of those who fell upon the field of battle, and labored to secure some of the grain which was now ripe. But companies of Indians infested the country, who took prisoners, shot men who were laboring in the fields, and stole horses and cattle.

In September, Colonel Hartley, of the Pennsylvania line, led an expedition of two hundred men against the savages, and destroyed their towns at Tioga and Sheshequin. The Indians had fled in haste, leaving some plunder, which Colonel Hartley secured. On his march down the river he was attacked by two hundred warriors below Wyalusing, and, after a sharp encounter, they were repulsed with loss. See *Colonel Hartley's Report—Penn. Archives*, 1778.

But the savages followed almost upon the heels of Hartley's men, and resumed their work of murder, kidnapping, and plunder.

Immediately after Colonel Hartley's expedition in 1779, General Washington took measures to carry out a plan, which had been under consultation, of sending a powerful armament into the country of the Six Nations, to destroy their towns and chastise them for their incursions upon the frontier settlements, and the cruelties and barbarities which they had perpetrated. The expedition was committed to the charge of General Sullivan, who collected his forces at Wilkesbarre, and thence transported his artillery and baggage up the river in boats, and forming a junction with a division of the army under the command of General Clinton, at Tioga Point, proceeded to the prosecution of the objects of the expedition. Colonel John Butler at the head of the British and Tories, and Brant in command of the Indians, made a stand, a little below Newtown, on the Chemung River, with fifteen hundred or two thousand men, but were routed with considerable loss, and left the Indian towns, and the fields loaded with fruit, to be overrun and desolated by an avenging foe.

"Not a moment of delay was allowed. Being now in the Indian country, hundreds of fields, teeming with corn, beans, and other vegetables, were laid waste with rigid severity. Every house, hut, and wigwam was consumed. Cultivated in rude Indian fashion for centuries, orchards abounded, and near a town between the Seneca and Cayuga Lakes there were fifteen hundred peach-trees, bending under ripe and ripening fruit: all were cut down. The besom of destruction swept, if with regret and pity, still with firm hand, through all their fair fields and fertile plains. Deeply were they made to drink of the bitter chalice they had so often forced remorselessly to the lips of the frontier settlers within their reach. Some idea of the extent of country inhabited by the Indians, the number of their towns, and the great quantity of produce to be destroyed, may be formed, when it is stated that an army of four thousand men were employed, without a day's (except indispensable) remission, from the 29th of August until the 28th of September, in accomplishing the work of destruction. The farthest northwest extent of General Sullivan's advance was to Genesee Castle, at the large flats on the beautiful river of that name."—*Miner's History*, p. 271, 272.

But, notwithstanding the success of General Sullivan's expedition, it did not result in the security of Wyoming from the incursions of the savages. Still, parties of Indians continued their visits, and from time to time exercised their propensities for plundering, kidnapping, and murder. For three years the settlement was in a constant state of alarm, and many strange and interesting incidents marked its history. The capture and escape of Thomas Bennet and Lebbeus Hammond, of Pike, Vancampen, and Rogers; the kidnapping and late discovery of Frances Slocum, with a multitude of other events as full of romance as any of the scenes found in the writings of Sir Walter Scott, are detailed in subsequent chapters.

"The number of lives actually lost in Wyoming during the war it is impossible to estimate with certainty; probably three hundred, being one in ten of the inhabitants, or exceeding one third of the adult male population at the commencement of the war. Connecticut, to have suffered in the same proportion, would have lost near twenty-three thousand, and the

United Colonies three hundred thousand."—*Miner's History.*

Upon the termination of the war with Great Britain, the supreme executive council of Pennsylvania presented a petition to Congress, praying for a hearing touching the difficulties with Connecticut in relation to the title to the lands upon the Susquehanna. To this Connecticut promptly responded, and the question was submitted to an arbitration agreed upon by the parties, and assembled in Trenton, N. J., in December, 1782. The following was the decision:

"We are unanimously of opinion that Connecticut has no right to the lands in controversy.

"We are also unanimously of opinion that the jurisdiction and pre-emption of all the territory lying within the charter of Pennsylvania, and now claimed by the State of Connecticut, do of right belong to the State of Pennsylvania."—*Ibid.*, p. 308.

Of this decision the people of Wyoming did not complain, fully expecting to be "quieted in their possessions" under the government of Pennsylvania. They supposed their individual claims to the right of pre-emption had not been submitted nor adjudicated, and with them, as things stood, it was not a matter of much importance whether they were to be subject to the jurisdiction of Pennsylvania or Connecticut, provided they might remain in the peaceable possession of their lands. But from the proceedings which followed, the settlers soon found that the object of Pennsylvania was their utter expulsion from the homes which had already cost them infinite vexation and much precious blood. There was an affectation of conditions of compromise, but they resolved themselves into these points:

"1st. Pledges to be given, such as could not admit of denial or evasion, for their obedience.

"2d. A disclaimer in writing, publicly, plainly, and unequivocally given, of all claims to their lands held under title from Connecticut. Then follow the merciful terms.

"3d. The settler to take a lease of half his farm for about eleven months, giving up possession at once of the other half. On the first of April following to abandon claims, home, possession, to his adversary.

"4th. The widows of those who had fallen by the savages to be indulged in half their possessions a year longer.

"And 5th. The Rev. Mr. Johnson to be allowed to occupy his grounds (under disclaimer and lease, of course) for two years."—*Miner's History*, p. 324, 325.

The settlers remonstrated, and stood firmly to their positions. The agents of the government of Pennsylvania proceeded to constitute townships, and take possession of the lands. The settlers were not subdued by the dangers and troubles through which they had passed. Though war had diminished and weakened them, they were not prepared tamely to submit to downright usurpation and oppression. The soil which had drunk the blood of their dear friends—fathers, brothers, and sons—was too sacred to be lightly abandoned. Their homes they were determined to hold, peaceably if they could, forcibly if they must. Seeing themselves likely to fail of maintaining their rights, the law being in the hands of those interested, they seized their old rusty guns and hurled defiance at their oppressors. Colonel Butler, Colonel Jenkins, and Colonel Franklin led on the Connecticut people in the maintenance of their rights, always exhausting negotiation and diplomacy before they had recourse to forcible measures. Colonel Armstrong, the author of the famous "Newburg Letters," was commissioned to visit the scene of strife, with an armed force of four hundred men, and *restore peace.* Finding the Pennamites and Yankees in the field in the attitude of war, he required both parties to give up their arms and cease hostilities, promising "impartial justice and protection." The Yankees feared "treachery," but Colonel Armstrong "pledging his faith as a soldier and his honor as a gentleman" that the opposite party should also be disarmed, they finally submitted.

"They paraded, were ordered to 'ground arms;' they were then commanded, 'Right about—march ten steps—halt—right about!' which they obeyed; when Colonel Armstrong ordered his men to advance and take up the grounded arms. Thus far was according to their expectations; but their surprise was merged in bitterest mortification when Colonel Armstrong gave rapid orders, as rapidly obeyed, to surround the disarmed settlers, and make them all prisoners: resistance was vain, and escape hopeless. Not a musket was taken from Patterson's forces, but they beheld the successful treachery of Colonel Armstrong with unrestrained delight and taunting exultation. A soldier's faith should be unsullied as the judicial ermine—the pledged honor of a gentleman more sacred than life. Both were basely violated, and language is too poor to paint in proper colors the detestable deed."—*Miner.*

The poor fellows were now bound with cords, and hurried off, some to Easton, others to Northumberland, and thrown into prison. Armstrong returned to Philadelphia to herald his triumph; but, to his great mortification, he almost immediately learned that most of the Yankees were released on bail, and were again in the field. Skirmishes now ensued, and lives were lost on both sides.

A sympathy was now quite general in Pennsylvania for the settlers. Armstrong's perfidy was known and execrated, and when he returned to Wyoming, having been authorized to raise a force sufficient to reduce the Yankees, he could only bring into the field about one hundred men. In an assault upon a party who occupied three block-houses at Tuttle's Creek he was repulsed, and one of his subalterns, a Captain Bolen, was killed. This was the last blood that was spilled in these unfortunate conflicts. September 15, 1784, the Legislative Assembly of Pennsylvania " ordered the settlers to be restored to their possessions."

A portion of the settlers had, by means of the oppressive measures of Pennsylvania, become wholly disaffected with her; and, led on by Colonel Franklin, a most active and able political agitator, they made a stand against the jurisdiction of Pennsylvania, and actually commenced incipient measures for the organization of the disputed territory into a new state. The settlers were now themselves divided into two factions; one under the influence of Colonel Pickering, who acted under the authority of Pennsylvania, and the other led on by Colonel Franklin, who acted partly for himself and partly for the dear people. The feud was, however, finally terminated by the apprehension and imprisonment of Franklin, who, after he had lain in jail in Philadelphia for several months, so far lost his ardor as to ask pardon of the Legislature, and promise allegiance to the state, which promise he for many years faithfully fulfilled. So terminated all the wars of the Valley of Wyoming.

ITS HISTORY. 67

COLONEL PICKERING.

After the termination of the wars, Wyoming became a pleasant, flourishing rural district under the jurisdiction of Pennsylvania, and its inhabitants soon attained not only competency, but many of them wealth and opulence.

> "Look now abroad: another race has filled
>     These populous borders; wide the wood recedes,
>   And towns shoot up, and fertile realms are tilled;
>     The land is full of harvests and green meads;
>   Streams numberless, that many a fountain feeds,
>     Shine, disembowered, and give to sun and breeze
>   Their virgin matins; the full region leads
>     New colonies forth, that toward the western seas
>   Spread like a rapid flame among the autumnal trees."
>
> BRYANT.

Their commercial operations were carried on by a laborious process, but they were remunerative. Colonel Holenback and others, who commenced life with little or nothing, amassed fortunes by trading with the settlers and the Indians scattered through the wilderness between Niagara and Philadelphia. Things moved on in a quiet way, and business was pursued by its ancient channels until it was found that Wyoming and Lackawanna valleys constituted one of the richest basins of anthracite coal in the State of Pennsylvania. Eastern capital finally became enlisted, and, together with home resources, has originated a vast trade, which has changed the whole course of business. Agriculture is now a mere circumstance in the business interests of the country.

Until within a few years Wyoming was as much like "The Happy Valley" in Rasselas as could well be imagined. The only modes of access to the great world were either by the river, which was never properly navigable, or across the eastern mountains, over an almost impassable road. Thanks to modern improvements, every thing is now changed. The spell is broken. The dark silence of the past has given place to the bustle of business, the shriek of the locomotive, and the thunder of the cars. Instead of a full week's travel between this secluded spot and New York or Philadelphia, only a few hours are now occupied by the journey.

From the present point of business, activity, and progress, we propose to lead the reader back to the primitive simplicity of the first settlers—to take a brief view of their struggles and perils—their conflicts with the wild beasts, the wild Indians, and with each other. The history of no portion of our great country is more replete with curious incidents and romantic adventures than the history of Wyoming. Every foot of the soil is rendered classic by some historic fact or some curious legend. Bloody conflicts, hair-breadth escapes, starvations, heart-breaks, love adventures, prodigies of heroism, and miracles of endurance, mark every page of the early history of Wyoming, and are associated with every one of her ancient localities.

Our object shall be to introduce to the reader some of the tellers of the wondrous tales of the olden time. They shall now speak for themselves. Their own simple stories, told, as nearly as may be, in their own language, is the desideratum which we propose to supply, and for which our materials are quite ample.

Novelists and poets have strained their imagination to render the scenery and the scenes of Wyoming enchanting to their readers, while facts and incidents have been sleeping here, or have been but partially understood, which are really more wonderful than the fruitful brains of these writers were able to conceive. The truth, told without affectation after the excitements of the strange scenes described have long since passed away will be found to outstrip fiction in exciting interest.

Perhaps the brightest gem to be found among the poetical effusions of Thomas Campbell is his "Gertrude of Wyoming." There is much that is truthful in his pictures, some few things which are false, but nothing overdrawn. One of our own poets, who had gazed upon the objects and scenes of the valley for himself, makes the following beautiful allusion to Campbell's Gertrude in a strain not below the poetic beauty of that poem:

"I then but dreamed: thou art before me now,
  In life, a vision of the brain no more.
I've stood upon the wooded mountain's brow,
  That beetles high thy lovely valley o'er.

Nature hath made thee lovelier than the power
  Even of Campbell's pen hath pictured: he
Had woven, had he gazed one sunny hour
  Upon thy smiling vale, its scenery.

With more of truth, and made each rock and tree
   Known like old friends, and greeted from afar:
And there are tales of sad reality
   In the dark legends of thy border war,
With woes of deeper tint than his own Gertrude's are."

HALLECK.

## II.

### BRANT AND HIS TORY ASSOCIATES.

"But this is not a time"—he started up,
  And smote his breast with wo-denouncing hand—
"This is no time to fill the joyous cup;
  The mammoth comes—the foe—the monster Brant,
With all his howling, desolating band;
  These eyes have seen their blade and burning pine
Awake at once, and silence half your land.
  Red is the cup they drink, but not with wine;
Awake and watch to-night, or see no morning shine."
CAMPBELL'S Gertrude.

JOSEPH BRANT was a Mohawk sachem. He has been represented as a half-breed, but Colonel Stone

makes it appear quite probable that he was a full-blooded Indian. He was born in the western woods, somewhere within the bounds of the present State of Ohio, while his parents were upon a hunting expedition. His Indian name was *Thay-en-da-ne-gea*. Sir William Johnson held a peculiar relation to the Brant family. Molly Brant was a beautiful squaw, and, when about sixteen, upon a regimental parade—upon a banter on her part—had been allowed by an officer to spring upon his horse behind him, and, with her blanket and black tresses streaming in the air, to fly over the ground, to the great amusement of the spectators. Sir William was present, and was so charmed with the creature that he took her to his house. Colonel Stone says that she became "his wife," and that her "descendants from Sir William Johnson compose some of the most respectable and intelligent families in Upper Canada at this day." Mr. Campbell calls Molly Brant Sir William's "mistress," and in the "Documentary History of New York" she is called his "housekeeper." In all the records we have consulted she is called by her maiden name, "Molly Brant," which would seem to be against the idea of her regular and lawful marriage to Sir William Johnson.*

Joseph, a younger brother of Molly Brant, was most naturally taken under the patronage of Sir William; and, as the baronet took great interest in the civilization and improvement of the Indians, it is not strange that he took measures for the education of his *protégé*. The Rev. Mr. Wheelock had established a school at Lebanon, Connecticut, for the education of Indian boys. Joseph was sent to this school with several other Indian boys, and was, in the English sense, so *clever*, and made such progress as to receive high commendation

---

* Mr. Lossing informs us that Sir William married Molly Brant just before his death, to legitimatize his children.

from his teachers, and to be employed as an interpreter. He even assisted in translating St. Mark's Gospel into Mohawk. The correspondence between Sir William Johnson and Dr. Wheelock in relation to the subject of this brief sketch is preserved in the Documentary History of New York, and is well worth perusing. In 1763, Molly Brant, moved by prejudice against the New Englanders, caused a letter to be written to Joseph, in Sir William's name, in which he was requested to return home. Dr. Wheelock was much displeased at this, and wrote a letter of remonstrance to Sir William upon the subject, but it was of no use. Sir William's "housekeeper" could not be denied, and Joseph, becoming discontented, came back to take a prominent position among the Iroquois, and to be a powerful ally of the Johnsons and of the crown of Great Britain.

In 1777 Brant came down from the north with a band of his Mohawks, and made his headquarters at Ocquaga and Unadilla, and at the latter place General Herkimer sought and obtained an interview with the Mohawk chief, with a view to employing the influence of a former acquaintance and an old friendship to bring him over to the cause of the colonies. General Herkimer had with him about three hundred men, and, after some ceremonies, met Brant at Unadilla. The interview was civil, but fruitless. Brant told the general that, for the sake of old friendship, he would not harm him. But the chief was not to be satisfied without displaying his force; and, upon a signal, five hundred warriors darted from their concealment and gave the war-whoop. The "old neighbors" then separated to meet only once more, and that upon the battle-field.

The next we hear of Brant is at the battle of Oriskany, on the 6th of August. The conduct of the Indians and Tories toward the prisoners which fell into their hands on this occasion was marked by the most unparalleled ferocity. A surgeon of General Herkimer's brigade of militia, by the name of Moses Younglove, made an affidavit, which is now in the office of the Secretary of State, in which he makes the most terrible disclosures. He was made a prisoner, and was "brought to Mr. Butler, Sen."—Colonel John Butler—"who demanded of him what he was fighting for; to which he answered, 'He fought for the liberty that God and nature gave him, and to defend himself and dearest connections from the massacre of savages.' To which Butler replied, 'You are a d—d impudent rebel;' and, so saying, immediately turned to the savages, encouraging them to kill him, and saying, if they did not, this deponent and the other prisoners should be hanged on a gallows then preparing." "Six or seven" persons were killed at one time, at the instance of a wounded Tory. "Those of the prisoners who were delivered up to the provost guards were kept without victuals for many days, and had neither clothes, blankets, shelter, nor fire, while the guards were ordered not to use any violence in protecting them from the savages, who came every day in large companies, with knives, feeling of the prisoners to know who was fattest; that they dragged one of the prisoners out of the guard, with the most lamentable cries, tortured him for a long time, and this deponent was informed, by both Tories and Indians, that they ate him, as they did another on an island in Lake Ontario, by bones found there, newly picked, just after they had crossed the lake with the prisoners." St. Leger had offered twenty dollars for every American scalp, which, of course, furnished the Indians with a motive for killing the prisoners. Younglove was finally doomed to the fire, and was likely to be fed upon by the savages. He was fastened to a stake on the bank of the river, and while preparations were being made for the burning, the bank providentially caved off, and he was carried down the angry current, and was taken up far below by another party of Indians, who took him to the west, where he was obliged to run the gauntlet. After this he was adopted by an Indian, put on the Indian habit, and remained among the Indians until he was exchanged. Dr. Younglove lived to old age, and died a few years since in the city of Hudson, much respected. His story is perfectly reliable.—See *Campbell's Border Warfare*, p. 114–116.

Now, when these atrocities were perpetrated, where was Joseph Brant? He was at the head of the Indians who were in the battle of Oriskany, and who tortured and devoured the prisoners there taken. If he was present, these barbarous transactions were permitted, if not ordered by him; but if he left the prisoners at the disposal of the fiends whom he had the honor to command in the battle, and simply retired out of sight, the whole iniquitous and fiendish system of torture, and murder, and cannibalism which followed was at least by his connivance, and at his responsibility. Dr. Younglove in after years published a historical poem, in which, referring to Brant, he represents him as

"By malice urged to every barbarous art,
Of cruel temper, but of coward heart."

In 1778 the operations of the royal forces on the border were put in charge of Colonel John Butler and "Captain Brant." Two projects were set on foot:

one was surprising the small garrisons and cutting off the settlements in Tryon County, and the other the destruction of the settlement at Wyoming, on the Susquehanna. The first of these enterprises was to be taken in hand by Brant, and the second by Butler. Early in the spring Brant collected a considerable force at Ocquaga. The settlers at Unadilla and in the neighborhood removed to Cherry Valley, and located themselves within the fortification which had been raised by the order of General La Fayette. Brant, with a party of Indians, soon visited Cherry Valley, with a view to making prisoners of some of the principal inhabitants. While skulking about in the woods he intercepted Lieutenant Wormwood, and shot and scalped him with his own hand. Wormwood was a gallant young officer, and an only son of a respectable resident of Palatine. He had been to Cherry Valley, and was on his return home. The agonized father, as he bent over the mangled corpse of his beloved son, poured out a flood of tears, exclaiming, "Brant! cruel, cruel Brant!" After giving this relation, Mr. Campbell remarks, "Tears started in many eyes which scarcely knew how to weep." Brant and this young officer had been personal friends, and he is said to have lamented his death, having mistaken him for a Continental officer. This was a cold-blooded murder, in whatever aspect it is regarded, and it was all that Captain Brant achieved on this expedition, with the exception of his making a prisoner of Peter Sitz, who was in company with Lieutenant Wormwood.

In the month of June, Brant, with a party, visited Springfield, burned the houses of the inhabitants, and carried away several prisoners. He left the women and children in a house to shift for themselves—an act which has been noted as an evidence of his great humanity. It must be conceded that Brant did not seem to delight in torturing and murdering helpless women and children; whether it was because he had a spark of kindness in his bosom, or because he considered it mean and cowardly, we shall not attempt to determine.

Captain Brant now concentrated his forces at Unadilla, and received constant accessions of Tories, who were more savage than the savages themselves. A reward being offered to any person who would gain satisfactory knowledge of Brant's proceedings, Captain M'Kean volunteered to undertake the enterprise. He took with him five brave men, and proceeded down one of the branches of the Susquehanna. He came upon the track of the chief about twenty miles from Cherry Valley, in the town of Laurens. A Quaker by the name of Sleeper informed him that Brant had been at his house that day, with fifty men, and advised him to keep out of his way. M'Kean, having satisfied himself of the condition of things in that quarter, returned, but not until he had left behind him evidence of his visit. He wrote a letter to Brant, charging him with his predatory and murderous incursions upon the unoffending settlers, and challenging him to single combat, or to meet, in fair fight, an equal number of the patriots with his Indians, telling him that if he would come to Cherry Valley they would make him a *goose*— referring to his name. This letter he fastened in a stick, and placed in an Indian path; Brant received it, and referred to it subsequently.

Some time in June, Brant, with four hundred Indians, met a party of regular troops and Schoharie militia on the upper branch of the Cobelskill. There were only forty-five of our men; twenty-one escaped, twenty-two were killed, and two were taken prisoners.

In July, a small settlement, situated west of the German Flats, was destroyed by Brant. Some of the people were murdered, and others were made prisoners, while their goods were either destroyed or carried away. In August, the German Flats was visited by the chief, with three hundred Tories and one hundred and fifty Indians, who ravaged the whole country, burning all the buildings, and plundering every thing which was movable. Most of the people had taken refuge in Forts Herkimer and Dayton, and, consequently, no great number of prisoners and scalps were taken.

Schoharie and the surrounding settlements were the objects of the constant and persevering onsets of the Indians and Tories. Colonel Vrooman had the command of the fort at Schoharie, and was contented with merely defending it, without protecting the inhabitants. Colonel Harper was not satisfied with this mode of proceeding, and ran the hazard of a journey alone on horseback to Albany in quest of aid. He put up at a Tory tavern on Fox's Creek, and locked his door. Soon a loud rap at his door alarmed him. He arose, and, placing his sword and pistols on his bed, demanded what was wanted. "We want to see Colonel Harper," was the answer. He opened his door, and four Tories presented themselves. "Step an inch over that mark, and you are dead men," said Colonel Harper. After a little conversation, they left the brave colonel to himself. In the morning he mounted his horse and went on. An Indian followed him, whom Colonel Harper several times frightened out of his purpose by presenting his pistol. Upon representing to the commanding officer at Albany the distressed condition of the people at Schoharie, a squadron of horse was immediately provided, and, by a forced march, lit upon the enemy the next morning; "and the first knowledge that the people had that any relief was expected, they heard a tremendous shrieking and yelling; and, looking out, they saw Colonel Harper, with his troop of horse, welting up the enemy. The men in the fort rushed out and joined in the attack, and the country was soon cleared of the enemy."—*Campbell.*

Mr. Campbell publishes an "exact transcript" of a letter from Brant, which is quite characteristic, and has some historical importance. We here give it in full:

"Tunadilla, July 9, 1778.

"SIR,—I understand by the Indians that was at your house last week, that one Smith lives near with you, has little more corn to spare. I should be much obliged to you, if you would be so kind as to try to get as much corn as Smith can spare; he has sent me five skipples already, of which I am much obliged to him, and will see him paid, and would be very glad if you could spare one or two of your men to join us, especially Elias. I would be glad to see him, and I wish you could send me as many guns you have, as I know you have no use for them, if you have any; as I mean now to fight the cruel rebels as well as I can: whatever you will able to sent'd me you must sent'd by the bearer.

"I am your sincere friend and humble servant,

"JOSEPH BRANT.

"To Mr. Carr.

"P.S.—I heard that Cherry Valley people is very

bold, and intended to make nothing of us; they call us wild geese, but I know the contrary.

"Jos. B."

Captain Walter N. Butler owed the Tryon County patriots a special spite on account of his imprisonment in Albany, an account of which we have given in another connection; and, by way of taking vengeance upon them, he planned an expedition against Cherry Valley. He procured from his father, Colonel John Butler, the command of a portion of his regiment, called "Butler's Rangers," together with the liberty of employing the Indians who were under the command of Brant. Captain Butler took up the line of march early in November, and met Brant, with his men, on their way to Niagara for winter quarters. At first Brant was indignant at being made second to Walter Butler, and refused to join the expedition. Matters were, however, pacified between the Indian and the Tory, and they proceeded. Colonel Alden, who had command of the fort at Cherry Valley, was repeatedly admonished of the probability of an attack by the Indians and Tories, but he regarded the event as wholly improbable, and took no precautions against it. On the eleventh, the enemy stole upon the town early in the morning, in a snow-storm, and took the place by surprise. The officers were quartered in private houses, and the wily foe, having learned their localities by a prisoner, sent forward separate parties to surround the houses and take them. Lieutenant Colonel Stacy was made a prisoner; and Colonel Alden made his escape from the house, and was pursued, tomahawked, and scalped. He was one of the first victims of his criminal skepticism and consequent neglect of duty.

The enemy now rushed upon the citizens, and commenced an indiscriminate murder of men, women, and children. Female helplessness, infantile innocence, or entire neutrality in the struggle was no defense against the savage Indians and the still more savage Tories. The Wells family, who had been entirely neutral, male and female, old and young, with the exception of a boy who was not at home, were all destroyed. A Tory boasted that he shot Mr. Wells when he was at prayer. Rev. Mr. Dunlop, an old gentleman, was made a prisoner, and robbed of his wig and a portion of his clothing, and was hurried off, shivering with the cold. A few were reserved for the purpose of exchange; among these were the wife of Colonel Campbell and his four children. The town was fired, and was soon reduced to a heap of smouldering ruins.

The historians record some generous acts on the part of Brant on this occasion. He interfered in behalf of some women and children, and prevented their massacre. "On the day of the massacre he inquired of some of the prisoners where his friend Captain M'Kean was. They informed him that he had probably gone to the Mohawk River with his family. 'He sent me a challenge once,' said Brant; 'I have now come to accept it. He is a fine soldier thus to retreat.' They answered, 'Captain M'Kean would not turn his back upon an enemy when there was any probability of success.' 'I know it; he is a brave man, and I would have given more to have taken him than any other man in Cherry Valley, but I would not have hurt a hair of his head.'"—*Campbell.* It has been supposed that the humanity of Brant on this occasion was a mere ruse, to show off by contrast the savage barbarity of Butler, against whom he harbored a prejudice, and this seems to us by no means an uncharitable conclusion.

The diabolical malice of Walter N. Butler had no bounds. He was so thoroughly determined to make a clean riddance of all the "rebels," that numbers of neutrals and some of the friends of the royal cause were cut to pieces, lest some of the "rebels," under the false pretense of neutrality or friendship, should escape. He acted upon the maxim that it was better to destroy friends than to let enemies escape.—See *Campbell*, p. 144.

The garrison held out, and a re-enforcement of two hundred militia, on the day following, drove the scattering parties of Indians and Tories from the neighborhood. They kept their position until the next summer, when they joined General Clinton in his march into the Indian country with General Sullivan.

Cherry Valley was a scene of desolation, and exhibited every where the saddest mementoes of heartless cruelty. Mr. Campbell says: "The mangled remains of those who had been killed were brought in, and received as decent an interment as circumstances would permit. The most wanton acts of cruelty had been committed, but the detail is too horrible, and I will not pursue it further. The whole settlement exhibited an aspect of entire and complete desolation. The cocks crew from the tops of the forest trees, and the dogs howled through the fields and woods. The inhabitants who escaped, with the prisoners who were set at liberty, abandoned the settlement."

Some of those scenes we often heard described in our childhood by those who witnessed them. We were raised in old Tryon County, in Middlefield, equidistant from Cherry Valley and Cooperstown. The settlement in Middlefield, then called "Newtown Martin," was destroyed, and the people scattered. Some of them lived to return and spend the remainder of their lives on the soil which had been stained with the blood of their relatives and neighbors. Old Mrs. Writer—who used to be called "Aunt Recter"—once related to our excellent mother, while we sat by her side, the story of her captivity and sufferings. She was stripped of all her clothing except her chemise and under-skirt. There was a most beautiful girl of her acquaintance who was the admiration of all. As Mrs. Writer— then Miss Cook—was hurried along by her captors, she saw a stout Indian cut the throat of the beautiful girl referred to a few steps before her. As she passed she saw her in her death-struggle. Her nose, her ears, her eyelids, and her breasts were cut off, and her rosy cheeks were deeply gashed. All this barbarous mangling of the poor girl was inflicted while she was alive, as a matter of sport and derision. Could fiends have devised deeds of such abominable atrocity?

When the company encamped a large belt of scalps was brought to her, and she was ordered to dress them, being instructed by the squaws. The process consisted in stretching them — spatting them between her hands, and then laying them out to dry. Every scalp, as she took it up, reminded her of some friend or acquaintance. She finally took up one which she thought was her mother's. It was the scalp of a female, and she almost knew to a certainty that it was covered with the very hair which she had so often combed and dressed. She wept; but the lifted tomahawk, and manipulations which indicated that her own scalp would soon come off, dried up her tears. Her mother, however, had not been killed. She lived to a great age, and died near the head of Otsego Lake. She was called "Aunt Molly M'Allum," and Mrs. Writer was half sister to Daniel M'Allum, the captive boy of whom we have elsewhere spoken.

Colonel Campbell, whose wife and children were made prisoners by Butler and Brant, in our childhood we often saw on horseback, on his way to and from Cooperstown, or upon a visit to his sons, two of whom, William and Samuel, lived in Middlefield; and one thing we remember, especially, attracted our attention: when we doffed our hat and made our best bow to the colonel as he passed, he always made a graceful bow in return. His son, Dr. William Campbell, was a most estimable man and a polished gentleman. He was the uncle of Honorable William W. Campbell, the historian of Tryon County. This brief paragraph of personal matters we hope will be excused, as it may not be considered wholly out of place.

In 1779 we find Colonel Butler and Brant opposing General Sullivan, and decently whipped on the Chemung. The Tory and the Indian chief fled to Niagara to get out of harm's way for that time, and to prepare for another marauding expedition when occasion might offer. The massacres of Wyoming and Cherry Valley were amply avenged. The Indians who were collected about Niagara in the winter of 1779–80, having lost all their crops in the lake country, and having none but salt provisions, a thing to which they were not accustomed, died of scurvy in great numbers.

In August, 1781, Major Ross and Walter Butler came down from Canada into the Mohawk Valley with six hundred and seven Tories and Indians. Colonels Willett and Harper met them near Johnstown with about five hundred militia, and put them to rout. The retreating Indian and Tory army fled to the northwest. Ross, with a portion of his men, escaped, but Butler was not so fortunate. He was pursued by a company of Oneida Indians, and on coming to West Canada Creek, about fifteen miles from the village of Herkimer, he swam his horse, and, upon reaching the shore, he turned his back upon his pursuers, who had just come up to the creek, and defiantly and insultingly slapped his hip, when one of the party took deliberate aim, and brought the vaunting Tory to the ground. The Indian dropped his rifle and blanket and swam the creek, and on coming up to Butler he found him wounded. He now craved the mercy which he had so often denied to helpless women and children—he most piteously begged for his life; but the Indian warrior sprang upon him like a tiger, and with his lifted tomahawk, shouted out, "Sherry Valley—remember Sherry Valley!" and he buried his tomahawk in his brains, and tore his scalp from his head while his death-struggle was upon him. The miserable man might well have died with the words of Adonibezeck in his mouth, "As I have done, so hath God requited me." He had no burial, but his body was left to rot above ground, or to be devoured by wild beasts. The place where he crossed the creek is called "Butler's Ford" to this day. This was the last incursion made into Tryon County, and it had a very appropriate winding up in the death, by the hand of an Indian, of one of the most cruel of the class of white men who stimulated the Indians to the diabolical cruelties perpetrated on the frontier.

Colonel Stone, in his "Border Wars," has preserved a letter from Walter Butler vindicating himself, and his father, and the Indians too—why did he not include the Tories?—from the charge of "cruelties." The letter is directed to General Clinton, and is dated "Niagara, February 18, 1779." In this letter Captain Butler says, "We deny any *cruelties* to have been committed *at Wyoming*, either by whites or Indians." He rests his vindication upon the fact that "not a man, woman, or child was hurt after the capitulation, or a woman or child before it, and none taken into captivity." Now what does all this prove, more than that the "cruelties" attending the Wyoming massacre *might have been greater than they were?* How many men were cruelly tortured the day *before* "the capitulation?" The apology seems to proceed upon the ground that the cold-blooded torture of "*men in arms*" is not cruel, especially if it took place before "the capitulation." What was the reason that none were tortured "after the capitulation?" Simply because there were none left, or next to none, to torture. Captain Butler avoids the points of complaint. These are, 1. That the prisoners taken upon the battle-field were tortured by the Indians, or barbarously murdered, in cold blood, by the Tories. 2. That the defenseless people in the fort, women and children not excepted, were plundered of their food and clothing, and left to perish with hunger and exposure. And, finally, that the articles of capitulation were wholly and cruelly disregarded *before Colonel Butler had left the ground.*

Next, Captain Butler proceeds to vindicate himself and the Indians from the charge of "cruelties" at "Cherry Valley;" and his principal justification is—for here he does not deny the facts—that "Colonel Denison and his people appeared again in arms, with Colonel Hartley, after a solemn capitulation and engagement not to bear arms during the war." Here the vindication wholly ignores the fact that the capitulation was made a nullity by Colonel Butler, and, of course, was not obligatory on the other party.

We shall not farther tax the reader's time and patience with refutations of the sophisms of this famous letter. Colonel Stone, in the largeness of his charity, calls it a "straightforward, manly letter." We regard it as a "straightforward" evasion, with nothing "manly" about it. The bad temper and barefaced falsehoods of the letter constitute another illustration, in addition to the many which the histories record, of the cowardly cruelty and meanness of Walter N. Butler, one of the Tory leaders in the border wars. Brant, although bad enough—ay, quite too bad for endurance—was almost a saint when compared with the younger Butler. Thanks to his imprisonment in Albany that the Wyoming massacre was not aggravated by manifold more horrors than it has been our painful task to record.

### WAS BRANT AT THE WYOMING MASSACRE?

The question of Brant's presence at the battle of Wyoming has been much discussed and differently decided. An impression that Brant was at the head of the Indians on that occasion has long been strong and quite general among the people of Wyoming—the impression originating from the old settlers and actors in that fatal and ill-advised encounter. Mr. Chapman, the first historian of Wyoming, in accordance with the popular tradition, asserts Brant's presence and lead on the occasion. Mr. Campbell, the historian of Tryon County, takes the same view of the question; while Thomas Campbell, the poet, with our own poets, Halleck and Whittier, poetize in the same direction. The able biographer of Brant—Colonel Stone—takes the other side of the question; while Mr. Miner presents reasons *pro* and *con*, and leaves his readers to judge of their force for themselves.

Colonel Stone rests the cause upon the denial of Brant, and the credibility of Indian and Tory witnesses. It seems rather strange that the ingenious author did not address himself to the task of proving an *alibi*, a thing which it may be supposed was very possible at the time he collected his materials. John Franklin once said in relation to Colonel Stone's witnesses, "You won't make such witnesses believed in old Wyoming: people there would take their *lives*, but never the *words* of Indians and Tories." The argument of the too partial biographer of Brant was also questioned by others besides the people of "old Wyoming." A review of "The Life of Brant" in the *Democratic Review*, supposed to have been written by the Hon. Caleb Cushing, controverts the author's positions, and shows their inconclusiveness. In 1846, in an article in the *Methodist Quarterly*, we took the same ground.

It is reasonable to ask where Brant was on the 3d of July, 1778, if he was not, as usual, at Colonel John Butler's elbow. He was with him the previous year at the battle of Oriskany, and the year following on the Chemung, when General Sullivan marched into the lake country. They were often united in border warfare, Butler commanding the Tories, and Brant the Indians. These questions are entitled to fair consideration and a satisfactory answer, and we shall now look at them with candor.

After much examination of the subject, we have reached the conclusion that during the entire summer of 1778 Brant was in the Valley of the Mohawk and on the head waters of the Susquehanna—at his head-quarters at Ocquaga or Unadilla, and, consequently, that he was not in the Valley of Wyoming at the time of the battle. In June the historians tell us that Brant and his Indians burned the settlement at Springfield, near the head of Otsego Lake.

Taking another step in advance, we certainly find Brant at Unadilla on the 9th of July, from an authentic letter of his published by Mr. Campbell, which we have copied above. This letter relates to supplies for his men, and acknowledges the receipt of corn from a Mr. Smith. We will now connect this fact with another. C. L. Ward, Esq., in an address delivered at the Pioneer Festival held in Owego on the 22d of February, 1855, asserted that the younger Brant had shown him "a receipt, in the handwriting of his father, for money paid for corn and other provisions, dated on the 5th day of July, 1778, two days after the battle, and while the British forces were in Wyoming." This receipt harmonizes exactly with the letter to Pursifer Carr, dated the 9th, which refers to transactions of the same class. It may farther be observed that Unadilla is the only locality where Brant would be likely to purchase supplies for his men at the date of the receipt. There he had his head-quarters, and when he visited other places he plundered provisions in abundance, and was under no necessity of purchasing of Tories. The chief could not have come from Wyoming after the battle on the 3d in time to be in negotiation for supplies in Unadilla on the 5th. The facts above established quite conclusively prove the alibi.

We next refer to a dispatch from Colonel Guy Johnson to Lord George Germaine, dated New York, 10th September, 1778. The following is the portion of the dispatch which relates to the question in hand:

"Your lordship will have heard before this can reach you of the successful incursions of the Indians and Loyalists from the northward. In conformity to the instructions I conveyed to my officers, they assembled their force early in May, and one division, under one of my deputies (Mr. Butler), proceeded down the Susquehanna, destroying the forts and settlements at Wyoming, augmenting their number with many Loyalists, and alarming all the country, while another division, under Mr. Brant, the Indian chief, cut off 294 men near Schoharie, and destroyed the adjacent settlements, with several magazines from whence the rebels had derived great resources, thereby affording encouragement and opportunity to many friends of government to join them."—*Documents relating to the Colonial History of the State of New York*, vol. viii., p. 752.

This dispatch shows clearly that Brant led the Indians in the incursions upon the settlements in the Mohawk Valley and on the head waters of the Susquehanna, while Butler made his raid upon Wyoming. Brant must consequently be identified with the hostile movements of the Indians and Tories which we have sketched above. There was, indeed, so far as we have yet been able to ascertain, no one engagement in which that "chief cut off 294 men" during the space of time embraced in Colonel Johnson's dispatch. The colonel must embrace all the persons killed in the small actions which occurred in the Mohawk Valley, and all the murders of the savages committed through the various settlements during the months of June, July, and August. The colonel's dispatch was probably based upon a report from Brant of the number of scalps taken *during the summer:* if this is not the explanation of the matter, we are at present unable to give any that would be likely to be satisfactory.

This document clearly proves that Brant was in the Valley of the Mohawk while Butler was in the Valley of Wyoming.

Another fact we have to adduce is that of a certificate of protection, given to one of the settlers, dated "Westmoreland, July 5th, 1778," and signed by "John Butler" and "Kayenguaurton." Colonel Butler varies the orthography of this name, probably from mere carelessness, and we have followed him. Colonel Stone and Mr. Lossing give us the name of this chief thus— "Gi-en-gwa-toh, which signifies, *He who goes in the smoke.*" Butler styles himself "Superintendent of the Six Nations," and his associate is called "the Chief of the Seneca Nation." The name of the chief is evidently written by Colonel Butler, but the outlines of a turtle—🐢—at the left of the name, signifying that the chief belonged to the turtle tribe of the Seneca nation, was probably executed by the chief himself.

This document has every internal evidence of authenticity. We have examined it with great care, and have no doubt of its having been written by Colonel Butler at the date which it bears, and signed, so far as he was able to sign it, by the chief who led on the Indians in the battle. It is in the hands of a literary friend, who kindly allowed us to examine it. No one will doubt that if Joseph Brant had been the leader of the Indians on the occasion of the battle, his name would have been attached to the document in his own handwriting.

Finally, we adduce the report of Colonel John Butler to Colonel Bolton, never before published, as in itself absolutely conclusive. In this report he says the Indians were led on by a Seneca chief by the name of *Gucingeracton*.

For these reasons, each of which alone is sufficient to satisfy any unprejudiced mind, we hope it will be considered as settled that Brant had no part in the Wyoming massacre.

The historians generally, both English and American, set down "the famous Mohawk chief Brant" as the ferocious leader of the Indians at the Wyoming massacre, and, so far as appears, Brant took no pains to correct the general impression. Thomas Campbell, the poet, in his Gertrude, in the lines at the head of this sketch, assumes the truth of the tale, and calls the chief "the monster Brant." After the war had closed, Brant settled in Canada, and died there. In 1822, his son, "John Brant, Esq., of Grand River," visited England, and made it a point to convince the poet that his father was not at Wyoming at all, and that, instead of being a "monster," he was a humane, brave, and a magnanimous foe. The first point he doubtless established, and the second the poet conceded, albeit, after yielding to the proof, he proceeds to refute it. Mr. Campbell, the historian, publishes the letter of Mr. Campbell, the poet, to John Brant, Esq., in his Appendix. We would copy this letter if it were not that its length and the irrelevancy of the greater portion of it make it inexpedient. The letter is dated "London, January, 1822." It acknowledges the receipt of certain "documents" forwarded by Mr. John Brant, and proceeds in an apologetic strain, of which the following brief paragraph may be considered as an expression of the spirit, and as an exponent of the sense:

"In short, I imbibed my conception of your father from accounts of him that were published when I was scarcely out of my cradle. And if there were any public, direct, and specific challenge to those accounts in England ten years ago, I am yet to learn where they existed."

Now we yield the point of Brant's immediate connection with the Wyoming massacre, but we are sorry not to be able as fully to yield to the claim made for him in certain quarters to more than common humanity and magnanimity. Little more evidence is needed to put those claims into doubt than the facts presented in Colonel Stone's apologetic life of the great Mohawk chief. The "cruelties" perpetrated in the Mohawk Valley during the years 1777 and 1778, where Brant was continually present, and where he was the presiding genius, are, if possible, more revolting than those perpetrated at Wyoming. In Wyoming the women and children were not murdered after the capitulation of the fort, but in Cherry Valley no sex or age was spared. We are aware that it is said that Walter Butler had command on that occasion. Yes, and Walter Butler says that "*the Indians*" perpetrated the "cruelties" at Cherry Valley, for the reason that, "being charged by their enemies with what they never had done, and threatened by them, they had determined to convince you that it was not fear which had prevented them." Now, as each party accuses the other, and no one doubts but both had a part in those "cruelties," it is but historical justice to divide the responsibilities between them. In fact, the steps of Brant, wherever he went, were red with the blood, not only of men, but of "*women and children.*" He sometimes did spare them, but at other times *he did not;* and, indeed, the former was the exception, and the latter the rule.

What, then, is gained by the friends of the chief when they have proved that he was not at the Wyoming massacre? Absolutely nothing; for his Mohawks and Tories were engaged in the same, and even greater "cruelties," in the valley of the Mohawk, and upon the head waters of the Susquehanna and the Delaware at the same time, and during the remainder of the war.

It will not be unfair now to direct the attention of the reader to a few instances of Brant's "cruelties."

The first instance we would refer to is the murder of his former friend, Lieutenant Wormwood, an account of which we have given.

Another instance is related by Mr. Campbell, as follows: "He often said that, during the war, he had killed but one man in cool blood, and that act he ever after regretted. He said he had taken a man prisoner, and was examining him; the prisoner hesitated, and, as he thought, equivocated. Enraged at what he considered obstinacy, he struck him down. It turned out that the man's apparent obstinacy arose from a natural hesitancy of speech." This case is distinctly described and specially marked.

Still another instance is clearly distinguished from the foregoing. It is related by Mr. Weld, a European traveler. In a skirmish with a body of American troops Brant was wounded in the heel, but the Americans, in the end, were defeated, and an officer taken prisoner. The officer, after having delivered up his sword, entered into conversation with Sir John Johnson, when Brant stole slyly behind them and laid the officer low with a blow of his hatchet. Sir John was indignant, and he resented the treachery in the warmest terms. Brant listened to him without concern, and, when he had concluded, told him that he was sorry for his displeasure, but that his heel was exceedingly painful at the moment, but, since he had avenged himself upon the only chief of the party which they had taken, it was much less painful than it had been before.—See *Border Warfare*, p. 249, 250.

Mr. Campbell had heard another version of this story, in which "it was stated that an officer was killed to prevent his being retaken by the Americans, who were in pursuit of the Indians." This story which the historian had heard may have been another instance still of Brant's cruelty, for it differs from either of the preceding relations. Indeed, the three descriptions above given can not be different versions of the same fact. The reasons for the murder are unlike each other, and are wholly incompatible, and the circumstances are equally various and inconsistent with the idea of their having occurred in the self-same case. It is in vain to try to

"Wash the Ethiop white."

One cold-blooded, unprovoked murder is enough to characterize a moral "monster" — many acts of the same class certainly do not relieve the case. We may judge the conduct of the chief too severely. Of this the reader will make up his mind in view of all the facts. All we aim at is historical justice; and this, at all hazards, we shall labor to secure.

Colonel John Butler, when the Revolutionary struggle came on, was a government functionary under Sir William Johnson, and after Sir William's death he became warmly attached to Sir John and Colonel Guy Johnson. When he fled with the Johnsons to Canada, his family fell into the hands of the patriots, and were exchanged for the wife and children of Colonel Campbell, of Cherry Valley. He was exceedingly active in the border conflicts. He commanded a regiment of Rangers in conjunction with Brant and his Mohawks, and was a fearful scourge to the patriots of Tryon County. He marched at the head of his Rangers, and a motley mass of Tories and Indians, upon Wyoming in 1778, and was there implicated in the most savage barbarities. His report of the transactions of that expedition, which we have given to the reader in another place, is a disgrace to civilization and humanity. He accompanied Sir John Johnson in his murderous onslaught upon the Mohawk and Schoharie settlements in 1780. His old residence is situated in

THE BUTLER HOUSE.

the Mohawk Valley, near Fonda. His property was confiscated by an act of the New York Legislature, but was amply reimbursed by the British government. He succeeded Guy Johnson as Indian Agent, with a salary of $2000 per annum, and was granted a pension, as a military officer, of $1000 in addition. He lost caste with the high-minded British officers on account of his savage cruelties in the border war, and particularly in Wyoming. It is said that on that account Sir Frederick Haldemand, then Governor of Canada, refused to see him.—See *Lossing's Field-Book*.

It is claimed that Colonel Butler was not so infamously cruel as his son Walter, and that he might have dictated more severe terms to Colonel Denison and the settlers in Forty Fort after the battle. All this we admit, and yet it is not saying much in favor of the great Tory leader. There may be many shades between the brutal and diabolical cruelties of Walter Butler and the modified savageism of Brant which are still at a vast distance from the laws of civilized warfare, and which are entitled to little respect from the historian. No man knew better the character of the warfare carried on by Tories and Indians than Colonel John Butler. He set on these bloodhounds, and, in some instances at least, encouraged them to do their worst. Prisoners of war and the wounded, while begging for quarter, were cruelly tortured, after the battles of Oriskany and Wyoming, under his immediate command. What great relief to the character of the Tory is it to say that he did not order the old men, women, and children in Forty Fort to be butchered? He might almost as well have done it, for he allowed them to be plundered of their food and clothing, and driven to the mountains to starve and be devoured by wild beasts. Sure enough, "The tender mercies of the wicked are cruel."

After the war Colonel Butler settled in Canada, and lived till about the year 1800, when he went to his accounts. He applied to the British government to be *knighted*, but failed, as we judge from the fact that we have never seen him dignified with the title of *Sir*.

He is not, even by historians but too tender of his reputation, called *Sir* John Butler, but simply Colonel Butler. An interesting anecdote touching his efforts to secure the honors of knighthood we shall insert in another connection.

## III.

### COLONEL MATTHIAS HOLLENBACK.

THE materials for the following sketch of one of the leading characters concerned in the stirring events of the history of Wyoming are derived partly from our own personal knowledge of the man, but principally from members of his family who are now living. To Mrs. H. D. ALEXANDER, Colonel Hollenback's *stepdaughter*, we are indebted for the greatest portion of the facts; and we owe many thanks to her granddaughter, *Miss E. P. Alexander*, for a beautiful manuscript, in which these facts are neatly and comprehensively written down. We have found little occasion for alteration in the manuscript, excepting in cases in which the statements have to be somewhat modified in view of other information. We have also to acknowledge our obligations to Hon. G. M. Hollenback, only son of Colonel Hollenback. Mrs. Alexander's father was killed in the battle when she was but a few weeks old, and Colonel Hollenback subsequently married her mother. Her knowledge of the history and incidents in the life of Colonel Hollenback is more complete than that of any person now living, and her recollections of facts and conversations of ancient date are exceedingly clear and definite. She has stored away in her memory a vast mass of facts which she learned from her mother and her stepfather in relation to the days of Wyoming's troubles. A portion of them are here given to the public. Many more might have been incorporated in this sketch did our space permit.

What we give may be relied upon with the utmost confidence.

Matthias Hollenback was born on the Swatara Creek, at Jonestown, Lebanon County, then Lancaster, Pennsylvania, on the 17th day of February, A.D. 1752. He was the second son of John Hollenback and Eleanor Jones, a lady of Welsh descent: his paternal grandfather came from Germany.

Mr. Hollenback came to Wyoming in 1769, in a company of forty young men from that part of the country. They were Stuarts, Espys, Youngs, and others, and they came with the intention of settling and becoming citizens under Connecticut laws, and aiding the Yankees in keeping possession of the country. They became entitled to lands under Connecticut claims, which they drew after they had been a short time in the valley. When Mr. Hollenback came to Wyoming he was about seventeen years of age; for enterprise, foresight, and force of character he was, however, "a man, every inch of him." The company encamped where Mauch Chunk is now situated; and, after the coal interest had called into existence a thriving town there, Colonel Hollenback often humorously remarked that he ought to put in a claim to that place, for he was first in possession. The forty adventurers came into Wyoming through a notch of the mountain in what is now Hanover; and when the beautiful valley first broke upon their sight, young Hollenback, the youngest of the company, threw up his hat, and screamed out, "Hurrah! that's the place for me." His companions laughed, one of them remarking, "Never mind, Mat; he'll do well enough."

The first land owned by Mr. Hollenback was the

tract now owned by the Lazarus family in Buttonwood, in Hanover Township.

He immediately commenced business as a merchant, having brought a small stock of goods with him. His first store was at or near the Block-house, at the mouth of Mill Creek. The stock comprised such articles as were then actually needed by the settlers, such as groceries, ammunition, etc. He did not continue long at Mill Creek, but came to Wilkesbarre; and, having purchased a lot on what is now the west side of the public square, built a large frame house for a store and dwelling, and considered himself permanently established, having brought on his younger brother John, and sister Mary Ann, to live with him; the one took charge of his business in his many absences, and the other managed his household.

His goods were purchased in Philadelphia, taken in wagons to Middletown on the Susquehanna, and then transported by water. The first method of transportation was by Indian canoes; and he literally "paddled his own canoe" up the winding, rapid Susquehanna the whole distance, 150 miles, many times before he was able to procure a more capacious vessel and to employ men to manage it. Then he purchased a Durham boat, which he kept steadily employed. At this period, the present road leading through the swamp was but a single bridle-path.

Mr. Hollenback, in his business enterprises, was prospered in a remarkable manner, and soon acquired distinction, and was promoted to positions of public trust and responsibility.

His first military commission is now before us, and is dated "17th day of October, in the 15th year of the reign of our sovereign lord, GEORGE the Third, King of Great Britain, &c., *Annoque Domini* 1775." It is an ensign's commission in the "trained band in the 24th regiment in his majesty's colony of Connecticut.

On the 26th of August, 1776, he was appointed by Congress to serve as ensign in Captain Durkee's company of "minute-men," a band raised for the protection of the people in the Valley; but when the Wyoming companies were ordered to join General Washington's army, he went with his companions in arms to the post of danger. Mr. Hollenback was with the army in New Jersey in 1776 and 1777, and fought in several battles. He was in the battles of Millstone, Trenton, Princeton, and Germantown. That he was a man of more than ordinary courage and tact is evident from the fact that he was more than once employed by Washington as a runner to visit the frontier settlements and outposts, and report their danger or safety. About the close of 1777, the face of things beginning to wear a terrifying appearance in Wyoming, many of the men who were with the army came home, and among them was Mr. Hollenback. Those who remained were transferred to the command of Captain Simon Spaulding.

After leaving the army, Mr. Hollenback not only addressed himself to his own affairs, but also kept a vigilant eye on events of public interest; and, with the natural sagacity for which he was remarkable, saw omens of the danger and trial which were in a brief space of time so fearfully realized, holding himself in readiness for action the moment that the war-cry should sound its dread call to the strife.

About the last day of June or the first day of July, 1778, the people of the Valley, learning that the enemy were on their way down the river, and that there was danger of being surprised by them, sent out scouting-parties to observe and report the movements of the Indians and Tories. The last scouts who went up were Hollenback, and a man whose name is not now known. They proceeded fifteen or sixteen miles directly up the river, and found the trail of the Indians, which led across the mountain; and also found the bodies of the two young Hardings, who had just been killed, being freshly scalped and much mutilated. They found a canoe, in which they embarked, bringing the murdered men with them, and returned down the river to Jenkins's Fort, where they were met by the survivors of the Harding family. The men who were killed had gone up for the purpose of hoeing corn, and had taken their arms with them, but were surprised by the Indians, some killed, and the rest taken prisoners, with the exception of a boy who hid himself in the river and escaped.

The man who was with Mr. Hollenback was so overcome by the sight of his dead friends that he begged to be put on shore, declaring that he would die with fear if he staid in the canoe. Mr. Hollenback endeavored to prevail on him to stay, but at length landed him, and came in alone to the fort; and upon arriving there reported that it would be useless to send out more scouts, as the foe were so near at hand, and all the men they had were needed where they were; that the allied fiends were rapidly approaching the Valley, and in great strength compared with those who were to resist them.

Forty Fort, on the west side of the river, was the place of rendezvous for the patriots, and they now began to collect in earnest, coming to the fort from Wilkesbarre and the country below, mustering all who were able to take part in the fight, and some of them bringing their families. This was on Thursday, 2d of July.

On Friday morning they marched from the fort in order to give battle to the foe, under the principal command of Colonel Zebulon Butler, an officer belonging to the standing army, who was here at the time on leave of absence, and had been requested to take the command by Colonel Nathan Denison, which he did, taking charge of the right wing, Denison taking the left.

Upon issuing from the fort, they moved toward a high bank or rise of ground above Shoemaker's, where Colonel Butler proposed to halt, and form the army to better advantage for giving the enemy battle, thinking it a good position for them to take, and, if possible, maintain. But Captain Lazarus Stuart opposed the plan, declaring that if Butler did not move on and take a stand farther up, *he would report him at headquarters as a coward.* Butler replied that he did not fear to go, but that it was throwing away an advantageous position, and they would have cause to repent it; and so the event proved. Mrs. Alexander says:*
"In passing the house of Mr. Sutton, they were met by him and requested to halt, he telling them that, as the day was very sultry, he had made some hasty preparation for their refreshment, by setting out a table in his house with pails of *water* and cups to drink from, and that all were in readiness for them. His kindness was very acceptable, and the men were formed into companies of twelve, and, by marching in order around

---

* What is here related must have taken place just before the little army left the fort, as Mrs. Bedford distinctly informs us that Mr. Sutton and his family were at the time in the fort.

the table, drank, many of them, their last draught of fair water. There was *one bottle of rum* given, but it was hardly tasted. This was told me by Mrs. Sutton when we went to be present at the raising of the bones of the slain in 1832, and proposed to erect a monument to commemorate the massacre. So the infamous report, which has been current for some years past, and told for truth by men who had no interest in or regard for the good name of our fathers, that those martyrs who fell on the day of Wyoming's doom were under the influence of rum, is a base lie! and admits of no milder name. Those true men were driven to death and flight, not by force of liquor, but by fearful odds, and the combined force of *four hundred Tories* and *five hundred Indian demons* thirsting and eager for their blood. That devoted band of *three hundred and fifty*, who went out to battle for all that was dear to them, were of too strong a mould to be led into the satisfaction of an unholy thirst for *rum*, and their descendants should fight as valiantly to remove the foul stain from their names as *they* did upon that fatal day when all was lost but honor."

As the little army marched up the plains, they were met by a white flag, the signal of a truce, which, instead of advancing, began to recede, and, strange as it may seem, the patriots followed it. Mr. Hollenback, who was at that time acting as one of Colonel Butler's lieutenants, opposed this measure, and proposed halting and considering the unmilitary action of the flag. But Colonel Butler had resolved upon his measures, influenced by the banters of the fighting party, and he thought it was too late to hesitate. The enemy gave way on the right as our men commenced the action. For a brief space the fortunes of the day seemed to be on our side. "But Butler perceiving," says Mrs. Alexander, "the enemy to be pressing on Denison's wing, sent him the order to *flank* on the left wing, and be ready to receive their shock. Denison, mistaking the order for that of retreat, and unused to military tactics, gave the word to 'Retreat a little,' instead of '*Fall back and flank out.*' It was necessary for them to fall back, as there was a swamp to be avoided. Rufus Bennet, who was near Denison at the time, told me this, and that it was the want of Denison using the proper military terms, more than his fright, that caused the order to be so construed, by which means our men were thrown into confusion, and totally unprepared for the terrible slaughter that awaited them, as they broke and turned to fly upon hearing the order. Colonel Butler endeavored to rally them, but they were so panic-stricken that the effort was without effect, and the enemy had possession of the field.

"Our men took to flight, such of them as had escaped death on the field, and the Indians, in full chase, commenced their work of slaughter."

The substance of the following account of Mr. Hollenback's escape has been furnished by his son, Hon. George M. Hollenback, of Wilkesbarre.

Mr. Hollenback was fighting on the right wing, beside Captain Durkee. The firing having ceased on the left, Captain Durkee requested him to run around the smoke and learn the cause. He returned with the answer, "The left wing is all broken up; the men are flying, and the Indians are killing them in all directions;" adding, "Captain Durkee, we must look out, or we shall soon be surrounded." At this moment the captain was shot in the thigh, and fell, exclaiming, 'Hollenback, for God's sake save me!' His faithful brother in arms seized the wounded hero and carried him some distance toward the river, the murderous savages being in hot pursuit. About to be overtaken, he was obliged to leave the unhappy man and run for his life. The Indians scalped Captain Durkee. Three or four pursued Hollenback, who had but a few moments the start. The fearful race was for a mile and a half down the river toward Monocasy Island. Hollenback intended to cross the rift at the head of the island. Seeing, however, that point full of his hunted comrades, and the Indians tomahawking them in the river, he changed his mind. The Indians close upon him, at a point some sixty rods above the point of the island, he suddenly sprang from the bank of the river among the willows into a bank of sand.

He had thrown off his clothing in the chase, retaining, however, some Continental money and a bill of exchange. These he put in his hat, and a piece of gold in his mouth, and plunged into the river. The Indians immediately commenced firing at him. The balls struck the water on both sides of him. He dove and swam under water as long as he could hold his breath. Rising again to the surface, he swam for his life, dodging under the water at the flash of the gun. In one instance he was not quite quick enough. A ball grazed his skin, when he opened his mouth and lost his piece of gold. He, however, retained his hat, his Continental money, and bill of exchange. He reached the eastern shore, and, supposing himself to be shot, he felt for the ball-hole, but found none. Entirely destitute of clothing, he reached the top of the bank, and entered the woods at what was called Cooper's Swamp. He there met Solomon Bennet, who had come out of the battle ahead of him. Bennet had his hunting-shirt and pantaloons, and Hollenback begged him to divide, which, with the characteristic generosity of a patriot and a soldier, he promptly did, giving him the hunting-shirt, and retaining the pantaloons for himself.

Remaining in the swamp about an hour to rest, our hero then made the best of his way through the woods, over the hills, avoiding all paths; exhausted by his prodigious efforts, and scratched with briers, he reached his home about one o'clock on the morning of the 4th of July.

The noble citizen soldier sought no permanent repose or exemption from the common danger. He remained at his own house only long enough to put on some clothing, and walked directly to Fort Wyoming, the site of the present old court-house. He announced his name at the gate, heard it repeated within: "Hollenback has come!" was the joyful exclamation. "No, no," responded the familiar voice of Nathan Carey, "you'll never see Hollenback again. He was on the right wing. I am sure he is killed." The gate was opened, however, and Hollenback stepped in. It being dark, and there being no candles, Nathan Carey lit a pine knot to see if it was really Hollenback, and then, overwhelmed with joy, embraced him with a brother's affection.

At four o'clock, this heroic man, without waiting to sleep a wink, pushed out on an Indian path, braving all dangers, to meet Spaulding with his seventy men, with a view of getting them into Wyoming Fort, to hold it against their savage foes. He met them at Bear Creek, but Captain Spaulding declined the hazard. Hollenback, however, so far prevailed as to induce fifteen or twenty of the men to accompany him, and on reaching the slope of the mountain near "Prospect Rock," he discovered his own house on fire; and a greater calamity soon appeared. The savages were in possession of the fort. Seeing all lost, he promptly directed his energies to the relief of the sufferers. He had procured from Spaulding's commissary all the provisions he could pack on his horse, and, following the fugitives, mostly women and children, he overtook them and fed them through the wilderness. He went to the Wind-Gap, and at Heller's and Easton followed grubbing a few weeks at twenty-five cents per day. He then returned to the Valley and set about repairing his loss. His credit at Philadelphia being good, he obtained a few goods, and began the world anew.

We now return to a few circumstances narrated by Mrs. Alexander, which occurred upon his reaching his house on the night of the fatal 3d of July.

When it was known that he had returned, every one was eager to question him concerning the fate of the day, and one Betsy Smith came in great haste to make inquiries after some of her friends, but was unable to speak with him, being met by his servant Jeanie, who demanded of her, "Could she na let the mon alane, gin his claithes were put on?" when Miss Smith tendered her apologies, not knowing the state of his *entrée* into town.

Jeanie was a lass from the land o' cakes, and was always spoken of as "Scotch Jeanie." Mr. Hollenback had paid her passage-money from the old country, as was quite customary in those days; and Jeanie not only worked out the amount, but remained in his family for some time, very much trusted, and was the last to leave his house, saying that she would stay and protect her master's property as long as she could.

After a little relaxation, Mr. Hollenback visited Spaulding's company to obtain, if possible, some men to return to Wyoming with him. Spaulding opposed his returning then, and ordered him into the ranks. He obliged him to stay there, near the Delaware, for nearly six weeks. At length he, with Lieutenant Jenkins, John Carey, and others, to the number of fifteen, came back to Pittston to learn what they could of the enemy's movements. In looking about, they observed a smoke issuing from the old block-house on the other side of the river, and a canoe moored near it, of which they concluded to possess themselves. Hollenback swam over, took the "dug-out," and was fired at, but not hit. They then started for Wilkesbarre, some in the canoe, the others on foot. Among the latter, Carey, Jenkins, and Hollenback.

On the way down they came upon a party of Indians who were driving a yoke of oxen loaded with plunder. Jenkins, being the superior officer of the party, ordered to "Halt!" but Hollenback shouted, "Rush on!" and, with Carey at his heels, flew after the Indians, who fled, leaving their booty, which the party took, and came on to the fort in Wilkesbarre.

Then, hearing of some disturbance in the lower part of Hanover, they asked Butler to let them have some more men, and they would go down and see about it. They wanted a company, but only got fifteen, making thirty in all. They proceeded down as far as Alden's, or Forge Creek, now Lee's, to Commer's Mill, where they found the Indians had been plundering, but had not got over the river. They were in a canoe. The party divided, and followed them on each side of the creek to its mouth, where they surprised and fired on them: one appeared to reel, as if to fall in the river, but recovered himself, being only wounded. The Indians left the plunder which they had taken at the mill; it consisted of a bag of flour, a bag of cucumbers, a bag of meat, a pair of boots, and a hat, all of which the men brought up to town with them.

The remains of the slain were collected and buried in a common grave, on the 22d of October. In relation to that event, Mrs. Alexander remarks: "I have conversed with several, besides Mr. Hollenback, who were present at the burial, and recognized many of the dead, though it was hard to identify them, as they had lain so long in the hot sun, and had been scalped and otherwise mutilated. Mr. Cooper, who afterward lived at the 'Plains,' told my mother, the late Mrs. Matthias Hollenback, that he saw my father, Cyprian Hebberd, her first husband, interred with the others.

"My father had gone up with the others on the 2d of July from Hanover, where he resided, and had left my mother, with her parents and friends, in Stuart's block-house, in Buttonwood, giving her all the money he had at the time, between sixteen and seventeen pounds, a good horse and saddle for her to ride, and another to be led, as he was certain they would be obliged to flee. I was then an infant of about two weeks old, having been born on the 18th of June.

"Father had an idea that he would not return, and accordingly made the best preparation he could for the welfare of his family in case he should not. He was in the Hanover company, who were stationed in the left wing, under command of Colonel Denison; and, after the fatal order of retreat had been given, seeing that it was useless to remain upon the field, he joined the others in the flight to the river. He was a very active man, and remarkably agile. Samuel Carey, who was with him, has told me that he would certainly have made his escape, but that, in running through a field of tall rye, instead of springing over it, he broke it down to make the way easier for his fugitive companions, and by so doing retarded his own flight, and was overtaken by the Indians and surrounded. Carey managed to reach the river and get into the water; but my father, exhausted with running and breaking down the grain, was just stepping in, when a stalwart Indian overtook him, and, plunging a spear into him, gave him his death-wound. He fell in the edge of the water, in sight of Carey, who told me the fact. Carey was taken prisoner by the Indians, and remained with them five years in captivity.

"The night of the 3d of July, Halldron, a tenant of my father's, came to the block-house in Buttonwood, and told the party there that they must leave it, as the Indians would be upon them before morning. But my grandmother, Mrs. Burritt, said she did not think they would be along before the third day after; nor were they. However, the party set out immediately, and proceeded two miles, then halted, and waited the rising of the moon, the night being very dark; then set out on their journey again, and were three days and nights in getting to Fort Allen, now Allentown, on the Lehigh. The second night there was a child born in the camp, the son of Mrs. Morris, whose husband was in the battle, but escaped.

"When they reached the Lehigh a man came over the river to meet them, riding a powerful horse, and bringing a bag of biscuit and two large jugs of milk, with which he fed them, and also helping such as had no horses of their own to cross the river, by taking two at a time on his own horse, and fording them over.

"The party had suffered much for want of water on the road, and when they got to the Lehigh both man and beast were eager to quench their thirst. The horse my mother rode put down its head so suddenly as to jerk the bridle from her hand, and I, whom she carried in her bridle-arm, was thrown from her grasp, and but for her catching my clothes quick as thought, I had closed a brief life by drowning in the Lehigh.

"The route which was taken by the fugitive party was called the 'Warrior's Path,' and led from Wyoming to Fort Allen. Some vestiges of it still exist, and it is noted in the old surveys and maps. The party were three weeks on the road from Wyoming to Connecticut, the place of their destination."

Mr. Hollenback was for a time so discouraged by the turn of affairs in Wyoming and the unsettled state of things there, that he left and went to Easton, where he lived with some of his acquaintances, but did not remain long. He was calculated for a life of activity and business, and was ill at ease while he was not actively and profitably employed. As his interests were all in Wyoming, he returned, built another house and store—still standing in Wilkesbarre—and once more embarked in mercantile pursuits, taking into partnership a Mr. Hagaman. As was the case before, the man was remarkably successful, extending his business, enlarging his influence, and increasing rapidly his pecuniary resources.

The inhabitants of Wyoming had hardly become settled after the trouble with the Indians when the Pennamite feud again broke out, in which Mr. Hollenback took an active part on the Yankee side. He rendered the New England people good service, not so much in fighting as by giving those who did fight the "aid and comfort" they needed—affording them at his establishment powder, lead, and provisions. A party of Yankees retired to the mountain for safety, and constructed under a hanging rock a rude fortification, calling it "Lillapie," or Fort Lillapie. To this hiding-place Mr. Hollenback frequently sent a stock of ammunition and eatables by trusty adherents to the cause, and assisted the party in various other ways. These civil wars very much retarded the progress of the country, and we now can hardly imagine the amount of trouble attendant on them. Much mischief was done by the Pennamites in the exercise of their authority, and many people were killed in the various skirmishes. Colonel Pickering came here, on the part of the Pennsylvanians, to adjust matters between them and the Yankees, but the affair was a tedious one, and a long time elapsed before its conclusion. The Yankees finally adopted Pennsylvania laws, and their lands were resurveyed and apportioned again under Pennsylvania warrants.

After the establishment of peace between the United States and Great Britain, Mr. Hollenback made the experiment of going with a large drove of cattle to Niagara. On arriving there he was taken prisoner by the British and Indians, they not having been informed officially of peace being made between the two nations. They kept him six weeks, until the intelligence was received, after which his captors purchased his cattle, and he realized a large profit. He made considerable money by this trip, and was encouraged to keep up the trade.

Determined to extend his business operations, he bought lands at Tioga Point—now Athens—and Newtown—now Elmira—where he established stores in order to trade with the Indians, and laid in a stock, at both places, of such articles as would attract their custom, and for which they would exchange their furs and peltries.

On one occasion he took a number of men with him, and went up to their town, on the Seneca Lake, to make arrangements with them and obtain their trade. But the Indians were suspicious that the party had come for the purpose of surveying and taking away their lands, and consequently made them all prisoners. All their baggage underwent a thorough search to see if there was a compass with the party, and Mr. Hollenback always thought that, had one been discovered, they would have paid the penalty with their lives. They counciled, and came to the conclusion at least to kill him, as he led the party, and even sent some distance for a young brave to come and kill the "Shinnewany." Mr. Hollenback said he felt somewhat alarmed, but took care not to manifest the fact; and when the chief entered the wigwam, he returned his steady and fixed gaze with one equally as steady. He rose and extended his hand; the chief had his tomahawk raised for instant use, and had, without doubt, intended to dispatch him; but his coolness and friendly bearing had its effect, and the brave gave him to understand that he need not fear, and seemed willing to hear what he had to say. After having conferred with him, and finding that his was a peaceful errand, that he had no idea of getting their lands, but wished to trade with them, he set him and his party at liberty, and agreed to influence his tribe to bring their trade and furs to Newtown. The result was their good-will and continued trade for many years after.

He went many times to Niagara with cattle, and

once collected a large drove, which he intrusted to a young man to take there; the fellow sold the cattle, and ran off with the money, Mr. Hollenback losing the whole.

In 1783, a treaty between the whites and Indians was held at Newtown. Mr. Hollenback had been employed by the government to furnish the Indians with all they required while they were there. In this operation he made about a thousand pounds. Colonel Pickering was the person who treated with them, and was so much of a favorite that they complimented him by giving him a name which, in English, means "the side of a mountain."

The famous John Jacob Astor was at this time doing business in Philadelphia, where Mr. Hollenback made his acquaintance as a customer. In 1789, by arrangement, Astor accompanied his friend from Wilkesbarre, up the Susquehanna, and so on to Canada. On the way they crossed the outlet of the Seneca, which was much swollen by a heavy rain, in which act Astor came near losing his life. He was not then accustomed to fording streams on horseback, and in the middle of the stream his head became unsteady. Hollenback, seeing Astor reel in his saddle, by a glancing stroke with the butt of his whip dashed the water in his face, and, at the same time, struck him under his chin, and roared out, "Look up, Astor!" He recovered himself, and came out of the imminent peril without harm.

It was this journey which made Astor's fortune. He saw the vast profits which could be made in the fur trade, and commenced his operations in that line. He made an effort to get his friend Hollenback to go to New York and engage in business with him; but the latter had settled his plans for life, already having considerable real estate in the Susquehanna Valley, and was not to be diverted from his purpose. These veteran traders met in New York in 1824 for the first time after their separation in Canada, and talked over their early adventures to their mutual gratification. "Hollenback, have you any sons?" inquired Astor. "I have one," was the answer. "Send him to me, and I will take care of him." "I thank you, sir; he can take care of himself," replied Colonel Hollenback.

The last trip which Mr. Hollenback made to Niagara was in 1792; and, after selling out his stock and concluding his business there, he made the discovery that the Indians were preparing to waylay and rob him on his return home. Such being the case, he laid his plans warily to elude them. His own horse being lame, he exchanged it with the landlord for another; had it taken into the woods at night and shod; and, all things being in readiness, he, with several others, started under cover of the night to pass through woods, and swamps, and over rivers, back to Pennsylvania.

There was with them an aged Dunker minister, named Rothruck, who was ill and poorly clad, and on foot. He had taken out cattle to sell in order to pay for his farm, and succeeded in getting bills of exchange for them. Mr. Hollenback was very kind to him, and helped him on as far as Owego, telling him to wait there until some rafts came down the river, and then to go to his house, and his wife would "nurse him up again." He did so, and Mrs. Hollenback clothed him, and ministered to his wants. When the wagons went down to Philadelphia for goods, he was put in one of them, and safely transported to the city, where Mr.

Hollenback got his bills negotiated, and sent him home rejoicing.

At one of the halting-places on the route the party found the vestiges of a man's clothes hanging on some bushes near a spring, and other indications of foul play with some one. They proved to be the clothes of a man—Mr. Street—who had left Niagara before them with about $2000, and had here been waylaid and murdered by a man whose name was Gale. Mr. Hollenback afterward found out the murderer, and succeeded in putting officers on his track: he was taken and hung.

Before leaving Niagara, he found that part of a notorious band of highwaymen, well known at the time and much feared—"The Doanes and Tomblesons"—were there, and also watching him closely. He ascertained that it was their purpose to follow him, and wait until he had stopped at all his trading stations, returned home, and set out again to purchase goods in Philadelphia, then to attack and rob him, as he would then have a large sum of money, and be the kind of prey they sought.

But he was too sagacious and brave to fall into their hands, though he came very near it. Soon after coming home he started for the city, and passed over the greater part of the distance before any thing occurred to alarm him. Upon riding along a sandy track in the woods one night, he heard some slight sound, and finally whispers in the bush, and his name was mentioned. Certain that he was dogged, he made all speed, and reached a sort of tavern, and disguising himself as much as possible, and also feigning drunkenness, he dismounted, and began to look about to see what kind of place it was. Seeing many strange-looking men about, and not liking the appearance of things, he did not remain long; but, before he left, he noticed a party of odd-looking fellows arrive from the same direction which he had come, who were evidently the ones he had heard in the woods, and answered well to the description of the Doanes, etc. He reached that same night another house kept by a widow, where they were in great alarm for fear of a descent by the Doanes, who were then filling the country with dread. Having taken supper, he retired to his apartment, got out his pistols, and watched the night long instead of sleeping. He arrived at the city the next day, and deposited his funds safely in the hands of Mr. Dorsie, his banker, thus escaping the Doanes and Tomblesons, who found in him too much courage and tact for their purposes.

Mr. Hollenback finally became more settled, and no longer went out on such toilsome and hazardous journeys, but remained more at home, still pursuing his business with energy and success. The mercantile business he kept up until the end of his life, and always prospered in it: his store was for many years the best in Wilkesbarre.

He was made justice of the peace after the establishment of the jurisdiction of Pennsylvania in Wyoming, and, when the new Constitution was formed, was appointed associate judge of Luzerne County courts, in which capacity he served until the time of his death, which event occurred on the 18th day of February, 1829, the day after he was seventy-seven years old. His commission as associate judge is dated "in the year of our Lord one thousand seven hundred and ninety one," under the administration of Governor Mifflin. His first commission as lieutenant colonel is dated 1787, another is dated 1792, and still another

1793. These commissions are all preserved, and are upon our table. The first of them was given by the executive council of Pennsylvania, and contains the autograph of Dr. Franklin.

When Jackson was running for President, he determined to vote for him, considering him the man most eligible for that high and honorable office. Being quite ill, he went to the polls in his carriage, and the judges came out and received his vote, the last one he ever gave. This was in November, 1828.

Colonel Hollenback always took great interest in religious affairs and the welfare of the Church. He gave largely toward building the first church built in Wilkesbarre, and was generally punctual in his attendance upon the services, never absenting himself when it was convenient to attend. His house was the home of ministers, and his hand always open to them.

He was, in many respects, an extraordinary man. There was no such word as failure in his vocabulary. He had courage and sagacity both equal to any thing in his line. In all his business relations he was a pattern of punctuality and fidelity to public trusts and private confidence.

Mrs. Alexander says: "My mother was a few months his senior. She was, in all respects, a suitable helpmeet for him, and during his long absences took the entire charge of his affairs. His confidence in her was great, he never doubting her ability. Her benevolence was remarkable, and evinced itself in more than one instance. She was the friend of the poor and needy, and, until the close of her long life, practiced that kindness and sympathy toward her fellow-creatures which her enlarged means admitted of, and her memory is held in grateful remembrance by many who are now living; and very many more, who, like her, have long since gone to 'that undiscovered country from whose bourne no traveler returns,' and can not now speak save through their descendants, were once the objects of her kind consideration. Both Judge Hollenback and his wife took an active interest in all that related to the settlement of this valley, and the stirring events of its history. They lived to see it in prosperity, and entirely recovered from the terrible blow which so nearly blotted its white settlers from existence, when they departed peacefully at the Master's summons. My mother lived some years after Father Hollenback's death. She was born the 19th of November, 1750, in Huntington, Connecticut, and died July 21st, 1833, in her eighty-third year."

Judge Hollenback was a character; he was emphatically a man for the times. He never knew fear; and that he was not reckless may be inferred from the fact that, amid the perils of his eventful life, he was never wrecked. He was brave, but not headlong. He calculated upon consequences with great precision. He was sometimes accused of obstinacy; he certainly had great firmness. Fierce and unprincipled opposition would wake up in him the *old soldier*, and he was a terrible foe. His perseverance and his power of endurance were almost beyond precedent. He took all his journeys on horseback, and his range of business was from Niagara to Philadelphia. Between Wyoming and the New York state-line he owned immense quantities of wild land. He often visited his lands personally and alone, traveling for days, and even weeks, through the wilds of Northern Pennsylvania, and being as much at home in the wilderness, without a path, as in his counting-room. When night over-

F

took him, he turned into the nearest human habitation, be it ever so humble, and made himself at home. He said to the man of the house, "Give my horse a peck of oats, or four quarts of corn;" and, entering the dwelling, perhaps a small log cabin, his language would be, "Good woman, I want a dish of mush and milk." Taking his seat while his supper was being made ready, quite likely he would fall asleep in his chair. His "mush and milk" disposed of, he perhaps asked for a blanket, and flung himself down on the floor, with his head upon his saddle-bags, and slept sweetly until daylight, when he was off. In his travels he often lay out in the woods upon the ground, covered only by the rose blanket upon which he rode.

In 1824–5, when traveling an extensive district, embracing a portion of Northern Pennsylvania and Southern New York, we often fell in with the veteran pioneer. He rode a large sorrel horse—a low-carriaged animal, but a fine racker. He would ride that animal from forty to sixty miles in a day. He often took refreshing naps on horseback, during which his horse would move quietly along, but, when he awoke to consciousness, his sagacious animal soon understood that an increase of speed was expected.

Judge Hollenback was full of life, humorous, even jocose, and fond of repartee. He was good company, full of anecdote, and was a considerable wit. He liked a good joke even when it was against himself. When free from the cares of business, he would unbend himself, and, walking back and forth across the floor, would amuse his friends, young and old, by telling stories. "Once," said he, on such an occasion, "when a lad, I crossed a grave-yard in the night, and thought I was not afraid until I made a false step and tumbled down among the graves. I was then so frightened that I bawled like a calf. I jumped up, and ran for life, thinking the ghosts were close at my heels." On one occasion, having been overtaken on the mountains by an awful thunder-storm, he said he paused under a great tree, and the thunder and the lightning were so terrible that he feared and quaked; and feeling that he ought to pray, he could think of nothing to say but " Now I lay me down to sleep," etc.

As for pride of equipage, Judge Hollenback had none. His dress was neat, but plain. He lived in a plain, old-fashioned, low frame house, planned for the purposes both of a dwelling and a store. He owned

no splendid carriage and plated harness, but traveled either on foot or upon horseback, with his saddle attired with a blanket, or a sheepskin tanned with the wool on.

Colonel Hollenback was as true-hearted a patriot as ever breathed. When the Revolutionary struggle commenced he held a military commission under the government of King George the Third, and every motive which could be presented to an aspiring and a mercenary mind was urged as a reason for his espousing the royal cause. His patriotic feelings spurned the whole. He "threw up" his royal commission, and, as soon as his services were called for, he accepted one from the Continental Congress, in the most gloomy period of the Revolutionary struggle. His sympathy for the sufferers, and his energy in supplying their wants upon the occasion of that melancholy exodus of the settlers of the 4th of July, 1778, have been referred to. We have often heard the survivors of that terrible flight dwell with enthusiasm upon Hollenback's services and manner on that occasion. His horse was loaded with bread and biscuits. He flung a loaf to one group and then to another, with his usual salutation, "God bless you! Keep up good courage; you will reach the settlement in safety," and words of like import. His timely supplies, his courage, his genial, earnest spirit, were largely instrumental in the deliverance of scores of the fugitives from death in the wilderness.

An anecdote was related to Mr. G. M. Hollenback by the late Judge Scott which furnishes a good illustration of the character of our subject. After the war was over, and Colonel John Butler was reposing upon his honors in Canada, he made application to the British government to be admitted to the honor of knighthood. His reputation had suffered in England, as well as in America, from the accounts which had been published of his cruelties in Wyoming. It was judged by his friends that if he could obtain a certificate from one of the officers who was present on the American side in that unequal conflict, to the effect that Colonel Butler's conduct was humane and soldier-like on the occasion, his application would succeed. Accordingly, a suitable messenger—a bland English gentleman—was dispatched to Wyoming. Colonel Hollenback was the man to be addressed. The agent of Butler called upon the old soldier at his office and opened the matter, taking from his pocket a parchment beautifully executed, only wanting the signature. Colonel Hollenback read it carefully; then, looking the gentleman in the eye, asked, "Do you expect me to sign this?" "Yes, sir, if you please," was the answer. "I shall not do it, for it is not true." Butler's agent urged the matter respectfully but earnestly, but the reply was reiterated, "It is not a word of it true, sir— I say, sir, it is a big lie." The dernier resort was finally reached, and that was to "a purse of gold." This was a match flung into the magazine. The fiery soul of the old patriot could no longer keep itself within due bounds. "Gold! gold!" he thundered out, with voice enough to reach the outskirts of his regiment, if he had been upon the battle-field, "your king has not got gold enough to buy me, sir." Then, loading the poor, disappointed agent with a volley of epithets, he pointed to the door, and said, "There, sir, is the door; let me never see you again upon this business." The gentleman was almost petrified, but made out to steer his course between the door-posts, and so disappeared, considering himself rather fortunate, as well he might, that he was permitted to make his exit without help. A man whom gold could not buy was probably to him a strange spectacle.

The stirring enterprise, the untiring energy, and the thorough business habits of Judge Hollenback exerted a vast influence upon the progress and elevation of the country. He found business for many poor laborres; he furnished supplies to multitudes of new settlers; he took an active part in the early public improvements; he kept in circulation a large capital; and he was a living—almost ever-present—example of industry and economy. Not Wyoming alone, but the whole country between Wilkesbarre and Elmira, owes much of its early development and present prosperity to the business arrangements and the indomitable perseverance of Matthias Hollenback.

Colonel Hollenback was employed by Robert Morris, the agent of Louis the Sixteenth, to provide a place of retreat for the royal household at some secluded spot on the Susquehanna. This was in 1793. He accordingly purchased twelve hundred acres of land lying in Bradford County, Pennsylvania, and embracing the locality where Frenchtown was subsequently built. The unfortunate monarch, however, never occupied this asylum in the wilds of Pennsylvania, albeit many of his subjects did. Louis Philippe, the late " King of the French," in 1795 came through "the Wind-Gap" on horseback, and lodged in Wilkesbarre in "the old red tavern," on the river bank, then kept by James Morgan, and subsequently known as "the old Arndt Hotel," and then made his way up to Frenchtown. All this is true; but our soil is none the bet-

ter for having been owned by falling monarchs, or even trod by the feet of royal fugitives. Louis Philippe, like Colonel Hollenback, learned in America to sleep on "the soft side of a board," a practice which he never wholly abandoned.

*Resolutions passed by the Officers of the Court and Members of the Bar:*

"At a meeting of the officers of the court and members of the bar of the County of Luzerne, held in the borough of Wilkesbarre, on Thursday, the 19th inst., the following resolutions were submitted, and unanimously adopted:

"*Resolved*, That we have heard with regret the death of the venerable Matthias Hollenback, one of the associate judges of the courts of this county, and that in testimony of his memory we will wear crape upon the left arm for thirty days.

"*Resolved*, That we will attend the funeral of the deceased on Saturday next, from his late residence in this borough.

"*Resolved*, That we deeply sympathize with the widow and family of the deceased in their late bereavement, and that a committee be appointed to present them with a copy of these proceedings, and to make arrangements for the funeral.

"February 19, 1829."

The following communication, copied from the Susquehanna Democrat, was written by the Hon. David Scott.

"Friday, February 27th, 1829.

"The Hon. Matthias Hollenback, whose death was announced in your paper of last week, was born of

German parentage, in Hanover, upon the Swatara, then Lancaster, now Lebanon County, Pennsylvania. Here he was inured to all the sufferings and privations incident to a frontier settlement at that early day. Possessed of a firm and vigorous constitution, and endued by nature with a strong, active, and enterprising mind, at the age of seventeen he joined the first adventurous party who came to make a permanent settlement, under the authority of Connecticut, in the Valley of Wyoming. This was in the autumn of 1769. From this period the history of his long and eventful life is identified with the history of this part of the country.

"In the controversy between Pennsylvania and Connecticut he actively and firmly adhered to the latter, under whose auspices he had embarked his youthful fortunes, and whose claims he regarded as paramount to every other, until the right of soil and the right of jurisdiction to the country were decreed, by a competent tribunal, to be in the former. From that moment he yielded obedience to the Constitution and laws of Pennsylvania, and contributed all in his power to quiet the turbulent, and to reconcile the disaffected to the legitimate authorities.

"This dispute between Pennsylvania and Connecticut had assumed all the characteristics of a civil war, and, notwithstanding the conciliatory recommendations and remonstrances of the Continental Congress, it was continued during the Revolutionary struggle. While the poor and destitute settlers were suffering on the one side from the common enemies of the country—the British, the savage Indians, and the worse than savage Tories—they were attacked on the other, and endured equal distress, by military parties under the authority of Pennsylvania.

"Thus surrounded with difficulties and dangers calculated to appall the stoutest heart—at a period, too, when many good but timid men doubted, hesitated, and feared, young Hollenback, in want of every thing but personal courage and patriotic feeling, was approached by one of those agents of the mother-country whose bland and fascinating manners, and duplicity of heart, marked him out as a fit emissary for 'treason, stratagem, and spoil.' On the one hand, the efforts making to free the country from British dominion was represented as entirely hopeless, and that, upon failure, poverty, shame, and death every where awaited the active partisan; on the other, by espousing the cause of the British king, money, office, and honor would be immediately conferred, and a life of ease and independence secured. The youth stood firm. He was not to be allured from the path of duty. He had taken his resolution, staked his all upon the issue, and was willing to abide the result.

"In 1776—perhaps the following year—two companies were raised in Wyoming, in one of which young Hollenback was appointed a lieutenant. He was active and successful in filling up and preparing his company for active service, and shortly after joined the army, under General Washington, in the State of New Jersey. His merits were soon discovered and properly appreciated by the general, who frequently consulted him in relation to the frontier settlements, and the means of defending them against the incursions of the enemy. He participated in all the sufferings of our half-fed and half-clothed troops during a winter campaign in the State of New Jersey, and was on several occasions employed by the general in the execution of confidential agencies.

"Such was the patriotism and spirit of the Wyoming settlers, that, during a short period, when they were not immediately threatened with attacks from the enemy, almost every efficient man among them joined the regular army, and left their families without protection. This calm portended a storm. The defenseless state of the frontier invited aggression. The Valley again began to suffer from the tomahawk, scalping-knife, and firebrand, and early in 1778 it was discovered that a horde of British, Indians, and Tories were collecting upon the Susquehanna frontier, and preparing to pour down upon the Valley of Wyoming, and exterminate the defenseless settlers. The officers from Wyoming urged the general to send a force for its protection, or to permit the two companies drawn from this settlement to return, for the purpose of defending their aged and helpless parents, wives, and children; but such was the situation of the army that no adequate force could be spared. An intense anxiety was felt among the officers: some obtained furloughs, and some resigned and returned to the Valley. Every preparation was made in their power to repel their invaders. About 350 men marched out to meet the enemy: they were drawn into an ambuscade. The result is known; Wyoming was reduced to widowhood and orphanage. About fifty only escaped that disastrous battle, of whom the subject of this notice was one.

"Articles of capitulation, in which security and protection of life were stipulated, were no sooner signed than they were violated on the part of the faithless and bloodthirsty enemy. What property could not be carried away was burned and destroyed, and the remnant of the settlers were driven, naked and houseless, to the surrounding mountains. Lieutenant Hollenback, whose property was all destroyed, still clung to the Valley, and participated in all its sufferings till the conclusion of the war.

"Upon the settlement of the controversy between Pennsylvania and Connecticut, and upon the promulgation of the laws of Pennsylvania in the disputed territory in 1786, Mr. Hollenback was chosen and appointed one of the justices of the courts of Luzerne County; and upon the adoption of the new Constitution he was reappointed an associate judge, which office he sustained with reputation till the time of his decease. He was honored with the command of a regiment by his fellow-citizens—a military office, being almost the only one in Pennsylvania compatible with that of a judge.

"In all the great political struggles which have agitated the country, Judge Hollenback was always actively and firmly attached to the cause of the people. In the recent conflict, although most of those around him with whom he had been accustomed to act entertained different views, and although he was exceedingly enfeebled by disease, he procured himself to be carried to the poll, and there, for the last time, exercised the right of suffrage in favor of the distinguished individual who has succeeded to the presidency. He was firmly persuaded that the interests of the country demanded this preference, and he acted accordingly.*

* Colonel Hollenback's preference for General Jackson as a candidate for the presidency was natural, there being many strong points of character which the two men possessed in common. They were both old soldiers and men of the right grit, the true successors and representatives of the brave old knights of the days of chivalry. When Colonel Hollenback's carriage arrived before the court-house a scene occurred. The late General Isaac Bowman, standing upon the steps, with a full tone of voice said, "Colonel Hollenback, the

"It is believed that he was not a member of any Christian Church, but it is known that he reverenced the religion of the Cross. Throughout his life he contributed liberally to the support of that communion and its pastors, to which he was conscientiously attached, and it is feared it will long feel the want of his supporting hand.

"His life was a life of temperance, industry, and attention to his business, the full fruits of which he enjoyed, in almost uninterrupted health, until his last illness, and in an ample fortune. From the incidents of his life the young may draw useful lessons for the regulation of their conduct, and from his death all may learn that *man is mortal:* that neither riches, nor honors, nor virtue, nor age, can form any shield against the fell destroyer."

old soldier, who helped fight the battles of the Revolution, has left his bed to come and vote for General Jackson—the last vote which he will ever cast." The board of judges came out and took the vote. The feelings of the people were excited to a high pitch. "Hurrah for the old soldier!" "Hurrah for Jackson!" burst forth from the spectators in all directions. It is said that some who had already voted for the opposing candidate joined in the cheering, and others who came to do the same stepped up and cast their votes for "the hero of New Orleans."

## IV.

### INCIDENTS AND ADVENTURES RELATED BY MRS. MARTHA MYERS.

> "In winter's tedious nights sit by the fire
> With good old folks, and let them tell their tales
> Of woeful ages long ago betide."
> SHAKSPEARE.

THE matter contained in the present chapter was communicated to us, for the purpose of a permanent record, by Mrs. Myers, in the month of August, 1841. We have connected the personal incidents with the current history of the times to which they refer, and have often supplied dates. The facts are given, as nearly as possible, as Mrs. Myers related them, and rest upon her authority. That the reader may be able to form a correct judgment as to the amount of confidence which is to be placed in her stories, we here give endorsements which we are sure will be entirely satisfactory.

Hon. Charles Miner, the venerable historian of Wyoming, says: "Some years ago, when Professor Silliman was in the Valley, he visited Mrs. Myers, and I had the good fortune to be present at the interview. Mrs. Myers has been, and yet is, one of the clearest chroniclers of the early scenes. Though the light

> "'Revisits not those orbs, that roll in vain
> To find its piercing ray,'

the mental eye retains all its early power and lustre. Though now—1845—*eighty-two* years of age, it is a pleasure to sit by her side and hear

"'Of most disastrous chances—hair-breadth 'scapes,'" witnessed in her eventful youth."—*Histor. Append.,* p. 14, 16.

Mr. Lossing, after visiting Toby's Eddy, says: "Thence I rode to the residence of Mr. Myers, a son of the venerable lady already alluded to, where I passed an interesting hour with the living chronicle of the wars of Wyoming. I found her sitting in an easy-chair, peeling apples, and her welcome was as cheerful and as cordial as she could have given to a cherished friend. Her memory was clear, and she related the incidents of her girlhood with a perspicuity which evinced remarkable mental vigor. Although blindness has shut out the beautiful, and deprived her of much enjoyment, yet pious resignation, added to natural vivacity, makes her society extremely agreeable. 'I am like a withered stalk, whose flower hath fallen,' said she; 'but,' she added, with a pleasant smile, 'the fragrance still lingers.'"—*Field-Book,* vol. i., p. 371.

Colonel Stone says: "Near the site of the fort is the residence of Mrs. Myers, a widow lady of great age, but of clear mind and excellent memory, who is a survivor of the Wyoming invasion and the horrible scenes attending it. Mrs. Myers was the daughter of a Mr. Bennet, whose family was renowned in the domestic annals of Wyoming both for their patriotism and their courage."—*History of Wyoming,* p. 213.

This is the lady to whose story we now invite the attention of the reader.

Mrs. Myers's maiden name was Bennet. She was born in Scituate, Rhode Island, January 15, 1763. Her father's name was Thomas Bennet; her mother's maiden name was Martha Jackson. The same year on which Martha Bennet was born, a settlement of Connecticut people was commenced in Wyoming, and Mr. Bennet rented a valuable property in Rhode Island, and removed to the Delaware, near to Stroudsburg. He took quarters there with a company of people in a stone house, which was fortified and called a fort. Mr. Bennet's object was to settle in Wyoming, and accordingly he visited that famous locality, but, finding the Indians surly, he for the time abandoned the project.

The hostile savages kept close watch of the old castle, and gave the occupants no little annoyance. The armed men there sometimes assumed the offensive, and hunted down small parties of Indians who were strolling about the woods for purposes of murder and plunder. On one of these occasions a brave old colored man took the lead, and, discovering an Indian camp, he fired upon the unsuspecting party, and laid one of them dead upon the ground. The rest of them fled with great precipitation.

One instance of alarm at this fort terminated without bloodshed. In the dead of night a great stamping was heard around the fort, and it was presumed that a large company of mounted Indians had hemmed them in on every side. All hands within were soon broad awake and fully armed. Every man examined his priming, and was ready to make a deadly shot. They disposed their force as advantageously as possible, and sent a man to reconnoitre from the roof. It was soon found that the invading host was a company of loose horses in a nocturnal frolic. The alarm, of course, was turned into merriment.

The next year Mr. Bennet removed to Goshen, New York, and rented a farm for six years. He set his sons at work upon the farm, and took his gun, his axe, and hoe, and visited the much-coveted valley. Two attempts to effect a settlement in Wyoming were unsuccessful because of the hostility of the Indians, Mr. Bennet losing all his labor, but, more fortunate than some of the early settlers, escaping with his life.

In February, 1769, Mr. Bennet joined a company of New England people, forty in all, who built a fort on the west bank of the Susquehanna, which, in honor of the forty hardy adventurers, was called *Forty Fort*. This fort was designed as a place of security against the Indians, but, withal was to be a Yankee fortification, where, if need should require, the New England settlers would be able to take refuge from the Pennamites. Mr. Bennet selected a situation on the flats about a mile above the fort, and, clearing off a portion of it, put in some seed.

The following year, 1770, Mr. Bennet united with a new recruit of settlers, and paused at the mouth of the Lackawanna, where they built a block-house. Here they were all taken into custody by John Jennings, sheriff of Northampton County, Pennsylvania. As Sheriff Jennings was proceeding with his prisoners to Easton, "at Wyoming," probably Wilkesbarre, Mr. Bennet managed to escape, and returned to the east. This event took place in the summer, as in the month of September he was at the east.—See his affidavit in *Pennsylvania Archives*, vol. iv., p. 391.

In September Mr. Bennet made arrangements to remove his family to Wyoming. He had examined the ground; he understood all the hazards of the enterprise; his courage was equal to the danger, and the question was settled. As to property, he had now but little to lose, for he had sold his farm in Rhode Island on personal security, and both the purchaser and security had failed, and the whole was lost. What by industry and economy had been saved in Goshen, was now put into as compact a condition as possible, and loaded upon pack-horses, and the family commenced their march toward "the land of promise." The country now presented a striking contrast with the picture of Wyoming which was formed in the imaginations of Mr. Bennet's family. The grasshoppers had destroyed nearly all the vegetation, and the aspect was one of utter desolation.

They wound their way over the mountains and through the vales until they came to Shehola, on the west side of the Delaware, and here they were hospitably entertained by a Quaker by the name of Wires. The next morning "Friend Wires" accompanied the miniature caravan as far as "the little meadows," where they took refreshments. Mrs. Bennet was boiling some chocolate over a fire made by the side of a log. She seemed unusually sad. "I don't know," said she, "what I am about to meet: I think something pretty heavy." It was not long before several men came up from Wyoming—one bleeding from a wound made on his head by a club—and reported that the Pennamites had taken possession of the fort, and were resolved upon driving off all the New England settlers.

A consultation was now held upon the proper course to be pursued. Mr. Bennet was a man of cool courage, and he had made up his mind to try his fortunes upon the fertile soil of Wyoming, and he was not to be turned aside from that purpose by any thing but stern invincible necessity. He was bent upon going on; but what would he do with his family? Mrs. Bennet, who was not easily intimidated, said, "If it were not for the children, I would go along." "Friend Wires" said, "Leave the children with me; I will take care of them." Stimulated by the courage of Mr. Bennet and his wife, the two men who had fled from the country resolved to return and try their luck again.

Mr. Bennet was a great hunter, and the wild woods had more attractions for him than the old settled country at the east: for himself, he could live any where in the Susquehanna Mountains by the aid of his rifle and hunting-knife. Mrs. Bennet was not so cool as her husband, but was equally firm in her purposes, and unterrified by danger. The company thought to find shelter for the time being with a Mr. Chapman, who had built a mill at Mill Creek, and who had been a neighbor and a friend of the Bennet family in Goshen.

When Mr. and Mrs. Bennet reached Wyoming, they found the dispute between the New England and Pennsylvania settlers had already ripened into open war. Captain Ogden, the Pennamite leader, had built a block-house, which was called a fort, at the mouth of Mill Creek, and had in his company Deputy Sheriff Jennings. Mr. Bennet was a peaceable man, and did not enter at once into the war, but took possession of a small log house he had previously built on the flats, just above Forty Fort. The grain he had put in, before his return to Goshen in the spring, presented a most delightful prospect of an abundance of provisions for the following winter.

The Yankees—that is, the fighters—invested the block-house, when Ogden proposed a parley. But no sooner had the besiegers entered the block-house to hold a conversation with the besieged, than Jennings served a writ on them, in the name of the Commonwealth of Pennsylvania. They were thirty-seven in all; and they were all taken to Easton, a distance of sixty miles, to jail. They obtained bail, and immediately returned. Again they were captured and sent off to jail, and again they were released on bail, and returned. A re-enforcement of 270 or 280 Yankees, under the command of Captain Durkee, came on, and built a fort where Wilkesbarre now stands, which they named, in honor of their leader, Fort Durkee. The Yankees now held the ground, and proceeded to the work of clearing farms and building. "The children" were brought on from Shehola, and Mr. Bennet was comfortably ensconced in his log cabin with his family.

But a few months of quiet had passed before the Pennsylvanians came on with an augmented force, under the command of Ogden and Patterson, the latter bringing up the river in a boat a four-pounder. Ogden captured Captain Durkee, and put him in irons, and took possession of the fort.

The Yankees were now pillaged, and, as far as possible, driven from the country. The house and premises generally belonging to Mr. Bennet were robbed; grain, cattle, and every thing movable, which could be found, were taken from him, but he did not leave the valley.

The Pennsylvanians now considered their victory complete. Ogden went to Philadelphia, leaving a few men in the fort. In the mean time, Captain Lazarus Stuart came on with forty brave fellows, and drove out the small guard from the fort, took possession of the cannon, and turned the tide once more in favor of the Yankees. Mr. Bennet now took up quarters in Fort Durkee, both as a measure of safety and of comfort. Here Mrs. Bennet contracted an intimacy with Mrs. Manning and her daughters, who lived on the flats below the fort. Her husband, by education and profession, was a Friend, and yet, for some reason, he was called *Captain* Manning. The Manning family were Pennsylvanians, but were non-combatants, and, consequently, could contract friendly alliances with Yankee families.

In the winter of 1771, Ogden again made his appearance, and invested Fort Durkee. His brother Nathan was killed by a shot from the fort, Mrs. Bennet witnessing the event. Stuart, finding himself unable to hold out against the superior numbers of the Pennsylvanians, managed to steal away, when the Pennamites took possession.

Captain Ogden was terribly enraged by the death of his brother, and, seizing several prominent Yankees who happened to be in the fort, sent them to Philadelphia in irons, charged with being concerned in the murder. Mr. Bennet did not belong to Stuart's party of fighting men, but had taken shelter in the fort, with his family, when he considered their lives in imminent peril. Stuart, with his men, left the fort, and Mr. Bennet fell into Ogden's hands; and he, without the slightest reason, excepting that he was in the fort at the time, was one of the suspected parties, and was obliged to endure the sufferings and disgrace of a suspected felon for five months in jail in Philadelphia.

The explanation of this affair is to be found in the fact that an "inquisition" was held over the body of Nathan Ogden by Charles Stuart, January 21, 1771, by which it was found that said Ogden was shot by "a certain Lazarus Stuart." But on the back of the report of the inquest is found "a list of the rioters in the fort at Wyoming when Nathan Ogden was killed." There are forty-seven of these "rioters," embracing nearly all the respectable Yankee settlers then in the country. Thomas Bennet was among these so called "rioters," and was taken up as a party to the murder. The same evil befell several other individuals, and might have befallen any of the number upon the list. —See *Pennsylvania Archives*, vol. iv., p. 384.

Captain Manning had raised a fine crop of corn, which he had stored away in the garret of his log house. As he practiced upon the principles of non-resistance, he could neither be a good Pennamite nor a good Yankee, and the consequence was that he was often persecuted by both, as one or the other happened to be in power. When Ogden took possession of the fort, some of "the boys" laid a plan to rob Captain Manning of his corn. The old Quaker had two buxom girls, one of whom, it was suspected, had a lover among "the Pennsylvania boys," and it was supposed that this fact would account for certain secret communications which were made to the Mannings with regard to the movements of the Pennamites. By some means, no matter what, the family got wind of the plundering expedition, and were thrown into great perplexities. The old gentleman could not fight, and as to magistrates and courts there were none to resort to. While he sat in the corner brooding over his helpless condition, his two daughters, who were large, muscular, and courageous, hit upon a plan of defense; and, upon opening it to the good old *Friend*, it seemed to look so little like war and bloodshed that he gave it the sanction of his silence. The girls hung over the fire a large iron kettle, and filled it with water, which, when the assailants made their appearance before the door, was boiling hot. They then took an instrument, vulgarly called a squirt-gun, constructed of the barrel of an old musket, and through the chinks between the logs sent a jet of the boiling water into the face and eyes of the assailants. A few shots were enough to conquer the courage of the gallant band, who immediately took to their heels, and put themselves beyond the reach of the formidable engine so efficiently served. The assailants ran off frantic with pain, while the girls shook their sides with laughter; and the good old Quaker was scarcely suspected of a dereliction of principle, although no one doubted but that he enjoyed the battle-scene to a high degree.

The perpetual annoyances to which this quiet man was subjected induced him to resolve upon taking a position a little farther from the centre of action. He consequently constructed a rude cabin upon Lackawanna Island—now called Scofield's Island—near the head of the Valley. The cabin was built on each side of a large fallen tree, which lay high above the ground. The roof was made of peeled bark, and the tree constituted the ridge-pole. As the Mannings were about to ship their effects on board of a canoe, Mrs. Manning said to Mrs. Bennet, "Friend Bennet, come go with us to the island; the boys shall have as much ground as they can work, and there is room enough in the cabin for us both; thee shall take one side of the tree, and I will take the other." This was too good an offer to be despised. Fort Durkee was now in the hands of the Pennamites, and every few weeks they were running over the Valley, and giving the Yankees who had the courage to remain at their homes infinite trouble and vexation—not being particularly courteous even to the women, who had the assurance to stick to the stuff when their husbands were driven off or sent to prison. Under these circumstances, Mrs. Bennet gladly accepted the generous offer of her friend; and "the boys" also loaded their canoe, and the two families pushed up the stream in company, and arranged their scanty catalogue of furniture and fixtures in the cabin. The Bennet boys had managed to save some grain, which they concealed at the head of the island.

In the mean time Mr. Bennet had been discharged, and had returned worn out with his tedious imprisonment, and badly discouraged. Captain Zebulon Butler had come on with a new recruit of Yankees, and had shut up Ogden in the fort at Mill Creek, and cut off his supplies. This was in the spring of 1771. Ogden found it necessary to communicate with the Pennsylvania officials at Philadelphia, and, not willing to run the risk of sending a messenger, who would probably fall into the hands of the Yankees, resolved upon an ingenious and daring enterprise. He made his clothes into a bundle, and fastened his hat on the top of it, then tied to it a small cord some twenty feet long. Taking up his bundle, he walked out into the current, and floated down on his back ahead of his hat and clothes. Of course, this enterprise was undertaken in the night. The Yankee sentinels saw the suspicious-looking object, and riddled the hat with bullets, but Ogden escaped unhurt, and soon reached Philadelphia. He dashed about, and soon raised a quantity of provisions and a new company of recruits, commanded by Captain John Dick. They stealthily entered the Valley, and eagerly awaited a favorable opportunity of throwing themselves, with their pack-horses loaded with provisions, into the fort.

David Ogden, a brother of the captain, was one of the company, and learning that Thomas Bennet had returned from Philadelphia, and was with his family on Lackawanna Island, set off, with a small posse, in pursuit of him. The capture or murder of Bennet would be a clever little adventure while they were waiting for a few hours for a favorable opportunity to elude the besiegers and get into the fort. Ogden knew the ground perfectly, and easily eluded observation until he found his way to the bank of the river over against the island. The Mannings had received the intelligence of the arrival of Captains Ogden and Dick in the neighborhood of the fort, and of David Ogden's intended visit to the island. The young Pennamite lover had made occasional visits to the island, and nothing was kept from his lady friend that might be of any interest to the family.

When Ogden and his friends showed themselves upon the beach, Mrs. Manning said, "David Ogden is coming over the river. Bennet, thee must clear out or be killed." Mr. Bennet replied, "I may as well die one way as another. I have been in jail until I am worn out; they have robbed me of all I have in the world, and now let them kill me if they will." The women, however, roused him from his deep despondency by seizing him by the arms and shoving him out of the door just in time to make his escape. He hid himself in the thick undergrowth, while Ogden entered the cabin with the words, "Is Bennet here?" The answer was "No." Mrs. Bennet asked, "What do you want of him?" adding, "If you should find him, you would do no harm to him." "Where is he?" demanded Ogden, in an angry tone. Mrs. Manning replied, "He is not here." Ogden repeatedly swore that, if he could find him, he would shoot him. He went out and scoured the woods, but with no success. After informing Mrs. Manning that they intended to enter the fort the next morning before daybreak, and after satisfying their hunger with the good things of the cabin, they departed, but did not immediately leave the island. Judging rightly that Mr. Bennet would soon come forth from his concealment, they hid themselves within gunshot of the cabin. When it was supposed that Ogden and his men had crossed the main branch of the river, Mr. Bennet's sons went out and called him, and he came in. He sat down in a sad state of mind, and Martha seated herself in his lap, and flung her arms about his neck, and commenced caressing him, and condoling with him in view of his troubles and dangers; and the sympathy of the child in this instance was a substantial good, for it actually saved the life of the father. Ogden afterward said he intended to have shot Bennet, and should have done it but for the fear of killing the child. The judgment of charity is that it was not merely as a Yankee that Ogden had formed the deliberate purpose to take Mr. Bennet's life, but as an accessory to the death of his brother. But Mr. Bennet was in no way connected with that deed: its perpetrator afterward fell in the Indian battle, as several affidavits to be found in the archives of the state abundantly prove.

On being informed of Captain Ogden's intended entrance into the fort early the next morning, Mr. Bennet, upon the pretense of going out to catch some eels, in the evening crossed the river, and went down to the Yankee lines, and communicated the information. When the Pennsylvanians made a rush upon the besiegers just before day, they found them fully prepared for them. They lost their pack-horses and provisions. Several horses were shot down under their riders, and a number of the party were severely wounded. Cap-

G

tains Ogden and Dick succeeded in entering the fort with about twenty of their men, but they entered to find famine and despondency staring them in the face on every side, and to feel the mortification of having contributed a considerable stock of provisions to the Yankee force.

Captain Dick, in his report, says: "The information of our coming was received by the Yankees through a letter falling into their hands, with which an Indian was sent by Captain Ogden."—See *Miner's History*, p. 131. This was Captain Dick's supposition. The fact is, that the credit of giving the information to Captain Butler is due to Thomas Bennet.

The besieged Pennsylvanians, finding it impossible longer to hold out, capitulated, and left Wyoming. The Manning family had really been serviceable to the Yankee cause by their connection with the Bennet family, to whom they owed a hearty good-will, and from whom they kept no secret which might be serviceable to them or their friends, and yet they were not in the confidence of the Yankee leaders, who resolved to drive them from the country. In pursuance of this resolution, on the day of the capitulation, Captain Fuller, one of the Yankee officers, came to the island with a company of men, and coming up to the cabin, cried out, "What are you doing here, you Pennamites? Clear out, or I'll burn your cabin over your heads." Captain Manning paused not to reason with the fierce Yankee, but immediately commenced packing his goods and loading them in a canoe. He left Wyoming never to return. He settled upon the west branch of the Susquehanna.

Captain Fuller now said, "Bennet, you have suffered enough. Come down to Fort Lukins, and you shall have as good a lot as there is there." Mr. Bennet took his family down to the fort, but refused to take up his residence there. He fitted up an old horse-shed in Forty Fort, and made it a comfortable residence for those times and for that country, in which his family lived for more than two years. During this period Mrs. Bennet presented her husband with another daughter—the late Mrs. Tuttle, of Kingston—and Martha began to develop extraordinary skill at housework, and great power of endurance.

The tide had now turned in favor of the New England settlers, and large accessions were made to their numbers. Colonel Denison came in from Hartford, Connecticut, and took board with Mr. Bennet. He was married to Betsy Sill, this being the first match consummated among the settlers.

All this time the Indians were numerous, but very quiet. When Mr. Bennet was taken a prisoner to Philadelphia, some of them earnestly urged Mrs. Bennet to come with her children and live among them; evidently considering her life in danger from the Pennamites, they wished to afford her shelter and protection.

We have seen that Mr. Bennet had been sent to Philadelphia to jail as one of " the rioters in the fort at Wyoming, January 21st, 1771, when Nathan Ogden was murdered," but had been discharged after an imprisonment of five months. Another of these "rioters," as they were called, was a man by the name of William Speedy. He was somewhat in years, and was called " Old Speedy;" but his age could not abate the rigor of the Pennsylvania authorities, for they kept him in close confinement in Philadelphia for more than two years. How, where, or precisely when Speedy was captured and committed to jail we are not able to say, but his final examination must have taken place some time in the year 1775. Mrs. Myers says, when her sister Polly was two years old, and she was twelve, her mother was desired to go to Philadelphia as a witness in favor of Speedy, who was to be tried for the murder of Nathan Ogden. This journey Mrs. Bennet performed alone on horseback, a distance of 120 miles, most of the way through the wilderness. When she reached Philadelphia she found that the court had adjourned, and she then made a journey to Goshen and attended to some business. When the trial came on she was present, and her testimony cleared Speedy. He was wasted away to a mere skeleton. When he was discharged his joy and gratitude overleaped all bounds. He fell upon his knees before Mrs. Bennet, and almost worshiped her. "Get up, Speedy," said she; "I have done no more than any one ought to do for a fellow-creature." He kissed her hand and bathed it with tears. It is refreshing to find that in these stern and almost barbarous times the law of kindness and feelings of gratitude had not become utterly erased from the human mind.

Mrs. Bennet returned home after an absence of some weeks, during which Martha had been nurse, kitchen-maid, and governess. She brought water from a cold spring which boils up at the river's edge, below a high, steep bank. The child would scarcely ever consent to be left alone, and this made it necessary for Martha to carry her down to the spring, and bring her up on one arm, while she brought a pail of water with the other. She did the housework for the family, consisting of her father, three brothers, herself, and sister, including baking and washing, during her mother's absence. This, for a girl of her age, was no small task. She says, "It was a hard siege, but I had strength given me for the trial."

Three years of quiet in the settlement had resulted in a high degree of prosperity. Plenty had crowned the labor of the settlers, and there had been a large accession to their numbers from the New England States, not merely consisting of young, hardy adventurers, but the old and infirm came on, with their children and grandchildren, to spend the remnant of their days in "the beautiful valley," and to lay their bones beneath its green sod.

Mr. Bennet built a "double log house" on his land, which Mrs. Myers says "was then called a good house." "We removed," says she, "to our new house, raised good crops of grain, and had a fine stock of horses and cattle. We sold grain and bought articles of convenience from the Middletown boats. Father and brothers hunted beaver, bears, deer, raccoons, wild turkeys, etc., and we were in comfortable circumstances. Game was abundant at this period; we often saw wolves, bears, and deer swimming the river. One night a ferocious animal entered the yard, and so wounded one of the young cattle that it was found necessary to kill it. Father and brothers seized their guns when they heard the disturbance, but the savage beast bounded off just in time to save himself; they saw him escape, and, as near as they could judge from a mere glance, it was a panther."

In December of this year (1775) the famous expedition of Colonel Plunkett took place. The New England people prepared to give the colonel a warm reception at the head of the narrows, on both sides of the river. Mr. Bennet and his son Solomon were at the breastworks below Shawnee for two weeks, and Mrs. Bennet took down to them a horse-load of provisions at two different times. Men, old and young, boys and women, were all on hand to act their part in the defense of their homes. After an unsuccessful attempt to storm the Yankee works, the gallant colonel undertook to take his forces in a bateau across the river. The first boat-load, which, it is said, Colonel Plunkett commanded in person, was saluted by a brisk fire from the bushes by Lieutenant Stuart and his men, and one of the Pennamites was killed and several wounded. The gallant colonel lay down in the bottom of the boat, and ordered the men to push out into the river and go over the falls. The party in the boat and those left upon the west side of the river met at the foot of the rapids, and, upon consultation, concluded that it was so late in the season, and the ice was accumulating so fast, that "prudence would be the better part of valor," and the Pennamite army returned home with diminished numbers, no spoils, and no addition to their reputation for either tact or courage.

Colonel Plunkett and his band were sadly chagrined at their defeat. They had not the slightest doubts of success until they saw the impregnable position of the Yankees, and the spirit with which it was maintained. It is said that the wives of the officers bespoke, in advance, a portion of the plunder: one wanted a feather bed, another a silk dress, and another a smart Yankee girl for a servant. These anticipations were all blasted, and the only reasons which the adventurous officers had to give in justification of themselves was, that the wild Yankees had assembled in thousands, and filled the woods on both sides of the river; that they had availed themselves of the perpendicular ledge of rocks from which no force could dislodge them, and the river was rapidly filling up with ice. In all this the numbers of the Yankee force were vastly exaggerated; and as for the rest, a sagacious commander ought to have understood the ground beforehand.

The expedition of Colonel Plunkett terminates the first period of this unnatural war—a war which was not only a public calamity, but inflicted untold griefs upon persons and parties who pined and writhed under its consequences in private, who never troubled the public with their heart-crushing griefs. Young Lukins, son of the surveyor general, was at Sunbury at the time Plunkett set out for Wyoming, and he went with him merely for the romance of the thing. The poor fellow was killed. "His death," says Mrs. Myers, "was much lamented by the settlers: his father was a very worthy man, and was much respected."

. Mr. Miner gives an affecting incident of the death of another young man. He forced his way near the Yankee line; a Yankee marksman watched his opportunity, and shot him down. After the battle he visited the spot, and found a hat-band which he judged had been cut by the ball from his rifle. Going down the river with lumber many years afterward, he received the hospitalities of a fine old gentleman. The conversation turned upon the former troubles in Wyoming. "I lost a beloved son in the Plunkett invasion," said the father; and, producing the hat, said, "The bullet must have cut the band." The big tear stood in his eye while he held up the sad memento of his son's hapless fate. Of course, the scene was painful to the visitor, who declared that he never before realized the extent of the calamities of war. Ah! and this was a war between brothers—a feud in a family.

> "Brother with brother waged unnatural strife;
> Severed were all the charities of life:
> Two passions—virtues they assumed to be—
> Virtues they *were*—romantic loyalty,
> And stern, unyielding patriotism, possess'd
> Divided empire in the nation's breast;
> As though two hearts might in one body reign,
> And urge conflicting streams from vein to vein."
>
> JAMES MONTGOMERY.

## REVOLUTIONARY WAR—TROUBLE WITH THE INDIANS.

The expedition of Colonel Plunkett was the last effort of the proprietary government of the Colony of Pennsylvania to remove the New England people from Wyoming. The prospects of a rupture with the parent government now absolutely demanded union, and Congress passed resolutions recommending "that the contending parties immediately cease all hostilities, and avoid every appearance of force until the dispute could be legally decided." This wise recommendation had its influence upon the more considerate and prudent of both parties, while the common danger from the hostility of the savages suggested the folly and madness of the longer continuance of the feud. There was no difference of feeling between the Pennamites and Yankees upon the question of American liberty and independence.

On the 19th of April the battle of Lexington had been fought, and on the 17th of June that of Bunker Hill. The interest of these momentous events was felt in the wilds of Wyoming, as will be clearly seen by the records of certain public proceedings which are left upon the minutes of the town. Witness the following:

"At a meeting of yᵉ proprietors and settlers of yᵉ

town of Westmoreland, August 1, 1775, Mr. John Jenkins was chosen moderator for yᵉ work of yᵉ day. Voted, that this town does now vote that they will strictly observe and follow yᵉ rules and regulations of yᵉ honorable Continental Congress, now sitting at Philadelphia.

"*Resolved by this town*, That they are willing to make any accommodation with yᵉ Pennsylvania party that shall conduce to yᵉ best good of yᵉ whole, not infringing on yᵉ property of any person, and come in common cause of liberty in yᵉ defense of America, and that we will amicably give them yᵉ offer of joining in yᵉ proposals as soon as may be."

On the 8th of August, the same year, a meeting was held, made up of both New England and Pennsylvania people, at which a patriotic resolution was passed, which concluded with these words: "*And will unanimously join our brethren in America in the common cause of defending our liberty.*"

July 4th, 1776, the ever-memorable Declaration of American Independence was passed by the Continental Congress, and August 24th we find a town meeting "held in Westmoreland, Wilkesbarre District," at which "Colonel Z. Butler was chosen moderator," when it was voted "that it now becomes necessary for the inhabitants of this town to erect suitable forts as a defense against our common enemy." Forty Fort was ordered to be enlarged and strengthened. The people, old and young, made large contributions in labor to these necessary provisions for the common defense.

By order of Congress, "two companies on the Continental establishment" were raised "in the town of Westmoreland," to be "stationed in proper places for the defense of the inhabitants of said town and parts adjacent." Robert Durkee and Samuel Ransom were elected captains of these two companies. These companies consisted of something more than eighty men each, and they were made up of the strong young men of the settlement. At the critical period when our army had retreated across the Delaware, these companies were "ordered to join General Washington with all possible expedition." This order left Wyoming in a most defenseless condition. Nothing but the stern necessities of the Revolutionary cause could be offered as the slightest palliation of the cruelty and injustice of this measure. These companies were raised expressly for "the defense of the inhabitants" of Westmoreland "and parts adjacent," but they were now called to leave their mothers, wives, and sisters exposed to the incursions of the merciless savages, without any thing like adequate means of defense.

The Indians were evidently making preparations to identify themselves with the English cause. They all withdrew from Wyoming and went north. There were rumors of their intentions to cut off the settlement, which filled the minds of many with alarm. In the fall of 1777, Queen Esther came up the river with about a dozen Indians. She encamped at the mouth of Shoemaker's Creek, but a short distance from Mr. Bennet's residence. Mrs. Bennet, accompanied by Martha, visited the queen's camp and had considerable conversation with her. She asked her if it was true that the Indians were coming to kill us all. She shook her head and shed tears. Her head was gray, and she seemed to be old. She remained there about a fortnight.

Mrs. Myers says, "Not long after Queen Esther left

the Valley we heard rumors of violence committed at the north by parties of Indians which strolled over the country. These reports created great alarm among the people of Wyoming. In June, 1778, about two weeks before the battle, we had seven head of horses stray away. The boys going in pursuit of them asked me to go with them and pick cherries. We had not gone far into the woods before the boys saw some young hickories broken and twisted in a peculiar manner. One of them exclaimed, 'Oh, the Indians! The Indians have taken away the horses.' This turned out to be the fact. Upon our return we learned that the Indians had been at Peter Harris's, above Scofield's. Soon after the two Hardings were killed, and now we, with the settlers generally, moved into the fort. It was crowded full."

Colonel John Butler, a Tory leader, with an army of eight hundred, consisting of Indians, Tories, and British regulars, came down the river in boats and on rafts, and landed just above the head of the Valley, near Sutton's Mills. Colonel Denison, with a company of men, went up to reconnoitre, and found they had left the river and taken the mountain path. By this means he would avoid the danger of meeting the patriots in the Narrows, where his superior force would give him no advantage. The hostile army came into the Valley through a notch in the mountain opposite to Fort Wintermoot, a small fort which bore the name of a family of Tories, and was surrendered at once. A scouting party from Forty Fort was sent up to learn Butler's position and strength, and Finch was killed and Hewitt shot through the hand. This took place near where Shoemaker's Mills now stand, between the village of Wyoming and Carpenter's Notch. The next day a company went up and brought in Finch's body. After the battle the Indians referred to the circumstances, and said they could have killed the whole of both parties if they had chosen to do so. It is likely, however, this was a mere brag, and that really *fear* had something to do in the matter.

### THE BATTLE OF JULY 3, 1778.

The settlers had made strong representations of their perilous condition to General Washington, and prayed that at least the companies raised in the settlement might be sent to their aid, but all was in vain. They now had no hope but in their own small resources and the protection of Providence. The old men and boys which were left armed themselves as well as they could, and resolved to make a brave defense against the savage Indians and the still more savage Tories. The little army numbered about three hundred men, and was organized in six companies. There were grandfathers and grandsons in this army, some of them entirely untrained, and most of them unaccustomed to military discipline, and to the arrangements and evolutions of an army. Mr. Miner says, "There were about two hundred and thirty enrolled men, and seventy old people, boys, civil magistrates, and other volunteers."

Colonel Zebulon Butler had obtained leave of absence from the army, and came on in advance of the Wyoming companies, which were finally ordered to proceed to the scene of danger and alarm under Captain Spaulding. The command, by universal consent, was accorded to Colonel Butler. On the 3d of July, an Indian on horseback was seen at the mouth of Shoemaker's Creek, within sight of the fort. Upon finding that he was noticed he galloped off. Colonel John Butler now sent orders to the people in the fort to surrender, which was promptly refused.

The question was now mooted whether they should go out and fight the enemy on the plains above, or keep within the fort until re-enforcements should arrive. Captain Spaulding was coming on with an efficient, well-trained company, and Captain Franklin was on his way from Huntington with a company of volunteers, and it was the opinion of Colonels Butler and Denison that it was best to delay until the recruits should arrive. Captains Lazarus Stuart and William M'Karrican headed the party which were for marching out of the fort at once and meeting the foe. A warm debate upon the question followed, which closed with high words. The belligerent captains, perceiving that the majority was on their side, intimated that it was cowardice which influenced the views of the colonels, and that, if they should decline the command, they—the captains—would lead on the brave men who would volunteer to go out and flog Butler and his Indians. These insulting insinuations roused the spirit of Colonels Butler and Denison, and they resolved to hazard all upon the chances of a battle. Colonel Butler said, "We go into imminent danger; but, my boys, I can go as far as any of you." Those who were fierce for fight seemed to be under the impression that the enemy was about to retreat, or that they would run as soon as they saw danger. They were anxious to meet and punish the Indians while they were within reach, and to chase them out of the country. This, as they might have known, and as the event proved, was all erroneous. In this case, as in many others, hot-headed and reckless men prevailed against sober counsels.

The little army formed, and set out in the line of march in high spirits, with drums and fifes playing, and colors flying. Mr. Bennet was one of the "old men" who volunteered to defend the country. He, however, was so certain that the little army were about to be drawn into a snare and cut off, that he declared he would go with them no farther than "Tuttle's Creek"—the distance of one mile, or a little more—and he carried out his purpose. He left them at the creek, but his son Solomon went on. Soon after the little patriot army had left the fort, Major Durkee, Captain Ransom, and Lieutenant Pierce came up upon a gallop. They had left Captain Spaulding at Merwine's, about thirty miles from Wyoming, and hastened to the point of danger. Dashing into Mrs. Bennet's cabin, one sang out, "Can you give us a mouthful to eat?" They were furnished with a cold cut. Swallowing a few mouthfuls, they took a piece in their hand and pushed on. They left the fort never to look upon it again; they were all slain in the battle.

> "Whence is this rage? What spirit, say,
> To battle hurries me away?
> 'Tis Fancy, in her fiery car,
> Transports me to the thickest war,
> Where giant Terror stalks around,
> With sullen joy surveys the ground,
> And, pointing to the ensanguined field,
> Shakes his dreadful Gorgon shield."
> WHARTON.

When they came to Swetland's Hill, about one mile farther, it was reported that the invaders were flying, and they resolved to pursue them. They saw several straggling Indians, who, being fired upon, ran off as if terribly frightened. The enemy was lying in ambush, in three companies, disposed in the form of a crescent, extending from Fort Wintermoot in a westerly direction into the marsh which lies along at the foot of the mountain. Their advance line fell back upon the main body without much resistance. Their plan was well laid, and they had now succeeded in leading the little band into the trap which they had set for them. When the moment arrived to strike, the whole body of Indians and Tories opened a galling fire upon the patriot ranks, and cut down a large number. The noise of the musketry and the whistling of the bullets were terrible, but the wild yells of the savages were still more so. The men stood the first shock bravely, returning the fire with great spirit, but without much effect on the left wing, the enemy being covered by the steep slope which borders the marsh and a thick undergrowth. Colonel Denison, discovering that he was about to be outflanked and surrounded, ordered his wing to "fall back." This order was mistaken for an order to *retreat*, and confusion and a panic followed, which all the efforts of the officers failed to arrest. Every captain fell either at the head of his men, or deserted and alone. Colonels Butler and Denison rode along the line, and endeavored to rally their men until they were left nearly alone, and exposed to most imminent danger. But the day was lost, and every man made shift for himself as best he might. Some ran down the plains, some took to the mountain, but most fled in the direction of the river. Many were struck down with the tomahawk; and others were taken prisoners, and suffered a still more terrible fate.

When Thomas Bennet returned to the fort, he paced the bank of the river back and forth in the greatest excitement. When the firing began, he listened until he noticed the reports scattering down the plain. He then hastened to his cabin, exclaiming, "Our boys are beat; they will all be cut to pieces!" He was a man of strong nerves, but no stoic; he walked back and forth, and seemed all but distracted.

Colonels Butler and Denison, being mounted, came in first. A few of the fugitives came in in the course of the evening, but no news came to the Bennet family with regard to Solomon until the next day at about two o'clock, when he made his appearance, and gave an account of his escape. He was at the extreme right, in Captain Bidlack's company. When they came up to Fort Wintermoot it was in flames, and the hostile army lay just above. When the firing commenced he had twenty-two balls in his pouch, and he shot them all away but one. They drove the enemy about eighty rods, the dead, British regulars and Indians, lying strewed quite thick upon the ground. He used his own rifle, which would prime itself, and required no ramming down. He loaded quick, and took fair aim, and his man fell. When it was discovered that the Indians had turned Colonel Denison's left flank, and that our men were flying, it was now evident that the day was lost; then every man shifted for himself. Solomon Bennet steered his course toward the river; he gained the river bank against Monocasy Island, but a little in advance of several Indians who were in pursuit of him. He plunged into the river, and swam upon his back; the Indians fired upon him repeatedly, but, accurately watching their motions, he was always able to avoid the ball by dropping his head under the water at the moment they fired. The Indians seemed to enjoy the sport, indulging in a hearty laugh whenever young Bennet arose after dodging the ball. He reached the island, not knowing whether he was safe there from the merciless foe. He cautiously crept across the island, and then swam to the eastern shore. He was nearly exhausted, and, crawling up the bank on his hands and knees, he saw a naked man in the bushes, whom he recognized as Matthias Hollenback—the late Judge Hollenback, of Wilkesbarre. Bennet had crossed the river in his shirt and pants, and now he divided his scanty supply of clothes with his friend, loaning him one of his two garments, while he wore the other. Thus furnished, they found their way to the fort at Wilkesbarre.

When it was ascertained that arrangements were in progress for a capitulation, Solomon Bennet said, "I will never give myself up to an Indian." Mrs. Bennet then demanded, "What will you do, then?" and added, "You must clear out immediately." Mr. Bennet then expressed some doubts as to his fate, when Mrs. Bennet answered, "You must go too." Andrew, a lad about eleven years old, began to cry when the mother said, with emphasis, "And you must go too, for if we are killed you can do us no good." Accordingly, all three left for Stroudsburg. These are the simple facts; but the bitter grief which attended these trying circumstances has never been written. There were many such sad partings on that terrible day, and some much more aggravated. The depth of sorrow which filled the hearts of husbands and wives, parents and children, brothers and sisters, on that day and the day before, will only be brought to light by the revelations of the last Judgment. The parting of the Bennet family was brief, but the separation was long.

Colonel Butler left the fort upon the day of the battle, but not until he and Colonel Denison had agreed upon articles of capitulation, which were drawn up in

Mrs. Bennet's cabin. The table upon which those articles were written was preserved by Mrs. Myers until the day of her death, and is still in possession of the family. Mrs. Myers says, "Dr. Gustin went up to Fort Wintermoot with a white flag three times before the articles were fully agreed upon. They stipulated that the fort should be given up, but the inhabitants were not to be molested in their persons or property. The day but one after the battle, I think, Indian Butler, as he was called, marched his Indians into the fort in regular order, and, after drilling them a little, dismissed them. They ran about among the inhabitants, earnestly looking to see how they were situated, but for that day molested no one. Butler was a large, corpulent man, with a fair skin. I looked at him with astonishment, wondering how such a fine-looking man could come with the Indians to kill us.

"The next day the Indians began to plunder the people. Colonel Denison remained in our cabin, but when Butler came into the fort he sent for him, and they sat down by the table and entered into conversation. Colonel Denison remonstrated with him upon the subject of the aggressions of the Indians, urging that it was a breach of a most solemn engagement, such as are respected among all nations. Butler said, 'My men shall not molest the people. I will put a stop to it.' But when he went out of the fort the Indians resumed their plundering. Colonel Denison again sent for Butler, and again he came into our room and repeated his promises that it should cease. The Indians were quiet until the next day about two o'clock.

A large party then came into the fort, some of them drunk. Doctor Gustin wrestled and talked French with them. This was designed to divert them, but they again resumed their plundering. Toward night Butler came in again, and Colonel Denison had another conversation with him, earnestly chiding him for the breach of a solemn treaty. Butler finally waved his hand and said, 'To tell you the truth, I can do nothing with them.' Colonel Denison chid him severely, but received the same answer, 'I can do nothing with them.' The colonel then vehemently urged the articles of capitulation, and that they had not supposed it possible for him to allow so wicked a breach of faith on the part of his men. His final answer was as before, 'I tell you, sir, I can do nothing with them.' He then arose and left, and we saw no more of him. In fact, he left us to the tender mercies of the savages, without any regard to the articles which he had signed with his own hand.

"The Indians were now worse than ever. They came into our house, and a stout Indian claimed Colonel Denison's hunting-shirt, a very nice one, made of fine forty linen, with a double cape, fringed around the cape and wrists. The colonel objected; but, upon the Indian raising his tomahawk, and mother begging him to give it up, he consented. While she was unbuttoning the wristbands the colonel stepped back, and Polly Thornton, who sat by me, received a package of money from his pocket. It was the town money, in Continental bills; it afterward did the needy much good. The Indian, observing that something passed back to us, sang out, 'What's that?' 'You are taking the man's shirt,' replied mother. The hunting-shirt obtained, the Indian retired. Soon after another came in and demanded the colonel's new beaver hat. As in the former case, he objected; but, as in that instance, the lifted tomahawk and mother's entreaties brought him to terms.

"Our great chest, now in my possession, contained our valuable clothing. It was now robbed of all its contents. An Indian took mother's bonnet from her head and her shawl from her shoulders. She then covered her head with an old straw hat which was lying upon the ground. Captain Henry, an old Indian who had lived upon terms of intimacy with our family, and who was a prisoner in the fort when it was given up, came in with father's fine broadcloth coat on, which had been taken from the chest. He demanded, 'Where old Bennet?' Mother replied, 'Gone through the swamp to Stroudsburg.' 'Ah!' says he, stroking his sleeve, 'me old Bennet now. Where Solomon, that good marksman?' 'Gone to Stroudsburg.' 'Where Andrew, the little boy?' The same answer was given as before."

One circumstance Mrs. Myers—probably from motives of delicacy—does not relate, which has been communicated by another eye-witness. From the history thus far, it will be seen that Mrs. Bennet was a woman of great spirit, and an unusual amount of physical strength even for those times. She could stand being robbed by an Indian with a tomahawk in his hand, but she could not endure to have her clothing pulled from her person by an Indian *woman*. A filthy squaw undertook forcibly to deprive her of one of her garments, when the spirit of the Yankee woman, even by all the fearful circumstances by which she was surrounded, could not be held down. She drew her clenched hand, and gave the old hag a blow in the face which felled her to the ground. The squaw, recovering, grappled the pale-faced woman, but was soon worsted in the struggle. It was an anxious moment with the friends of Mrs. Bennet who were present. Would she be tomahawked on the spot? was the question revolved in every mind. That question was soon settled by a roar of laughter from the Indians, one of them patting her on the back with the complimentary words, "Good squaw." The vanquished old thief then sneaked off, woefully crestfallen. The masculine nerve of the women of those times seems to have been given them for the occasion, or which, perhaps, is a more truthful theory, were developed by the times. Circumstances originate characters. By a law of Providence, human nature adjusts itself to the circumstances by which it is surrounded. But let us proceed a little farther with Mrs. Myers's story in her own language.

"They took our feather beds, and, ripping open the ticks, flung out the feathers, and crammed in their plunder, consisting mostly of fine clothing, and, throwing them over their horses, went off. A squaw came riding up with ribbons stringing from her head over her horse's tail. Some of the squaws would have on two or three bonnets, generally back side before. One rode off astride of mother's side-saddle, that, too, wrong end foremost, and mother's scarlet cloak hanging before her, being tied at the back of her neck. We could not help laughing at the ridiculous figure she cut, in spite of the deep trouble which then all but overwhelmed us all.

"Few of the Tories came into the fort; but a young man by the name of Parshal Terry, who was in the battle under Butler, came in painted, and called to see his friends at their cabin. His brother had been in the battle on our side. He was shy, but was recognized.

"Indians came in who appeared to be friendly; they painted us, and tied white bands around our heads, as they said, that we might be known as prisoners of war, and not be in danger of being killed by strange Indians."

Something more than a week after the battle the houses throughout the settlement were fired. The smoke arose from all quarters at the same time. Soon after this, the widows of Timothy Pierce and John Murphy—their maiden name was Gore—with Ellis and Hannah Pierce—maiden ladies—requested Mrs. Bennet to visit the battle-ground with them, to see if they could identify the bodies of Pierce and Murphy. They found the bodies of the slain broiling in the hot sun, but so changed that they could not distinguish one from another. The husbands of the two young widows, and three brothers — Silas, Asa, and George Gore—lay upon the ensanguined field, but the heart-broken visitors had not even the poor satisfaction of identifying their remains. The company returned to the fort sick at heart, to have their imaginations haunted for long years with the awful spectacle which they had witnessed, of the mangled and wasting bodies of their neighbors, brothers, and husbands.

General Washington had projected an expedition into the Indian country effectually to chastise the savages, and to make an end of their incursions upon the frontier settlements. The people in the fort, not fully appreciating the time which would be necessary to prepare for such an expedition, entertained hopes of the arrival of the army of relief daily, and so remained there about two weeks. At the expiration of this period, Colonel Denison was making arrangements to go down the river in a canoe to bring up his family. Martha Bennet had lost all her best clothes, and found that it was necessary for her soon to make a move of some sort to replenish her exhausted wardrobe. She finally ventured to sob out, "If I could leave mother and sister, I would go with Colonel Denison down to Sunbury, to Captain Martin's, and work, and get me some clothes." Esquire Pierce, coming up, inquired into the cause of Martha's grief. Upon learning the facts, he addressed her in his quaint style: "Go along, gal, go along, and I'll take care of mother and child." She accordingly took passage in Colonel Denison's canoe, and arrived at Sunbury the next day. She found a company of between thirty and forty persons from the Valley quartered in a house. One of the company was Desdemona Marshall, the late Mrs. Wadsworth, of Huntington. Miss Bennet was received with great cordiality, and invited to remain with them, and be one of the household.

This family of fugitives, united by common sufferings and common dangers, was not to remain long together. There was a rumor of hostile Indians on the west branch of the Susquehanna, and a woman and a boy were tomahawked and scalped in the immediate neighborhood. Miss Bennet and others went to see them while they were yet alive. It was soon rumored that the Indians and Tories had again visited Wyoming, and all the settlers had left. A company commenced making preparations to go across the mountains to Stroudsburg, and Miss Bennet accepted an invitation to go with them. All the means of conveyance they had was a small cart drawn by a yoke of steers. There were some small children in the company, who were allowed to ride when they were tired, but as for the rest they all walked. Their journey was of the distance of about seventy-five miles, and nearly all the way through the wilderness, and crossing the high ridges which lie between the Susquehanna and the Delaware. The Misses Bennet and Marshall, with three other girls, outstripped the company, and saw nothing of them during the day. They became hungry, and turned aside and picked berries to satisfy the demands of nature. The path was exceedingly rough, and Miss Bennet's shoes gave out in consequence of the constant contact with stubs and sharp stones, and her feet were so injured as to leave blood behind them. "But," says she, "we made ourselves as happy as possible, amusing ourselves with singing songs and telling stories." They were constantly annoyed with fears of "the Indians," knowing that those dreadful scourges of the country might chance to cross their path at any moment. As the darkness of night began to approach, they met two men whom they first supposed to be Indians; but, perceiving them to be white men, they sung out, "How far is it to a house?" The answer was as cheering as it was cordial. "Two miles; be of good courage; we are hunting for some cows, and will soon be in." The young pedestrians soon arrived, and found the house guarded by several men. The family had gone, and most of the goods were removed. They made a supper of bread and milk, and lay down upon sacking bottoms from which the beds had been removed. They waited for the arrival of the company with great anxiety until about two o'clock in the morning, when, to their great joy, they arrived in safety.

The morning's light came, and our travelers were early on their way. They passed through Easton, where they bought provisions. That day "the girls" kept within sight of their companions in travel. The third day, at night, they arrived at Stroudsburg. Miss Bennet there met her mother and sister, but was greatly disappointed in not finding her father and brothers. Her brother Solomon had been to Middletown in pursuit of her, had returned that day, and set out immediately, with Colonel Butler and Captain Spaulding, for Wyoming. Mrs. Myers says, in relation to the events of that day, "One disappointment followed another in quick succession, and I seemed almost left without hope."

> "Come, Disappointment, come!
> Though from Hope's summit hurled,
> Still, rigid nurse, thou art forgiven,
> For thou, severe, wert sent from heaven
> To wean me from the world;
> To turn my eye
> From vanity,
> And point to scenes of bliss that never, never die."
>                                    HENRY KIRKE WHITE.

Soon after Martha Bennet left the fort, Indians came in, who seemed any thing but friendly and trustworthy. "More Indians come," said they, "right away; eat Yankees up." This tale was told undoubtedly to intimidate those of the settlers who still remained, and to frighten them away. Whatever was thought of it, the fact that parties of those hated, murderous, plundering wretches kept prowling about was a sufficient reason for the last white person to quit the Valley. Mrs. Bennet, with her child, came over the mountain in company with Major Pierce and his family, perhaps the last of the settlers who were left. The child, afterward Mrs. Tuttle, was then five years old, and she always recollected that dreadful journey. At that tender age she had to walk nearly the whole distance on foot, having no beasts of burden in the company. She remembered camping out, or rather lying on the ground, under the open heavens, in what has ever since been called "The Shades of Death." Hungry and weary, they laid themselves down upon the bare ground, and invoked oblivious sleep. Mrs. Bennet drew out a portion of her skirt, and told little Polly to lie on it as close to her as possible. Mrs. Tuttle lived to a great age, and we learned these facts from her mouth not long before her death.

It may be a matter of wonder how so many of the settlers subsisted in the fort for more than two weeks, after having been robbed of every thing by the Indians. This mystery is explained by a curious fact. There was a capacious cellar under a building in the fort where a considerable quantity of provisions was stored. When the Indians commenced the work of plundering, as a company of them approached this place of deposit, some witty individual sang out, with apparent concern, "Small-pox! small-pox!" The old brave who was on the lead grunted out "Oh!" and sheered off, the others following him; they jabbered in Indian, and looked back at the reputed "pock-house" with no little consternation. After this the Indians kept at a distance from the place, invariably going round it, and casting at it one of those significant Indian glances so indicative of a horror of being caught in some trap. The "wit" of our brave fathers and mothers did not always "come afterward," but often "hit the nail on the head," and stood them in stead when all other resources were utterly exhausted. This happy hit probably saved the lives of many of the settlers; for "humane" as the Tory leaders boasted of being, and "magnanimous" as some authorities contend that the "Red Man" is, not a hoof, nor a kernel, nor a morsel of bread or meat which the cruel invaders could either seize and carry away, or consume by fire, was left to the people to keep them from perishing with hunger.

Soon after the arrival of Major Pierce's company of fugitives, Mrs. Bennet heard a young Philadelphia lawyer uttering terrible threats against the Yankees, declaring that he would go to Wyoming with a company, and a Yankee should not set foot upon the ground. She immediately made it her business to communicate the matter to Colonel Butler. The very next day Colonel Butler and Captain Spaulding mustered their men and set off for Wyoming, preferring the hazard of meeting the Indians to that of allowing the Pennamites to take possession of the country.

The company saw no Indians, but every where met the sad traces of their ravages. The houses of the settlement were nearly all reduced to ashes, the crops were destroyed, and the horses, cattle, etc., were either killed or driven off. The beautiful and fruitful vale, which in the spring presented so charming a prospect of a rich harvest, was now the very picture of desolation. Colonel Butler and his company repaired to the battle-field, and gathered up the remains of those who were slain on the fatal 3d of July, and buried them in a common grave, where the monument now stands.

Mrs. Bennet and her daughters did not remain long at Stroudsburg, but went to Goshen, where they took up quarters with a Captain John Bull, "an old gray-headed man with a large family." Mrs. Bennet "did two days' work in one" at the spinning-wheel, while Martha "did housework for fifty cents a week." They made shirts and pants, and sent them to Wyoming to Mr. Bennet and the boys, who remained there, and worked their land and enlarged their clearing. The Revolutionary war was now in full blast; there were no manufactories in the country, and foreign goods were extremely scarce and dear. Mrs. Myers says that at this period they gave "fifty cents a yard for calico."

Early in the spring Mrs. Bennet went to "Bethlehem, ten miles below Litchfield," to her brother Samuel Jackson's. Captain Bull sent his son with a horse part of the way, and they "rode by turns." They remained among their friends "in Litchfield, Nobletown, and Canaan until the next spring." They frequently received intelligence from Wyoming, and finally began to meditate returning. In the fall Solomon Bennet came on with a horse to bring his mother and two sisters back to their loved and much-desired Wyoming home. Mrs. Bennet and her youngest daughter rode upon the horse, attended by Solomon, while Martha took passage in a sloop from Canaan to Newburg. They met at the latter place, and, passing Washington's camp, went on to Goshen. Here they purchased a yoke of oxen and a cart, and, loading upon this homely vehicle the fruits of Mrs. Bennet's and Martha's earnings, they commenced their slow march. They came by Stroudsburg, and thence through the road made by Sullivan's army; and, finally, Mr. Bennet's family, after more than two years' separation, were together again.

Mr. Bennet had fitted up "one of Sullivan's old barracks, just opposite to Wilkesbarre, for a house." They had an abundance of corn and garden vegetables, but no flour, as there was no grist-mill in the Valley. The only resort of the settlers, for the time, was to a *hominy block.* This was a block cut from the trunk of a large tree, hollowed, and set on end. The corn was put in the hollow, and bruised with a pestle hung upon a spring pole. Such was the demand for hominy that this rude mill was kept going day and night. The girls often worked the mill, and not unfrequently were obliged to wait long for their turn. There were now about thirty families in the settlement.

General Sullivan had left several companies in the garrison at Wilkesbarre, under the command of Colonel Moore. Among the officers were Captain Schott and Lieutenant Lawrence Myers, who married and settled in the country. The former married Naomi Sill, and the latter Sarah Gore. A store for the supply of the garrison was provided, and was under the directions of the commissary, William Stuart. He had flour, and, although none could be obtained from him for the labor of the men, yet Miss Bennet, being skillful in fine knitting and working lace, could procure it for her work. By knitting a pair of stockings and a pair of gloves for the commissary, and working a lace cap and some silk lace to trim a cloak for his lady, she procured one hundred pounds of flour. All this work she did "nights by pine-light, after spinning two sixteen-knotted skeins of flax." Besides all this, she "did much about house, and often had to work the hominy block." Her "rule was to go to bed at one or two o'clock in the morning." She says, "We were constantly afraid of the Indians, and the well-known cry of the sentinels, 'All's well!' which broke upon the stillness of the night during my nightly toils, was to me a most welcome and pleasant sound." She notices a little incident, small in itself, but significant and fruitful in its results. She says, "A company of us girls would often go out and gather five-finger-leaf for tea, and while on these little excursions we were guarded by the soldiers." Ah! indeed! "Guarded!" yes, and loved and wooed "by the soldiers," as the facts afterward proved.

Tea was proscribed because it was taxed by the British government, and could not easily be obtained, and when it could be had it was drunk stealthily. The people generally sought the best substitute which the soil afforded, and this, at best, was poor enough. Congress was obliged, for purposes of revenue, to lay a tax on many of the conveniences of life. Those who enjoyed the luxury of glass lights in their houses had to pay a tax on every pane. Mrs. Myers says that Lieutenant Van Horn, a Pennamite, for whom she certainly had no great respect, came around taking account of the windows which were in the hastily-built cabins of the settlers. Addressing her, he demanded, "How many lights have you in your house?" "Oh, plenty of lights," was the answer. "Look all around, and you will see for yourself," at the same time pointing to the chinks between the logs. The functionary becoming satisfied, from the evidence afforded by his own eyes, that there was not a pane of glass in the old barrack, soon took his leave.

Miss Martha, at this period, was one of the most efficient agents in supplying the necessaries of life to the family. We have seen that she procured flour for her work where it could not be obtained by the settlers "for either love or money." She procured meat in the same way. She knit a lace cap for an old Mrs. M'Clure, and procured of her three pigs, for which she had refused the cash. These animals grew, and turned to most excellent account.

Things had been so managed that most of the Pennamites belonged to the garrison; and some of the officers being of this class, the Yankee settlers were often subjected to petty annoyances. Mr. Bennet could procure no land to work under cover of the fort, and finally resolved to make an attempt to work his own land above Forty Fort. On the 27th of March, 1780, he commenced plowing within "the Ox-bow," a bend in the creek on the flats, between Elijah Shoemaker's and the river. His team consisted of a yoke of oxen and a horse. The boy Andrew rode upon the horse. When they came to the bend in the creek the horse seemed shy. Mr. Bennet said, "I fear all is not right. I think we will only go around once more." When they came again to the same point, four Indians sprung from the bushes, and one seized Mr. Bennet, and another took Andrew from the horse. The Indians hurried off their prisoners, and soon came up with two more Indians, having Lebbeus Hammond as a prisoner. Mr. Bennet exclaimed, "Hammond, are you here?" With downcast look, Hammond answered "Yes." An Indian mired Hammond's horse in the marsh and left him. They then took the old war-path over the mountain.

When Mr. Bennet left home, he told his wife that if he did not return by sundown she might conclude some harm had befallen him. Soon after sundown Mrs. Bennet gave the information at the fort that her husband and son had not returned, and desired that a party might be sent out in search of them. Mr. Hammond's wife was also alarmed on account of his failing to return as expected. Not knowing but that a large party of Indians had made a descent upon the Valley, it was thought not to be prudent to go out that night. They fired the alarm-gun, and waited till morning. A company then went out, and found Mr. Bennet's oxen and horse trembling with the cold, the weather having changed during the night. They followed on the track of the Indians to the top of the mountain, and then returned.

Mrs. Bennet and her remaining children were now left in a state of most cruel suspense for the space of six or seven days. Any supposition which contained the elements of probability was terrible almost beyond endurance. There were a few things possible between the worst presumption—and that was that the prisoners would be cruelly tortured to death—and the most favorable, which was, that they would be taken to Canada. Mr. Bennet was somewhat in years, and was afflicted with rheumatism, and it was most probable that he would break down under the hardships of his captivity, and fall a victim to savage cruelty. The barbarous tortures inflicted by the savages upon the helpless victims of their fiendish orgies were all like household words with Mrs. Bennet and her children. Their midnight dreams were occupied with the fearful tragedy of a cold-blooded massacre by the instrumentality of the tomahawk, the scalping-knife, and blazing pine knots. In their imaginations, the aged sire and his boy were often seen suffering the most excruciating tortures for hours, and then their bodies left to be devoured by wild beasts. All this was highly probable, and all the reasonings about it based on facts, which the settlers in the Valley of Wyoming had more perfect knowledge of than any other people upon earth.

In the midst of the gloom and despondency of the families of Mr. Bennet and Mr. Hammond, and the general impression that the prisoners would never return, three emaciated, limping, reeling figures were seen directing their course toward the fort at Wilkesbarre. Who could they be? As they came near, it was discovered that they were "the Bennets and Hammond." Their appearance almost seemed like a resurrection from the dead. The mystery was soon explained; they had arisen upon their captors at Meshoppen, and cut them to pieces, and had found their way back to the embraces of their families and friends. Their feet had been badly frozen, and the consequences were most painful. When the excitement of their flight was over, they scarcely had a spark of life left. Good nursing soon restored their physical strength, and Mr. Hammond and Andrew Bennet were able to get about in a few weeks; but Mr. Bennet's feet were so dreadfully injured by the frost that several of his toes came off at the first joint, and he was obliged to walk with crutches for more than a year, during most of which time he suffered indescribably, and required much attention. We shall give a particular account of the rising and escape of the Bennets and Hammond in a chapter by itself.

Mrs. Myers says: "We remained under cover of the fort another year. Solomon married the widow Upson: her maiden name was Stevens. Her husband was killed by the Indians. Upson, with another man and a boy, were in the woods making sugar. When the boy was out gathering sap, he saw the Indians come up slyly to the camp, and pour boiling sap into

Upson's mouth while he lay fast asleep on his back. The other man they tomahawked, and made a prisoner of the boy.

In the spring of 1781, Mr. Bennet, his son Solomon, and old Mr. Stevens each built a small log house on the flats near where Mr. Bennet's house stood before the battle. They raised fine crops, and had abundance until another calamity overtook them.

### THE ICE FLOOD.

"See how the noble river's swelling tide,
Augmented by the mountain's melting snows,
Breaks from its banks, and o'er the region flows."
BLACKMORE.

In March, 1784, the spring of "the hard winter," a heavy rain suddenly melted the vast burden of snow upon the mountains and plains, broke up the strong ice in the river, and formed it into dams in the narrows and at the head of the islands. At about two o'clock P.M., Colonel Denison and Esquire Myers came riding down the river on horseback. Seeing the three families apparently unapprised of their danger, one of them cried out, "Bennet, what are you about? The ice will soon be upon you in mountains." Mrs. Bennet had previously been urging her husband to take the family to the high bank across the creek. He, however, relied securely upon the tradition communicated to him from "the oldest Indians," that "the water had never been over these flats."

After the warning given by Colonel Denison and Esquire Myers, however, the old gentleman gave up his policy of inaction, and "began to stir about." The big canoe was loaded, and went off, carrying the old people and the children. The boys drove the cattle to Swetland's Hill, taking along the wagon and horses. They barely escaped, the water rising so rapidly that it came into the wagon-box just before they reached the hill. Martha staid at the house and assisted in loading the canoe, which Solomon Bennet and Uriah Stevens run back and forth between the house and the bank. As they were engaged packing up, the ice above gave way with a tremendous roar. Martha cried out, "Boys, we are gone!" She says, "In an instant we were in the canoe—I can not tell how—and were lifted up among the tops of the trees, and surrounded by cakes of strong ice. The boys rowed, and I pulled by the limbs of the trees; but, in spite of all we could do, we were driven down the stream rapidly. It was now dark, and our people, with lighted torches, came along the bank in the greatest anxiety of mind, frequently calling out, 'Where are you?' As we were swept along by the terrible current, and unable to make much headway in consequence of the obstructions occasioned by the ice, we saw the lights following along the bank, and occasionally heard our friends shout out, 'Keep up good courage; you will soon reach the shore.' We struggled for life, and at eleven or twelve o'clock at night we reached the shore. Uriah Stevens sprung upon a log which lay by the shore, and thence upon the ground. I followed him, but the moment I struck the log it rolled, and I was plunged under the water. I was fortunate enough to rise within reach of the young man, and he pulled me out. Solomon, in the canoe, was then driven out among the ice, and it was an hour or more before he reached the shore. My clothes were frozen on me, and I was badly chilled. I was obliged to walk half a mile in this condition before I could get to the fire."

Many of the houses of the settlers were carried entirely away. Mr. Bennet's house was taken down the stream some distance, and lodged against some trees near the creek. The other families lost their hogs and poultry. Seven head of young cattle which were driven to the hill were not contented to remain there, and were all drowned in an attempt to return. Mrs. Myers says, "Our wheat was in the chamber, and, although some of it was washed, we had plenty left. Our corn and meat were saved. Our potatoes and cabbage, being buried, remained undisturbed; so that, although our house was gone, we had plenty of provisions."

Mr. Bennet now hastily put up a temporary cabin, constructed of boards and blankets. Mrs. Myers says, "For seven weeks we lived all but out of doors, doing our cooking by a log before our miserable cabin. After this we occupied our new double log house, which stood near where Elijah Shoemaker now lives, and, by slow degrees, was improved so as to be comfortable."

RENEWAL OF THE PENNAMITE AND YANKEE WAR.

Mr. Bennet had just removed his family into his new house, while it was without chimney or chinking, when the old troubles between the two classes of settlers were revived. Armstrong and Van Horn, under the authority of the Legislative Council of Pennsylvania, had come on with a company of armed men, taken possession of the fort at Wilkesbarre, and proceeded to drive the New England people from the country by force and arms. Captain Swift, a Yankee, was wounded in an attempt to fire the fort, and was lodged at the widow Brockway's, at Tuttle's Creek. Many families were driven from their houses; among them were the widows Shoemaker and Lee, near neighbors to Mr. Bennet. In vain did they plead that their husbands had been slain by the Tories and Indians, and they were helpless and defenseless widows, and they could not leave their homes and take a long journey through the wilderness. Go they must, and they made the best of the necessity. They left a portion of their goods with Mrs. Bennet, and were taken to Wilkesbarre, and thence, with Esquire Lawrence Myers, Giles Slocum, and many others, were hurried on toward "the swamp." At Capouse, Myers and Slocum escaped, but the great mass of the persecuted people had no remedy but to submit to their fate. Mr. Miner says, "About five hundred men, women, and children, with scarce provisions to sustain life, plodded their weary way, mostly on foot, the road being impassable for wagons; mothers, carrying their infants, literally waded streams, the water reaching to their arm-pits, and at night slept on the naked earth, the heavens their canopy, with scarce clothes to cover them." What a reflection, this, upon Armstrong, Patterson, Van Horn, and Company!

Mr. Bennet and Colonel Denison escaped, and went up the river to Wyallusing. Mrs. Bennet stuck by the stuff. She had never yet left the Valley for the Pennamites, and she had made up her mind that she never would. She was not left, however, in the possession of her home without an effort to drive her away. Mrs. Myers says, "Van Horn and his *posse* came up, having pressed a Mr. Roberts, with his team, to carry off our goods. Van Horn ordered mother to clear out, but she firmly replied that she was in her own house, and she would not leave it for him or any body else. He ordered Andrew and me to put things upon the wagon, a service which we refused to render. Some of the men went to the corn-house, where there was a quantity of corn; but mother seized a hoe, and, presenting herself before the door, declared that she would knock the first man down who touched an ear of the corn. They looked astonished, and left her. They then began to look about the house, and they found the big chest belonging to the widows, which was so heavy that they found it hard to lift, and they threatened to break it open with an axe. They carried some of our things out of the house; but, before they had commenced loading up, they became alarmed lest they should be noticed by the Yankee boys, a company of whom were at the widow Brockway's, and they left rather hastily, charging mother to be ready to leave the next morning. When they left Roberts went about his business, and 'the boys' came and helped us return our things to their appropriate places. The Pennamites gave us no more interruption."

A few days after the above events had transpired, Miss Bennet went out to milk the cows very early—as she says, when she "could see the stars." John Satterlee came along, to whom she said, "Satterlee, what in the world are you doing so early?" He answered, "We have Dave Ogden out here in the woods." "Who has him?" demanded Miss Bennet. "Bill Slocum," was the answer. Said she, "Do let him go; he'll certainly kill you. Is he bound?" "No," was the answer. "Can you give me something to eat?" asked Satterlee. "Yes; but you must not tell where you got it," was the answer. A cold cut was set before him; and, after satisfying his hunger, he left, smiling. Miss Bennet charged him again and again, while he sat at the table, either to "let Ogden slip away or to bind him fast." Colonel Franklin, the Yankee leader, had his head-quarters at Mill Creek, on the opposite side of the river, whither Satterlee and Slocum were bound with their prisoner. They took him into a canoe at the mouth of Shoemaker's Creek, and pushed off. Ogden soon asked, "Boys, can you swim?" "No," was the answer. Ogden's arms were pinioned, but his feet were free. He upset the canoe, turned on his back, and easily shoved himself across the river. Slocum hung to the canoe, but poor Satterlee went down and was drowned. Ogden and Slocum came out on the bar opposite Forty Fort, and took different directions. Five of the finest young men in the settlement were killed during these terrible conflicts, among whom was William Smith, a young man of fine character, and much beloved.

"The boys" at the widow Brockway's had nearly exhausted their powder. Word came to Colonel Franklin, but it was a difficult matter to convey across the river the needed supply. Mrs. Kennedy—an old lady called Mother Kennedy—volunteered to convey the powder to the place where it was wanted. She tied it around her waist, under her dress, and brought it to Mr. Bennet's, whence it soon found its way up to the widow Brockway's.

Soon after this a large company, under the command of Captain Bolin, a fine-looking man, crossed the river from Wilkesbarre, and marched up toward the head-quarters of "the boys." The captain called at Mr. Bennet's, and asked for a drink of water. Miss Bennet heard him, with a great swell, say, "I'll dislodge them." They moved on toward the widow Brockway's; there were four houses there, built of hewed logs, so situated and provided with loop-holes as to constitute a formidable fortification. Martha Bennet was anxious for the result, and soon went around the corner of the house and listened. A brisk discharge of fire-arms soon commenced, but did not long continue. Bolin's company fired upon the block-houses, and were promptly answered. The redoubtable captain took his position behind a large tree, but the well-directed aim of some one of "the boys" inflicted upon him a mortal wound, and he soon expired. The company then fled down the flats, bearing the corpse of their captain.

When the hostile band were seen in full retreat, Miss Bennet made a visit to Mrs. Brockway's, and found no one at all hurt; but Mrs. Myers, afterward Mrs. Bidlack, being there for safety, said a ball passed just over her head. She returned with Miss Bennet, and spent the night. Mother Kennedy's powder did the work this time, and, in fact, terminated this unhappy war. Mrs. Myers says, "The widows Shoemaker and Lee soon returned, and we were no more molested. This awful civil war was finally ended, to the great joy of all who loved peace and valued human life."

The view which we present of the Pennamite and Yankee wars, it will be observed, is given from the Yankee stand-point, and often reflects discredit upon the other party. It must not, however, be understood that all the Pennsylvanians concerned in the wars are regarded as equally guilty, nor that there were none among them entirely innocent. The whole responsibility of the sanguinary proceedings, which occasioned so much suffering, rests upon the *land-jobbers;* they were the men who kept up the quarrel, while innocent parties on both sides suffered most severely.

With the termination of the last Pennamite and Yankee war Mrs. Myers's narration closes. What remains to be done is to give a more particular account of the conclusion of this unfortunate struggle, and a brief sketch of the subsequent history of the relater of the stories which we have endeavored faithfully to record.

The Pennamite and Yankee war was finally terminated on the principle of mutual concession, but not without great difficulty. At the close of the Revolutionary war, the "Superior Executive Council of Pennsylvania" petitioned Congress for a hearing in relation to the Connecticut claim, "agreeable to the ninth article of the Confederation." Connecticut promptly met the overture. A court was constituted by mutual consent, which held its session in Trenton, New Jersey. The decree was awarded, on the 30th of December, 1782, in favor of the jurisdiction of Pennsylvania. The Pennsylvanians, of course, were pleased, and the New England people made up their minds to submit to the decision. There was, however, still a question left open of vastly greater importance than the jurisdiction over the country; that question was *the right of the soil*. The Pennamites thenceforward made every effort to drive out the Yankees, and to possess their lands. A military force was employed to drive off "the intruders," and to take from them the fruit of their toils and sacrifices. Blood again began to flow, and there were prospects of a more terrible conflict than had yet taken place in the ill-stared valley. In the sanguinary conflicts which now occurred Swift was wounded, and Stevens and Smith were killed on the Yankee side, and Bolin and others fell on the side of the Pennamites. Untold hardships were inflicted upon the greatest portion of the settlers; they were absolutely driven out of the Valley by the point of the bayonet. They were driven through the swamp, that being the nearest way to Connecticut. This way consisted of sixty miles of wilderness, and it had to be traced on foot. Esquire Elisha Harding, one of the sufferers, gives the following graphic and touching account of the exodus: "It was a solemn scene: parents, their children crying for hunger; aged men on crutches—all urged forward by an armed force at our heels. The first night we encamped at Capouse, the second at Cobb's, the third at Little Meadow, so called. Cold, hungry, and drenched with rain, the poor women and children suffered much. The fourth night at Lackawack, fifth at Blooming-grove, sixth at Shehola; on the seventh arrived at the Delaware, where the people dispersed, some going up, and some down the river. I kept on east, and when I got to the top of Shongum Mountain, I looked back with this thought: Shall I abandon Wyoming forever? The reply was, No! oh no! there lie my murdered brothers and friends. Dear to me art thou, though a land of affliction. Every way looks gloomy except toward Wyoming. Poor, ragged, and distressed as I was, I had youth, health, and felt that my heart was whole. So I turned back to defend or die."—*Miner's History*, p. 346.

> "And oh! ye fountains, meadows, hills, and groves,
>   Think not of any severing of your loves:
>     I love the brooks which down their channels fret
> E'en more than when I tripped lightly as they.
> The innocent brightness of a new-born day
>     Is lovely yet;
> The clouds that gather round the setting sun
>   Do take a sober coloring from an eye
>   That hath kept watch o'er man's mortality:
> Another race hath been, and other palms are won."
> 
> WORDSWORTH.

Public sentiment in Pennsylvania condemned this brutal outrage upon the common laws of humanity, and the *land-sharks* who were concerned in it were compelled to modify their course. The Legislative Council of Pennsylvania found it necessary to adopt conciliatory measures, and finally put the New England people into peaceable possession of their homes, on terms which the considerate were willing to accept. There was an ultra Yankee party, which sprung up under the leadership of Colonel John Franklin, and they openly opposed the jurisdiction of Pennsylvania. A series of conflicts followed between Franklin and his party on the one hand, and Colonel Pickering, the government functionary, and his party on the other, during which Franklin, upon the charge of treason, was seized and sent in irons to Philadelphia; and, in retaliation, Pickering was abducted and carried off into the woods, and kept on short allowance among the musquitoes for near three weeks. Franklin was tamed by his long imprisonment of more than one year, and the people of Wyoming had rest.

It is a curious fact that, in all these troubles with the State of Pennsylvania, the Yankees had the sympathies of a multitude of the people in this state; and there were those who suffered in common with them, not only from Pennsylvania, but from various other states. The Shoemakers and M'Dowells were Pennsylvanians, and Esquire Lawrence Myers was from Maryland. No matter where they were from, to Connecticut they must go, and they were pushed off through the swamp. Myers escaped at Capouse, and "the widows," after the brave posse of "militia" had quit them at the Delaware, went down stream to their friends. The guilt of these people, it is presumed, consisted in their having formed alliances with the Yankees, or taken a Connecticut title for their lands. Myers had married a Yankee wife, and that was a sufficient reason why he should be marched off through the swamp toward Connecticut.

The Revolutionary war closed, and peace blessed all parts of the country except Wyoming. A five years' war between two parties which had contracted a bitter hatred for each other followed, in which property and life were sacrificed, and the bitter fruits of civil war made up a fearful harvest. But peace—welcome peace—finally came, and the wounds inflicted by the sanguinary scenes of those fearful times were gradually healed.

In the midst of the terrible conflicts and unexampled sufferings which we have been called to survey as we have passed through the preceding pages, there were tender greetings and matrimonial alliances. The brave girls of those times found means of access to the hearts of the brave lads, both in the army and among the hardy settlers. As, in the popular romances, love and murder hold prominence in the plot, and are closely related, so, in the history of Wyoming, these two antagonisms stand out in bold relief, and are traced in parallel lines. While the soldiers were guarding the girls in their excursions over the plains in quest of "five-finger-leaf," or the wild fruits which clustered in abundance in the thickets—while the thunder of the battle roared, and while old and young fled in dismay before the conquering foe, common danger and mutual sympathy engendered attachments. Glances were exchanged and hearts were won in the midst of civil commotions, while the groans of the slain were wafted upon the breeze.

> "In peace Love tunes the shepherd's reed,
> In war she mounts the warrior's steed;
> In halls in gay attire is seen,
> In hamlets dances on the green."
>
> Scott's *Lay of the last Minstrel.*

The tender emotions originating under the fitful circumstances of the times were often dissipated by the sad rumors which were too common to excite surprise. The cup of bliss was often dashed to the ground by the chances of war ere it touched the fevered lip. The affianced bade adieu to his loved one, to play the man for his country or his party, and never returned. His fall upon the battle-field or at the post of public duty sent to *one heart* a deeper thrill of sorrow than that which agonized the heart of the mother who bore him. The story of his fate for long years with that one would be the leading fact in the history of a most eventful period.

The picture which is but faintly drawn above is not an imaginary one. There were cases of the kind—there may have been many—there certainly was one. Martha Bennet and William Smith were solemnly pledged to each other through life, for weal or woe. Smith was shot in cold blood from the fort, when occupied by the Pennamites, while walking across the street in his shirt-sleeves in the evening, near the termination of that unnatural civil war. Miss Bennet was disconsolate, and for a considerable time thought to spend her life in a state of celibacy. William Smith was a son of the wife of Doctor William Hooker Smith by a former husband by the name of Smith. The death of Smith created a deep sensation among the settlers, and inflicted an incurable wound upon the hearts of a large and respectable circle of relations and friends. Martha Bennet—subsequently Mrs. Myers—was treated as a *sister* by the numerous family of Dr. Smith—daughters and sons—until they had all gone far down the vale of years.

In the great conflict for ascendency between John Franklin and Timothy Pickering, many of the leading spirits in the preceding conflicts on the Yankee side were for submission to the laws of Pennsylvania, and consequently arranged themselves on the side of Pickering. It was finally agreed to hold what, in modern parlance, would be called a great *mass meeting*, on the old battle-ground at Forty Fort, in May, 1787, and decide the question by popular vote. A stand was erected for the moderator, clerk, and speakers, and the hard-fisted settlers were assembled to listen to the propositions of the parties and the pleadings of the advocates. James Sutton, Esquire, was called to the chair. Colonel Pickering made an eloquent speech in favor of submission to the jurisdiction of Pennsylvania, giving the most ample assurances that the government would protect the settlers in all their rights as citizens, and that there should be no more harassing proceedings instituted against them. Colonel Franklin then arose and rehearsed the grievances of the settlers, and denounced "the pretended compromise" and all its supporters in the most unmeasured terms. The blood of the old Yankees was stirred. Some were on one side, and others on the other, but all were excited and determined on victory. The old argument of *physical force* was not yet quite out of date, and, in the absence of fire-arms, each man ran to the grove hard by and cut a club. Many blows were dealt out on both sides, but were so adroitly parried off that no heads were broken. There was a general melee. Esquire

THE MYERS HOUSE.

Sutton was driven from the stage and disappeared. Supposing that he was spirited away, and was about to be victimized by the hair-brained partisans of Franklin, a party scoured the woods and by-places, and found him, now left to himself. Colonel Hollenback cracked Colonel Franklin about the ears with his riding-whip, loading him with a volley of epithets. A rather informal vote *to sustain the laws of Pennsylvania and accept the proposed compromise* was passed, and the gathering dispersed.

A new-comer mingled in this scene. The reader has noticed the name of Lawrence Myers introduced on several occasions in the preceding narrative. The father of Esquire Myers removed, with his family, from Germany in the year 1760, and settled in Frederick, in the State of Maryland. He had four sons, Lawrence, Philip, Henry, and Michael. The two former served the country in the Revolutionary war in the Maryland line, and were in the battle of Germantown. Lawrence had come to Wyoming, and married, and become identified with the New England settlers. He was a man of spirit and enterprise, and was appointed deputy sheriff under the laws of Pennsylvania, and exercised his functions and his influence in quieting matters under the compromise. His brother Philip came on to Wyoming in 1785, and was present at "the club-fight." He had sought the hand of Martha Bennet, and they were joined in marriage July 15, 1787, he being aged 27, and she 25 years.

Mr. Thomas Bennet gave his son-in-law a town lot on the north line of old Forty Fort. On this he erected a comfortable house, constructed of yellow pine logs, hewed, and pointed with lime mortar, and lined on the inside. This old relic still stands, and, if no vio-

I

lence is done to it, with reasonable repairs may live to see the opening of the next century.

The storm of war had blown over, old grudges between the two classes of settlers were fast fading away, and society was assuming a condition of stability and prosperity.

>"Affliction's cloud, however dark,
>  Grows lighter by the lapse of years,
>And many a sorrow now we mark,
>  Once deeply felt, whose very tears
>Have left, as brighter scenes passed by,
>  Only a rainbow in the sky."
>
> Roscoe.

Mr. Myers purchased a lot of one hundred and fifty acres, extending from Forty Fort to the top of the mountain. He cleared up his farm, and raised a large family of children. Mrs. Myers's great force of character never forsook her. She possessed a strength of will and a firmness of nerve which carried her through dangers, sufferings, and toils enough to have broken down many ordinary women. For many years Mr. Myers kept a public house. His house being situated on an eddy in the Susquehanna, it was a great place of resort for the lumbermen bringing their pine lumber from the upper part of the Susquehanna and its tributaries, and taking it to the Baltimore and Philadelphia markets. The consequence was that Mr. Myers's house was thronged for weeks by the hardy "raftsmen" every spring. The house would often be literally jammed full, and nearly all the night would be occupied by all the help that could be raised in preparing for breakfast. But Mrs. Myers's resources never failed her; no one left her table without having had set before him an abundant supply of food, prepared in the best style of the times. She was an admirable housewife down to old age; and when her circumstances would have excused her from anxious care, from mere habit she governed the kitchen and directed all the cooking processes.

Mrs. Myers was a large-hearted, liberal woman. She had the poor always with her. Upon the town lots at Forty Fort were located a race of poor people—some of them idle, some intemperate, and many of them vicious. Whoever or whatever they were, worthy or unworthy of her charity, they were never turned away empty. Every day, summer and winter, poor, squalid, ragged, barefooted women and children were dismissed from her door with some of the necessaries of life. And she did not always wait for an application on the part of the needy. Often at dinner she would say, "Boys, I want to ride out this afternoon." No questions would be asked, but at the proper time the horse and carriage were ready, and often she was her own driver. She first ordered her bags and baskets of good things deposited in the carriage, and then off she went to make the heart of the needy glad. Mrs. Myers was no mean driver, even when she had become advanced in age. When between sixty and seventy years of age, she was left in the carriage, in the village of Kingston, by some male member of the family. In his absence the animal became restive, and set off at full speed. Instead of giving him a chance for a fair run up the plain, smooth road homeward, she obliged him to describe half a circle and come up against a heavy "pair of bars." The animal by this time had acquired a tremendous momentum, and in an attempt to scale the bars he went through them with a terrible crash; then, being in a barn-yard, his race ended. When a dozen men, who had started on the chase, came up, the old heroine was upon the seat, with the reins fast in her hands, with nothing about the carriage or harness injured at all. During the whole operation she had not uttered a word, excepting a moderate "whoa!" to the horse, and this she ceased to do when she found it of no use. Upon her return home she spoke of the event with perfect composure, attributing her safety entirely to the providence of God.

Mrs. Myers was left a widow on April 2, 1835. Mr. Myers had a protracted illness, and during his decline and gradual approach to the hour of his departure his ever-faithful and kind-hearted companion never left him, scarcely for a day, to the care of others. On renewing the fire one night, a spark of burning anthracite coal struck her eye near the pupil. This injury brought on cataract. She had scarcely lost the sight of one eye before the other began to fail, and she finally lost that, and the world was thenceforward shut out from her vision.

> "Thus with the year
> Seasons return, but not to me returns
> Day, or the sweet approach of ev'n or morn,
> Or sight of vernal bloom, or summer's rose,
> Or flocks, or herds, or human face divine;
> But clouds instead, and ever-during dark
> Surrounds me; from the cheerful ways of man
> Cut off, and for the book of knowledge fair
> Presented with a universal blank
> Of Nature's works, to me expunged and rased,
> And wisdom at one entrance quite shut out."
>
> MILTON.

She lived after this nearly sixteen years, an example of pious resignation, and an interesting instance of physical and intellectual vigor.

Mrs. Myers was visited by Professor Silliman previous to her blindness. Mr. Miner gives an account of the visit in his history. Colonel Stone and Mr. Lossing, in turn, with other interesting tourists and authors, called upon her, as the most accurate chronicler of the stirring and romantic events of the early history of Wyoming. All make honorable mention of her. Her accurate memory of the scenes which came under her own observation, and those which were matter of common report and universal belief in the olden time, is remarked with admiration by the authors above referred to. But those alone who had been accustomed to hear these events related for years are prepared fully to appreciate her extreme accuracy of recollection. Her children, who heard her stories hundreds of times, we will venture to say, never caught her in a single contradiction or a material variation in relating the same facts. She never obtruded her reminiscences upon unwilling ears, but, when requested — and this was often done — she was always prepared to recall the strange events of her life.

What was very extraordinary in the case of Mrs. Myers is that she continued, to the last point of life, to remember *recent* occurrences as well as those which transpired in the days of her youthful vigor. Her active habits made it unpleasant to her to remain long at the same place. She consequently itinerated around among her children, who were settled in the neighborhood. While at one of these places she learned, by overhearing conversation, and occasionally asking a question, all that was going on upon the premises; and when she removed to another place, she related all the domestic news, giving most accurate accounts of the whole course of business. Let it not be supposed, however, that she exposed the imperfections or weaknesses of one family circle to another. She never dwelt upon the faults of the absent; and, in speaking of one of her children to another, she always made every thing as fair as possible. No mother was ever more constant and earnest in the pursuit of the best means to establish and maintain a most cordial family feeling among her children.

Mr. Myers died at the old homestead, the house which he first occupied after his marriage, and in which all his children were born and reared. Mrs. Myers died at the house of her son-in-law, Madison F. Myers, on the old Lawrence Myers farm, January 3, 1851. She had been rather indisposed for a few days, and required special attention. Her daughter visited her room at about one o'clock in the morning, and, finding her awake, asked her how she was. She made no complaint, but urged her to retire and take some rest. Upon receiving a spoonful of liquid to moisten her lips, she said, "How good the Lord is." These were her last words. The daughter retired, and the nurse fell asleep. At early dawn she was found lifeless. The lamp of life had quietly expired, no evidence being left of the slightest struggle, or the unnatural motion of a muscle—twelve days short of eighty-nine years of age.

"Thrice welcome, Death!
That after many a painful, bleeding step,
Conducts us to our home, and lands us safe
On the long-wished-for shore. Prodigious change!
Our bane turned to a blessing! Death disarmed,
Loses his fellness quite: all thanks to Him
Who scourged the venom out. Sure the last end
Of the good man is peace! How calm his exit!
Night-dews fall not more gently to the ground,

Nor weary, worn-out winds expire so soft.
Behold him in the coming tide of life—
A life well spent, whose early care it was
His riper years should not upbraid his green:
By unperceived degrees he wears away,
Yet, like the sun, seems larger at his setting."
                                    ROBERT BLAIR.

## V.

#### SKETCHES AND INCIDENTS COMMUNICATED BY MRS. DEBORAH BEDFORD.

"Old men beheld, and did her reverence,
And bade their daughters look, and take from her
Example of their future life; the young
Admired, and new resolve of virtue made."—POLLOK.

MRS. BEDFORD, at the time of this writing, is living and enjoying comfortable health. She lives, as she has done since the death of her husband, with her son, Dr. Andrew Bedford, of Abington, Luzerne County, Pennsylvania. From early childhood she has maintained a character not only without reproach, but above suspicion. She is the oracle of her family circle, and is universally loved. She is one of the few instances which are seen in a century of a contented, happy, hopeful mind, which has borne the friction and sustained the hardships of eighty-five years. She joined the first Methodist society which was formed in Wyoming in 1788, only ten years after the Indian battle. Her memory of the events of the olden time is still quite perfect, and her relations are given with more emotion than is common to those of her years. There is a remarkably matter-of-fact, business style about the stories of the survivors of the old stirring and bloody times; but Mrs. Bedford seems to recall the fears, the hopes, the sorrows, and the joys of the scenes in which she mingled eighty years agone. Her sympathies are so deep that time has labored in vain to extinguish them. We are aware of the delicacy of writing of the living; thus much we have thought it proper to say, and we hope that the modest self-distrust, and desire to keep out of sight, which are characteristic of our venerated friend, will not so far influence her mind as that this just tribute to her virtues will cause her pain.

Mrs. Bedford was the daughter of James and Sarah Sutton, and was born February 8th, 1773, in North Castle, New York. Her father was engaged in merchandising, and, when British goods were interdicted, he sold his property and removed to Wyoming, in company with Dr. William Hooker Smith, his father-in-law. Dr. Samuel Gustin married Susan Smith, his wife's sister, studied medicine with Dr. Smith, and was assistant surgeon with him in the army.

Mr. Sutton settled on Jacob's Plains, on the east side of the Susquehanna, two miles above Wilkesbarre. Before the Indian troubles he removed to Exeter, on the west side of the river, about five miles above the head of the valley of Wyoming. Here he built a grist-mill and a saw-mill upon a stream which gushes from a notch of the mountain. His house was built in the steep hill-side, and the scenery around him was wild and picturesque. Mr. Sutton was possessed of unusual mechanical genius. He was not a carpenter by trade, but, aided by a Dictionary of Arts, he was able to do most of the work of planning and constructing his mills himself.

At this time the Indians were friendly, and often visited Mr. Sutton's house. A company of them, made up of both sexes, once came in and cut up various pranks which greatly amused the children. They danced before the looking-glass with long ribbons tied to their hair behind, and seemed to feel no restraint even in a house well fitted up and furnished. Mr.

Sutton and his lady seldom opposed their wishes, as they did not choose to offend them. An old Indian once having brought a grist to the mill, after Mr. Sutton had taken out the toll, when he thought himself unobserved, took the measure and put the toll back into the hopper. Mr. Sutton thought this an occasion for a little sternness. He charged the theft upon him, and again took the toll. The savage was sullen, but offered no resistance.

In the year 1777—the year before the battle—there was much talk of war with the Indians. Several persons were killed up the river, and others taken prisoners. Mr. Sutton and John Jenkins, afterward known as Colonel Jenkins, made a journey through the wilderness to Queen Esther's Flats, in order to procure the liberation of Mr. Ingersoll, who had been carried into captivity. The distance of Queen Esther's town from Wyoming was about ninety miles. The visitors were treated very courteously by the queen, and she was free in her communications with regard to the prospect of war. She said she was opposed to war; she wished the Indians and white people to live in peace with each other. Mr. Sutton belonged to the society of Friends, was a religious man, and talked with the queen religiously. She seemed to have correct views of religious and moral obligations.

They were invited to spend the night with the queen, and the true spirit of hospitality seemed to characterize all her communications and arrangements. In the course of the evening, however, things took a new turn, and the travelers, for a while, were at a loss what construction to put upon the indications outside. A company of Indians came before the house, and, seating themselves upon a log, began to sing "the war song." The old queen went out to them, and was engaged in an earnest conversation with them for a long time. When she came in she frankly told her guests that the Indians were determined to waylay and kill them, adding, with great emphasis, "I can do nothing with them. Now," said she, "you lie down until I call you." They did so; and when all was still in the town, she called them, and then said, "You must go down the river. Go down the bank, and take my canoe, and paddle it without noise. Lift the paddles up edgewise, so as to make no splash in the water, and you may get out of reach before the war-party find out which way you have gone." They slipped off and found the canoe, which the queen had particularly described, scrupulously followed her directions, and found their way home in safety.

The Indians which were prowling about now began to be ill-natured, and to exhibit signs of hatred to the settlers. On one occasion they made a war demonstration on the opposite side of the river, in full view from Mr. Sutton's house. There was a large company, and they were seen gathering pine knots for the whole day. They collected a vast pile, and when night came they set them on fire. The flame seemed to go up to the clouds, and sent out its glare over all the region round about. The Indians danced and whooped, sung and yelled, around the fire the whole night. The spectacle was most terrific.

In the spring of 1778, Mr. Sutton rented his premises in Exeter, and purchased a mill-seat in Kingston, in the place since called Hartsift's Hollow, one mile from Forty Fort. He sawed a quantity of lumber and made a raft. Then, putting on board the raft his family and all his valuables, they were floated down to

"Forty Fort Eddy." Mrs. Bedford says: "We lived in a shanty while our house was being built, and it was nearly finished, when we were overwhelmed with a tide of troubles. A malignant and contagious disease, called the putrid fever, broke out in the settlement. My grandmother Smith and aunt Gustin died of this disease. A young man who was at work upon our house also died, and my mother, two sisters, and myself caught the disease from him.

"The settlers now began to be apprehensive of an attack from the Indians, and many of them removed to the fort. My youngest sister died, and then our nurse left us and went into the fort with her parents. Doctors Smith and Gustin told us that there were so many sick in the fort that if we went there we would probably die; that those who were as near the fort as we were would do better to remain at their homes as long as they could do so with safety. It was then arranged that, if there should be a prospect of an attack, three alarm-guns should be fired at the fort. One day an old gray-headed Indian came and walked back and forth before our door several times. Father, supposing that there was a company of Indians on the hill, and, if the old Indian was molested, they would come and massacre us, gave him a loaf of bread, when he went away, and we saw no more of him."

One morning early the alarm-guns were fired, and Mr. Sutton went to the fort to ascertain the state of matters. When he left he ordered things to be put in a state of readiness to remove. He soon returned with an officer, a team, and a file of armed men. Mrs. Sutton was fast recovering; Deborah was much better, but not yet able to walk any distance; and the younger daughter was yet extremely low, and was carried upon a litter. Deborah was taken on a wheelbarrow by a young man by the name of Asa Gore, who belonged to Captain Stuart's company, and was afterward killed in the battle. They reached the fort, and the sick were laid on beds spread upon the floor.

Lieutenant Hamilton had been to General Washington's head-quarters, and most eloquently urged the necessity of immediate assistance being sent on to Wyoming. He pointed out the defenseless condition of the settlement, most of the effective force having been drawn away, and a remorseless horde of savages and Tories about to make a hostile demonstration upon them from the north. He had just returned, and he used his influence to prevail upon the companies which had assembled in the fort to remain there, and, if need be, to defend it until succor should be sent on from the army. But Captain Stuart threatened to withdraw his company if the commanding officers refused to go out and meet the enemy. They finally resolved to go out and fight. Stuart and his party were confident of success. They had no idea of the odds they would have to contend against, but were phrensied with the idea of shooting down a few scattered bands of Indians and Tories. Many of the people in the fort were not at all sensible of the awful hazards of the movement.

Dr. Smith and his family were in the fort at Wilkesbarre. A short time before the battle the doctor went to his house above the town to get some provisions. He undertook to boil some potatoes, and, as he was proceeding with this business, he imagined that something like a blanket was thrown over his head. He supposed it to be a warning from the spirit of his departed wife of some approaching evil. He looked out of the window, and saw several Indians standing on the top of the hill, looking toward the house. He went out at the back door and ran along the creek—Mill Creek—until he came to the river, and then proceeded on the beach, under cover of the river bank, and so reached the fort in safety.

We set down the above somewhat singular story without advancing any theory upon which it is to be explained. It was taken from the lips of Mrs. Bedford, and must be altogether authentic. Dr. Smith, during his latter years, was known to be somewhat skeptically inclined. The idea of a warning from the spirit of his departed wife proves that at the time he had strong convictions of the existence of disembodied spirits. Whether the serious circumstances by which he was then surrounded for the time dissipated his doubts, or the sense of personal security which supervened in after years overcame the convictions of earlier life, we are not prepared to say.

"On the 3d of July, 1778," says Mrs. Bedford, "our little army marched from Forty Fort to meet the enemy. Doctors Smith and Gustin went out mounted. When our men turned and fled, and the work of slaughter began, the doctors ran their horses, but were hotly pursued. The Indians were so near that a ball passed through Dr. Gustin's hat. They came in, and brought us the sad tidings that our men were beaten, and the Indians were pursuing them through the woods. My father, although a Quaker, believed it right to fight in self-defense, and would probably have been in the battle had it not been necessary for him to stay with the women and children, and to take care of the sick."

After the flag of truce had been sent up, and while the negotiations for the capitulation were in progress, a barrel of liquor which was in the fort was rolled down the bank and the head knocked in, that it might not fall into the hands of the Indians. When the Indians came into Mr. Sutton's cabin they marked those present as prisoners of war, and then proceeded to plunder them of their goods. Mr. Sutton, presuming too hastily that they would be left with the clothing which they had on, put on his wedding suit—a fine Quaker suit. Mrs. Sutton, a little more shrewd, left her best clothing in her trunks, and covered them up with rubbish, and so saved them from observation. The first "big Indian" that came along after Mr. Sutton had rigged himself up in his best stripped him of every article he had on excepting his shirt. How that rascally savage looked in his "fine Quaker suit," with his rifle, bullet-pouch, and powder-horn, and a string of scalps around his waist, may be imagined. It was no part of the policy of the Indians to have things in keeping according to the tastes of civilization.

It was now sufficiently evident that there was no safety for the settlers under the articles of capitulation. Butler left the Valley, and the Indians that lingered behind were under no manner of restraint. How Mr. Sutton was to dispose of his family was a question which had its serious difficulties. The youngest child was still very low, while Mrs. Sutton and Deborah were feeble, and the idea of a journey through the swamp was not to be admitted for a moment. Mr. Sutton's mechanical skill now came in play. He and Dr. Gustin set themselves at work to build a boat. They took timber and boards from deserted cabins, and drew out old nails which had ceased to be of any service where they were, and with such materials, "in nine days" they had completed and launched their craft. Trunks, boxes, and bundles were soon deposited in the boat, and the two families, fifteen persons all told, seated upon and among them. The ingenious and courageous navigators pushed off from the shore, and committed themselves and their families to the care of a gracious Providence upon the treacherous current of a river so obstructed by rocks and rapids as to be scarcely navigable in low water except by canoes.

Their hastily-built craft had been calked, but no tar or pitch could be obtained, and, consequently, it was found to leak considerably. They hauled up for repairs, or "to overhaul her," at Captain Stuart's place, in Hanover. The females went into the deserted mansion and took refreshments, while the men proceeded to "stop leaks." Poor Stuart was slain in the battle, or, as has been reported, tortured the day following, and his house was left desolate, but not yet consigned to the flames. Mrs. Bedford says that up to the time of their leaving the Valley nothing was said about the houses of the settlers being burned. She saw no smoke arising from burning houses, and heard no mention of it; but when she returned to the Valley she learned that the houses of the settlement had been consumed by fire soon after they left.

The difficulties which were overcome and the hazards which were run in this enterprise can now scarcely be estimated. Their craft was a slight flat-bottomed boat, constructed of materials not designed for such a purpose. Upon this frail vessel all the luggage which they dared venture to take on was piled up, and then fifteen persons, some of them sick, one utterly helpless, were seated among the luggage. And now what was before them? A rapid, crooked river, several considerable falls, at best of dangerous navigation, and, for aught that was known, many miles of the way they would be exposed to the merciless savages. It required courage and skill of no ordinary grade to execute successfully such an enterprise. Mrs. Bedford piously remarks, "We had a dangerous passage down the river, but the hand of Providence preserved us." We will here give a portion of her narrative in her own language.

"Just before night we came to a house on the bank of the river, where we were kindly received and furnished with supper. We thought to have remained here for the night, but, fearing the Indians, we concluded to trust the hand of Providence for a safe passage through the Nescopeck Falls, at dead of night, rather than run the risk of falling into the hands of the savages. We arrived safely at Northumberland the next morning. That day we learned that the woman and her two sons at the house where we took our supper, and where we thought to remain over night, were murdered by the Indians. Our apprehensions of danger were well founded, and, had we remained at that place, we should probably all have been either murdered or led into hopeless bondage.

"From Northumberland we went on to Middletown, but Dr. Gustin went to Carlisle, where he entered into practice.* We remained in Middletown more than two years. The town was full of 'Fleeters,' as we were called, and provisions were extremely scarce. We could procure none other than salt provisions, and for them we had to pay very high prices. Learning that

---

* An infant daughter of Dr. Gustin, who constituted one of the company in the boat, subsequently became the wife of the Rev. Mr. Snowden, a Presbyterian clergyman, and the mother of Hon. James Ross Snowden, well known in Pennsylvania as having occupied various important and responsible public positions.

there was a garrison established at Wilkesbarre for the defense of such of the inhabitants as wished to return to their possessions, we returned to the Valley. It was not without great sufferings and fatigue that we finally reached Wilkesbarre.

"Our grist-mill and house at Exeter were burned by the Indians and Tories. That the latter had a hand in the matter is evident from the fact that the mill-irons from both the grist-mill and saw-mill were all carried off, and they were things that the Indians would not take. Our house in Kingston had in some way escaped the flames, but had been stripped of its covering by our men to build barracks with in Wilkesbarre. We consequently had no materials with which to build us a house to live in. The ingenuity of my father, however, was equal to the emergency. He erected a frame, and filled it in between the posts with split wood, and plastered it with clay mortar on each side; he then made a wash of white clay, and washed it over with a brush, and gave it a very nice finish. My mother prepared some coloring matter, and ornamented the wall quite prettily. The house, when completed, was considered as really a fine thing. It stood in Wilkesbarre just above the fort, on ground occupied subsequently by Arnold Colt, Esq., and at present by Hon. John N. Cunningham.

"There was now no mill in the settlement. The officers and men in the garrison had flour which was brought in from below, but the people of the settlement pounded Indian corn in a hominy block, of which they made bread and mush, which was nutritious, and not disagreeable food. It was, however, difficult to procure this coarse breadstuff in sufficiency to meet the necessities of the people. The pestle was in motion night and day, each one who came taking his or her turn.

"My father now set himself at work to meet the pressing wants of the settlement by building a mill on Mill Creek, near the river. He found carpenters among the soldiers who assisted him, and the mill was soon put up. A sentry-box was constructed upon the top of the mill, where a watch was kept day and night, for the Indians were skulking about, plundering all they could lay their hands upon, and killing all who crossed their path. The mill was built of hewed logs, and was on land belonging to Obadiah Gore. During the Pennamite and Yankee squabbles it was seized by a certain person under a Pennsylvania title. My father was absent, having gone up the river for personal safety; my mother went up to the mill, and ordered the miller to clear out, informing him that the mill was her husband's property, and that she would have a company of men there immediately who would take him into custody. Just then three men rode up—one of them was Dr. Smith, my grandfather, and another was William Smith, who afterward was shot by the Pennamites—and the miller took the alarm and left. The mill stood and did good service to the settlement until the celebrated pumpkin flood, when it was carried away.*

* In October, 1786, a great flood occurred on the Susquehanna, which was the occasion of an immense amount of damage. The water was never known to rise so high except on the occasion of the great "ice flood." Mills, houses, barns, and stacks of hay and grain were swept away. Horses and cattle, pigs and poultry, in great numbers, were carried down the current. Corn-fields were cleared of such quantities of pumpkins that the raging current was completely speckled with them; hence the name—the "pumpkin flood." Wilkesbarre was partially inundated, great losses were sustained,

"The settlers returned in great numbers, but such was the exposure of the country to the savages at a distance from the fort that they crowded into Wilkesbarre until they were uncomfortably jammed together. Mr. Roswell Franklin, a brother of Colonel John Franklin, had a farm upon the flats below Wilkesbarre, not far from the fort. His wife said that she would go on to their farm if the Indians were as thick as the pine-trees. She carried out her purpose, but it cost her her life.

"Her daughter—a young woman—one day went to the spring for water, and was gone so long that Mrs. Franklin became alarmed, and sent some of the smaller children to see if they could find her. They soon came running back in a great fright, informing her that their sister was coming with a company of Indians. Mrs. Franklin had been confined but two weeks before. The Indians ordered her to get up and dress herself. Difficult as was the task, it had to be done. The Indians took what they wanted, and set off with the mother and her children. As they left, she saw an Indian take a shovelful of live coals from the fire and place it between two beds. The prisoners were taken to the woods.

"Mr. Franklin was plowing upon the flats between his house and the fort. He saw his house in flames, and, judging of the instruments of the mischief, unharnessed one of his horses, and rode to Wilkesbarre upon a jump. A company of men turned out and pursued the party, overtaking them on the mount-

and great suffering during the following winter was endured by the inhabitants of the ill-starred Valley in consequence of this fearful flood. It is a wonder that not more than one or two lives were lost.

am this side of Meshoppen.* The Indians were worsted, and the prisoners brought back, excepting Mrs. Franklin and her infant child.

"We saw people gathered on the outside of the fort, and, not knowing the cause, went down to ascertain what it was, and there we saw Miss Franklin, who related to us the whole story. She said, when our people came so near as to fire, they called on the prisoners to fall. They all fell; but her mother lifted up her head, and said, 'Your father is with them.' She said to her mother, 'Put down your head; there is an Indian coming to kill you.' He fired, and she breathed her last. After the first shot, our people called to the prisoners to come to them: they then ran to them, and the Indians which remained alive fled in every direction. Some one saw an Indian put Mrs. Franklin's child behind a log; but they must have removed it to another place, or carried it off, for it was not to be found. Miss Franklin said that when the Indians had built their fire at night, they would conduct themselves in the most brutal manner to the child and the mother. They would not let the mother nurse the child, and would often pinch the poor little creature to make it scream.

"Frederick Follett, at the time of the battle, was stabbed nine times, and scalped, and finally recovered. Several years afterward he called upon Dr. Smith to assist him in securing a pension. They made an appointment to meet at my father's house. The doctor examined his scars. He showed us where he was stabbed, and it was evident enough that he had been scalped. As to his being stabbed, he said it was done

* According to others, it was upon the Frenchtown Mountain, above Wyalusing.

by different Indians, each one giving him a stab in passing. He endured the scalping and stabbing without making a motion, that they might suppose him dead. When he was scalped, he supposed the next thing would be the tomahawk; but the attention of the Indian who did the deed being probably drawn in some other direction, he neglected this part of the operation. Those following on, supposing the work completed, contented themselves with piercing what they thought a dead man with their spears.

"A Mr. Corey, who had lost a son in the war, once came to my father's house some years afterward. We had been informed that he had learned the circumstances of his son's death. Upon my mother requesting him to tell us the story, he said, 'Mrs. Sutton, I will.' He then said that when the roll was called on the morning of the battle, he saw his son—a boy about fifteen years of age—standing in the ranks. He said, 'Silas, go back;' he answered, 'Father, I can do something.' He told him the second time to leave the ranks, and he went out of his sight. When they came into the action he saw his son by his side; it was then too late to send him away. This was the last he saw of him. A neighbor of his was taken prisoner, and subsequently returned, and gave him a description of the manner in which the boy came to his end. He said that after the battle some prisoners were encamped in the woods with the Indians and Tories, and that one of the Tories told the Indians that this boy was a captain of a company of boys that were being trained up to kill them. They then gathered a quantity of pine knots, and dug a hole in the ground, and set therein four bayonets with the points upward. They then lifted the boy up, and let him fall down on the bayonets, all of which pierced him, two just below his hips, and two near his shoulder-blades. They then built a slow fire under him with the pine knots, and thus tortured him until near daylight, when he expired.

"The witness of this horrible scene said that the poor fellow uttered the most heart-rending cries, but he durst not show the least emotion upon the occasion, not doubting but any manifestation of sympathy would subject him to the same fate. While the father was giving the relation, the big tears rolled from his eyes in quick succession. The whole story, and the manner of the old gentleman, are all now perfectly fresh in my recollection. These terrible scenes used to prey upon my thoughts, and harass me in my dreams, until they were imbedded in my very nature."

### PENNAMITE AND YANKEE WARS.

The scenes of the last Pennamite and Yankee war which Mrs. Bedford witnessed, or has related from her immediate family connections, are given pretty much in her own language, and contain several interesting incidents which are not in the histories, and which we have not learned from any other source.

"The wars between the Pennsylvania and New England people were terrible. Dr. Smith took sides with the Yankees in the first struggle before the war with the Indians. I remember to have heard it said that, when Colonel Plunkett was about to invade the settlement, the doctor harangued the people eloquently. He told them that every man who had no gun or sword must make swords of their scythes, and every boy who could lift a bush must be on hand. The spirit of the people was up; men, women, and children were all engaged in doing something. The old rusty guns and bayonets were scoured up, and those who had no guns took their scythes and attached them to poles, with which, in a close encounter, they could do terrible execution. Others seized their axes, hoes, picks, crowbars, and whatever they had which would serve the purpose of defense, or be useful in building breastworks. My father, Quaker as he was, shouldered his gun among the rest. They took their position at the foot of the valley, on both sides of the river, and when Plunkett, with his men, reached the head of Nanticoke Falls, they were met with a deadly fire, first from one side and then from the other. They looked up the mountain sides, and the waving boughs of hemlock, pine, and laurel, and the fearful yells and shouts which echoed from mountain top to mountain top, made a terrible impression on the minds of the assailants. The woods seemed to be alive, and the very trees in motion. The idea that thousands of the 'Green Mountain Boys' had come down from Vermont and New Hampshire seized the mind of the gallant colonel and his men, and they retreated without making a respectable effort to accomplish their object.

"After the Indian troubles began to abate, this unnatural war was resumed. One of my uncles lived in Forty Fort, and kept an open house for the accommodation of 'the Yankee Boys.' I kept house for him, and always had a supply of bread, meat, milk, and vegetables, and gave them free access to the pantry, where they would help themselves. The poor fellows would come in weary and hungry, set up their guns, and rush to the table like starving wolves.

"When Armstrong and Patterson came on, they commenced a series of efforts to drive the Yankees out of the country. One of their schemes was to burden the settlers with their men. They quartered their soldiers around among the people, and gave some one of them charge of the house. Six of Armstrong's men were quartered upon us, and the *meanest* one of the lot was put in charge of the house. He swelled and swaggered, and gave out orders with the authority of an absolute monarch. Mother was pleasant, and did the best for them she could, not wishing to offend them. Father thought he would leave the Valley, and he took a canoe load of our goods up to Black Walnut, intending to return and take his family, but he was taken sick there, and we heard nothing from him for near six months.

"Armstrong had a very bad felon, and applied to Dr. Smith for medical treatment. The doctor told him that he would not go into the fort to attend to his case, but if he would take board among the citizens he would do what he could for him. It was finally arranged that he should meet the doctor at our house. We gave him all the comforts which the house afforded, and his felon was soon cured. When the Yankees were all ordered off, Armstrong came to our house and said to my mother, 'Mrs. Sutton, you will not like to go with the rabble; you may stay a day or two, and then go at your leisure.' The gallant officer doubtless thought this indulgence an ample compensation for our attentions during his severe afflictions. Mother was about to be confined, and father was gone up the river, and she told him she could not go. 'Oh,' said he, 'you *must* go, but we will make it as agreeable for you as possible.' Soon after a file of armed men came in and ordered mother to clear out. When they left they said she might have fifteen min-

K

utes to leave in. She told them she could not go at all. Soon after they returned, and found mother lying on a bed on the floor. They told her to get up and be off immediately. She flung the clothing off, and, rising up, said, 'Here I am, take my life as soon as you please.' A ruffian pointed his bayonet at her, and swore he would kill her, taking a step toward her as though he would execute his threat, when one of them stepped up and turned his gun away, saying, 'Come along, and let the woman alone.'

"The Yankees were on Redoubt Hill, and our house was in range between that point and the fort, and they told us they should burn all the houses between the fort and the hill. They commenced firing the houses, and the bullets began to whistle around us. We then found we must flee, or lose our lives either by the bullets or the flames. We gathered up what we could carry and went to my uncle Bailey's—the location now occupied by Steele's hotel. Our house was burned and all there was left in it. We remained at my uncle's undisturbed.

"When father returned we removed across the river, and built a house in Forty Fort. Here we were during the conflict between Pickering and Franklin. When the people were called together to vote upon the question of submitting to the laws of Pennsylvania, my father was appointed moderator, and it devolved upon him to receive the votes and report the result. The Franklin men, beginning to doubt their strength, took father away, and carried him into the woods. A general *melee* followed. The men rushed into the thicket and cut clubs: it was an awful scene. The young hickories bent and fell before the great jack-knives of the men, and the heavy green clubs were lifted and brandished in all directions. Father was found and brought back; and, after a slight brush, in which no one was killed or very seriously injured, the men scattered and went home. Poor Franklin came along with his face bleeding from wounds received in the squabble.

"This was the winding-up of the civil wars of the famous Valley of Wyoming. Grievous and cruel wars and destructive floods desolated this lovely spot until many were driven to despair, and finally abandoned the place and settled elsewhere. Under the severe losses and untold hardships which we were compelled to endure from the causes which I have endeavored to describe, we had passed through a discipline which had its favorable influence through after-years. We were taught the vanity and uncertainty of all human things, and had received many lessons in relation to God's providential dealings.

"We returned to our place in Hartsift's Hollow, and remained there a while. Then my father, in connection with Dr. Smith, built a forge at Lackawanna; but, not succeeding as he desired in making iron, he returned to Exeter, where he and my mother both finished their earthly career.

"In 1788 I became interested in a new religious movement, commenced at Ross Hill, in Kingston, under the labors of Anning Owen. Nearly all my father's family fell under the same influence, and from that time we were identified with the Methodist Episcopal Church.

"In 1799, May 16th, I was married to Jacob Bedford, Esq. He died August 23d, 1849. I am now in my 85th year, July 13th, 1857."

## VI.

INCIDENTS OF THE WARS IN THE LACKAWANNA PORTION OF THE SETTLEMENT, RELATED BY MRS. MARTHA MARCY.

THE incidents recorded below have been communicated to us by the venerable JOSEPH MARCY, now—1858—seventy-one years of age. He is the only surviving son of the lady upon whose authority they are now transmitted.

Ebenezer Marcy came to the Valley from Fishkill, on the Hudson, and settled upon the lands now owned by his grandchildren, situated below the Lackawanna bridge, and about three miles above the village of Pittston. A block-house was built by the settlers in 1770 on the plain, in what is now called Upper Pittston. After the Indian troubles had subsided, Mr. Marcy took possession of his house, which by some strange providence had escaped the flames. It was "a double log house," built in the style of the times, with a "back wall," against which, during the cold season, a large fire, made of logs, was kept burning day and night. In the corner, near the fire, stood that necessary article of Yankee furniture, "the dye-tub," in which the "blue stockings" were "dyed in the wool" or "in the yarn." The dye-tub usually constituted a seat for some one, and it was upon this seat that the lad Joseph learned his lessons in the history of the olden time.

When Mrs. Marcy had visitors who wished to hear about the Indians and the Pennamites, Joseph would take his favorite seat, and listen with all the ears he had. After he had heard the stories a thousand and one times, they still produced the same excitement in his mind. He knew what was coming next, yet he listened, and gazed, and gaped with as much eagerness as if he had been listening to the romantic tales of a new novel. Ah! they were tales of the sufferings and adventures of his father, mother, brothers, and sisters. These stories he now relates with the greatest particularity, and seems as familiar with them as with any portion of his own history.

When John Butler arrived at Sutton's, he sent a scouting party down the river, who secured all the water-craft belonging to the Lackawanna people, and deposited them at the head of the island. The settlers at that point were consequently left without the means of crossing the Susquehanna, and this is the reason why several able-bodied and brave men were not in the battle, but were with their families in the fort on that fatal day. The fort consisted of a block-house, or probably three block-houses, surrounded by pickets made of split logs set in the ground and standing eight feet above the surface. Here the families who had settled on the Lackawanna, near its confluence with the Susquehanna, were quartered on the 3d of July, 1778.*

Soon after the tide of battle had turned against the patriots, a man who had been wounded in one foot,

---

\* The following "Articles of Capitulation for three Forts at Lacuwanack," dated "July 4, 1778," are published by Mr. Miner:

"ART. 1st. That the different commanders of the said forts do immediately deliver them up, with all the arms, ammunition, and stores in the said forts.

"ART. 2d. Major Butler promises that the lives of the men, women, and children be preserved entire."

and had managed to swim the river, brought over the sad tidings of the defeat and slaughter of the little army. After a few words upon the subject, he mounted a horse which belonged to Mr. Marcy, and laid his course across the mountains. All was stir, alarm, and confusion in the fort. The darkness of night came on, but not to hide from the eyes of the Lackawanna people the horrors of the scene which was being enacted on the west side of the Susquehanna. They saw across the river the Indians making preparations for their fiendish orgies. They kindled fires, and filled the air with their terrible yells. At length two prisoners were brought up. One was tied to a tree in a sitting posture, with his hands and feet bound to stakes driven in the ground, and a train of pine knots laid, extending some twelve feet, and terminating at his bowels. The farther end of the train was fired, and then the Indians commenced dancing around the poor creature, while the flame gradually approached him, and he was filled with the most indescribable horror at its progress. Splinters of pine knots were stuck into the flesh of the other and set on fire. The poor victims of savage cruelty shrieked, and called on God for help. Their wailings and the unearthly yells of the savages mingled together, and were wafted by the breeze across the plains, and echoed back from the hills. That was an awful night for the Lackawanna people. What would be their fate they could not foresee, but immediate flight was impossible. The best they could do was to throw themselves upon the mercy of the conquerors.

The morning came, and they raised a sheet upon a pole on the river bank. The "flag of truce" was discovered, and several British officers, attended by a

THE INDIAN TRIUMPH.

posse of Indians, came over and demolished the pickets around the block-house, and the Indians painted the prisoners. The people had hid their provisions in secret places; their flour and meal were concealed in hollow logs, and their meat was buried in the ground. A wretched old squaw soon came over, having *seventeen scalps* strung on a stick. She spoke broken English, and talked of being "dreadful tired," having, as she said, "been out all night *scalping the Yankees.*" A plan was soon set on foot still further to torture the feelings of the prisoners. An old mare belonging to Mr. Marcy was brought up, and Mrs. Marcy's side-saddle placed upon her back, with the hind part before, and the crupper tied in the mane. The squaw was then seated upon the saddle astride, a looking-glass being held in one hand and the string of scalps in the other. In this plight the animal was led by one Indian and driven by another back and forth before the fort, while the Indians hooted and laughed, and otherwise insulted the prisoners. There were men there who, if their wives and children had not been in the power of the savages, and they had had in hand their trusty rifles, would have sent a ball through the heart of the old limb of Satan, and run the hazard of dying the next moment. But, grinding their teeth, they smothered their wrath as well as they could.

Parties of the enemy went and collected the horses and cattle, and turned them into the fields of grain; this saved them the necessity of destroying the crops by other and more laborious means. The officers ordered the prisoners to milk the cows and bring in the milk for their use. It was soon found that, without a resort to some stratagem to save a portion of the milk, the children in the fort must starve; then the cows were left but half milked, and the operation was finished under cover of the night.

At evening the Indians made large fires of the pickets, and lay down before them, and soon fell into a dead sleep. This was the time for the prisoners to take their meal. The men stole away and finished milking the cows, while the women proceeded to bake their johnnycakes. The milk brought in and the cakes baked, the prisoners proceeded to take the only meal which they had the privilege of enjoying during the twenty-four hours. All this process of cooking and eating had to be conducted with the utmost silence and care. The prisoners were not cared for at all by the British officers, and could only furnish themselves and their helpless children with food, and avoid utter starvation, by stealth. Were not these British and Tories magnanimous conquerors?

On one occasion the prisoners were left by themselves, and the wife of Zebulon Marcy resolved upon trying to bake a loaf of light bread. Just as her loaf was well done, it was announced that "an Indian was coming." The loaf was rolled in a towel, and hid in the foot of the bed. The Indian came in, and, snuffing and looking about, he said, "Me want bread." One of the women replied, "We have none." Continuing his snuffing, he said, "Ah! me smell 'em;" and, going directly to the place where the loaf was deposited, he took it out. Mrs. Marcy cried, "You sha'n't have that bread: I want it to keep the children from starving;" and, springing forward, she seized the stolen loaf by one end, and in the contest it was broken in two, she retaining her half, while the Indian seemed satisfied with his portion. Well, thought the brave lady, "Half a loaf is better than no bread," and so it was.

Butler and his men left the Valley a few days after the battle, but parties of Indians were prowling about, plundering property, and burning the houses of the settlers as opportunity served and their feelings inclined them. About two weeks after the battle an Indian came to the fort and said, "Wild Indians come soon: kill Yankee and eat 'em." The settlers had gradually disappeared, and few besides the family of Ebenezer Marcy were left. Mrs. Marcy was in a delicate state of health, and, besides, was lame in her feet from rheumatism; but there seemed no alternative: she must undertake the journey across the mountains on foot.

Mr. Marcy's family consisted of himself, his wife, and five small children, the oldest a girl of eleven years of age. There was but one other individual in the company, and that was an old lady still more of a cripple than Mrs. Marcy. The exigencies of the journey would necessarily require covering at night, and hence the necessity of taking along blankets. Mr. Marcy was the only individual in the company who could carry any burden. He made a large bundle, in which he had carefully stowed away a family Bible, which Mr. Joseph Marcy has now in his possession, and preserves as a precious relic. It contains the family records, and settles some facts of public interest. All being ready, Mr. Marcy shouldered his burden, and ordered all hands to move on.

The little company commenced their perilous and doubtful journey probably on the 20th of July. Their course lay through Jacob's Plains, up Laurel Run to the path from Wilkesbarre to Stroudsburg, which they fell into on the mountain. They had nearly exhausted their provisions, and had to be put on short allowance. They fed themselves mostly on the twigs of sassafras bushes, roots, and berries. Mrs. Marcy had a cane in one hand and a spikenard root in the other, and would frequently take a little of the root in her mouth and chew it, swallowing the juice, making it serve, as she ever after maintained that it did, the double purpose of food and medicine. On the evening of the 22d of July, "on the Tobyhanna Hill," Mrs. Marcy was taken ill, and Mr. Marcy left her and the old lady, while he went forward a short distance with the children, and deposited them in the bushes. He then returned, and soon he was the father of another child. The new-comer was a daughter, and was welcomed and provided for as well as the circumstances would admit. Early in the morning Mrs. Marcy arose, and set off upon her journey with good courage, and, for her, at a brisk pace. The little piece of humanity which had been sent to them in the mountain was added to Mr. Marcy's burden, and that day they traveled the astonishing distance of *sixteen miles*, which brought them to Captain Spaulding's encampment. The captain kindly sent on two soldiers, each having a horse, to help on Mr. Marcy and his family as far as the Delaware.

When they came to "Dingman's Ferry," they asked for lodging, but were told in reply, by the good man of the house, that "the Wyoming people had eaten him out of house and home," and he could not keep them. Mrs. Marcy sat on a log before the door nursing her baby. "How old is that child?" asked the man. "Not quite two days," was the answer. "Good woman," said he, "you look tired; you ought not to go any farther, but I can not keep you." Then taking from a shelf a loaf of bread, he gave them "the half of a slice apiece," and said, "About two miles ahead you can get entertainment." They moved on, and found hospitality in the house of a farmer.

In the evening a man drove briskly by in the direction of the Delaware. It was a man whom Mr. Jonathan Spencer—Mrs. Marcy's father—had sent on to meet Mr. Marcy and his family. The man, learning at the ferry that he had passed the company, returned the next morning, and now the severest of the labors and trials of the pilgrims were ended. Eight days after the birth of her child Mrs. Marcy reached her father's house, near Fishkill, in much better condition, both physically and mentally, than could have been expected.

Mrs. Marcy "was very tired," and took her bed; but how long may it be supposed that she kept it? A month or two, with good nursing and skillful medical aid? No, indeed; it was only "for the greater part of the next day." The condition of her children brought her to her feet again after a few hours of rest. When they left the Valley their clothes were "mended up and were comfortable," but the long journey through the wilderness, often penetrating the thick brush and briers in quest of berries to save them from absolute starvation, reduced their garments to shreds and tatters. Mrs. Marcy's old friends and neighbors made large contributions in "old clothing," and "the girls" came in and helped her sew, and "in about a week" the little folks were all "decently clad."

The little "woods girl," as she was called, was an object of no little curiosity. Mrs. Marcy "felt thankful to God for her strange preservation and that of her infant, and for the deliverance of herself and family from the tomahawk and scalping-knife; and, in accordance with her feelings, she called her girl Thankful."

The child lived to the age of seventeen, and then died with measles.

The Marcys were among the persecuted Yankees during the Pennamite and Yankee wars. Mrs. Marcy used to tell a ludicrous story of some of Armstrong's men, who came up to Lackawanna in the way of fulfilling their mission. They seemed to be hard pressed for provisions. They found "an old sow with a litter of young pigs;" they butchered and devoured the whole family. Not yet satisfied, or desiring something in the line of poultry and eggs, they took "an old hen that had been setting seven days," and they cooked and devoured the hen and her stock of eggs. There must have been a little touch of the *savage* in these zealous votaries of the land-jobbers of Pennsylvania.

At the time Armstrong was disarming the Yankee settlers, two of his officers visited Lackawanna, and, entering Mr. Marcy's house, inquired for arms. There were seven guns in the house, which they proposed to disable by taking off the locks. Mrs. Marcy remonstrated against their proceedings, informing them that "the men folks" were not at home, and declaring that it was not handsome for them to take advantage of the circumstances. At that moment young John Carey, one of her boarders, came in. Seizing his rifle, he cocked it, and, pointing the muzzle toward the unwelcome visitors, he said, with a firm tone, "Stop your work, or you will have what there is in my rifle." The rifle was not loaded, but the threat was enough. The gallant subalterns turned about and left. The arms which were thus saved from being made useless subsequently did good service in the Yankee cause.

Mrs. Marcy outlived her husband, and finally died full of years and much respected.

## VII.

### MRS. SYLVIA SEYBOLT'S ACCOUNT OF THE BATTLE AND FLIGHT.

*[Taken from the Presbyterian.]*

Mrs. Sylvia Seybolt, who now resides with her son-in-law, Joshua Mullock, Esq., of Mount Hope, Orange County, New York, was one of the occupants of Forty Fort at the time of the massacre. She was then fourteen years old, making her now eighty-seven. In the spring of 1775, her father, Jedediah Stephens, with his family, consisting of five sons, five daughters, and two sons-in-law, removed from Canaan, Connecticut, and settled in the Valley of the Susquehanna. Here he prospered abundantly for a little more than three years, when this beautiful vale was laid waste.

During the progress of the Revolution, the boys residing in the Valley of the age of sixteen and under had voluntarily formed themselves into a military company, and had elected from their own number William Mason for their captain, and for lieutenant, Rufus Stephens, a brother of Mrs. Seybolt. These heroic boys formed part of that ill-fated band that left the fort under Colonel Zebulon Butler, and fell a prey to Tory and Indian barbarity. While the battle was raging, an Indian, pleased with the appearance of Mason, took him under his protection, intending to save his life; but, being afterward told by a Tory that he was captain of a rebel company, the Indians kindled a fire, and, with fiendish delight, placed him on it, and held him there with their bayonets until life was extinct. Lieutenant Stephens was found dead, his body being literally covered with bullet and tomahawk wounds.

An older brother, Jedediah Stephens, was among the few who escaped. While running toward the river, two Indians sprang suddenly out of the bushes and fired upon him, one bullet passing through his clothes between his side and arm. One of the Indians then commenced reloading his gun, while the other gave full chase. The latter soon overtook and attempted to seize him, but Stephens, eluding his grasp, felled him by a blow with the breech of his gun, and struck him a second blow after his fall, which doubtless killed him. He soon reached the river and plunged in; here he was again fired at, and again escaped unhurt. He swam across the river, and secreted himself under the boughs of a tree that had fallen into the water. In this shelter he remained until after dark, when he recrossed the river and entered the fort.

The next day after the surrender of the fort, an Indian, with a large knife in his hand, came up to Stephens, and, taking hold of him, says to him, "White brother, in the battle yesterday you killed my brother, now me kill you." Stephens denied, at the same time saying, "We are all good brothers now." The Indian then examined him thoroughly to see if he was not wounded; but, with all his thirst for vengeance, he failed to recognize him as the slayer of his brother, saying as he let him go, "Well, me don't know; he *look* like him."

While the plundering was in progress, Mrs. Seybolt saw an Indian break open her sister's trunk, in which he found a bottle of camphor. He took it up, and, smelling of it, asked if it was poison. The owner replied that it was not; he then made her taste it, after which he drank it off, and went and lay down by the river. The doctor was soon informed of the circumstance, and, on examining him, pronounced him in a dying state.

Five days after the massacre the survivors were ordered to leave the valley. They all set out on foot across the Great Swamp, in which they lay during two nights; on the third they arrived at Stroudsburg, near the Delaware. In this company was a sister of Mrs. Seybolt, with a child only two weeks old. From Stroudsburg they proceeded to the Hudson, near Newburg, where they obtained a conveyance as far as Sharon, Connecticut, in wagons employed in carrying provisions to the American army. From Sharon they again traveled on foot until they reached their former homes.

The incidents related above I received from the lips of Mrs. Seybolt a few days since, and as every thing connected with the Revolution is filled with interest, I hope they may prove acceptable to your readers. Although there is here and there a survivor of the Revolution, yet we must soon cease to hear these thrilling tales from the lips of those who were participants or eye-witnesses. May we prize as we should the precious boon of liberty which cost our forefathers so much suffering.—W. F. M.

## VIII.

#### THE CAPTIVE GIRL, FRANCES SLOCUM.

MAKING captives, particularly of children, and adopting them as their own, is one of the laws of Indian warfare. Usually the little captive is adopted by a mother who has lost a child. If a son falls in battle, or a daughter perishes by hunger or fatigue, or dies by disease, the vacancy, if possible, is supplied by some pale-faced prisoner, who is imagined to bear some distant resemblance to the lost one. An attachment formed in the mind of a savage female for a beautiful child which she had been accustomed to fondle in time of peace, has led to the capture of the coveted object when war has broken out. But it is probable that the main ground of this species of plunder is a part of the system of *cruel vengeance* with which the savage heart delights to glut itself for real or supposed wrongs. The uneducated minds of the Indians enter into no analysis of civil society, distinguishing between the innocent and the guilty, but lay to the charge of the whites in general all the wrongs which they may have received at the hands of individuals, and often, by the mode of redress here referred to, strike the innocent—even break the hearts of unoffending mothers. The savage mind condemns in the gross; and for robberies and murders inflicted on them by lawless banditti, heartless speculators, or oppressive governmental expatriation, they hold the white race, generally and singularly, responsible. Hence they take sweet vengeance upon all white individuals or communities, as occasion offers, for their numerous and grievous wrongs.

When a boy in our native town, near "the sources of the Susquehanna," in the State of New York, we knew a young man who was with the Indians from the commencement to the close of the Revolutionary war. He was the son of our father's next-door neighbor, and we were a close observer of his manners and habits, seeing him every day, and often spending hours, and even days, in his company. We often listened to his romantic story at our father's fireside, both from him and from his old mother.

Daniel M'Allum—ordinarily called Dan M'Allum, and Indian Dan—was stolen when he was two years and a half old from the head of Red Creek, Middlefield. Before the commencement of hostilities between the parent government and the colonies, an old squaw was in the habit of coming from an Indian camp in the swamp, which lay hard by, and spending hours with "Aunt Molly M'Allum," and caressing little Dan, showing him her trinkets, and allowing him to play with them. When the war broke out, the savage woman set her heart on making the child a prize. She was hid in the brush for days, waiting for an opportunity to effect her object. At length the little fellow was taken by his father to "the sugar-bush" in the month of March, and becoming weary, and wishing to go to his mother, he was put into the path to return alone to the house, which was only a few rods distant. The squaw slid from her hiding-place, seized her prey, and bore him away. The mother was at ease until near night, when her husband came in, and, to their great consternation, it was discovered that the child was spirited away, and the agency by which he had disappeared was shrewdly suspected. It might be that a wild beast had devoured him, but it was deemed more probable that he had fallen into the hands of the Indians. The woods were scoured, and the cry for help sent through the settlements, but all in vain. The Mohawks, and with them the squaw with her prize, had fled to the north, and the child was given up for lost.

At the close of the war he was a stout lad and a perfect Indian. When the prisoners were required to be given up, Dan said his old "Indian mother cried bitterly;" but there was no evading the requisition of the British authorities, and she made her preparations for the separation. She filled a little bag with parched corn and dried venison, and, putting it in his hand, she went with him near to the place where the prisoners were rendezvoused—either on the Mohawk River or at Cherry Valley, we are not certain which—and, pointing him out the way, she flung her blanket over her head, and turned about and ran. He paused, looked after her, and his heart almost came into his mouth. He maintained that no one could have felt deeper sorrow at burying his own mother. He could not endure the separation, and set off at full speed after her. She, however, managed to elude him, and he was found by some one in the path, giving boisterous vent to his sorrow, and was taken to the depôt of the prisoners, where his father found him and bore him to his mother.

And now another trial awaited the poor boy. The usages of civilization were like the chains of slavery to him. To wear pants and jacket, and sleep upon a bed, and to eat bread, and salt meat cooked in an iron pan —all this was so strange—every thing so unnatural, that he sighed and cried, and said a thousand times over, "Oh that I was again in the wild woods, chasing the deer and the bear, and enjoying the luxury of sleeping upon the ground, under a blanket, with my feet before a great warm fire!"

"Dan M'Allum," so long as we knew him, which was until we entered our eighteenth year, exhibited strong traits of Indian character. He was fond of hunting, loved rum, would have his Indian pow-wows, and, when under the influence of the intoxicating draught, his Indian whoop rang through the neighborhood, but excited no terror. Dan was not quarrelsome when sober, and when intoxicated he had neither the power nor tact of a warrior or a bully. When so drunk that he could not stand, he would ride his horse upon a run perfectly erect, and scarcely ever fell from his horse's back. Often have we heard the poor fellow say, apparently from the bottom of his heart, "I wish to God I had never left the Indians, for I was a good Indian, but I shall never make a white man." He finally married and settled, and his character became much modified by the kindly influences of home, and the independence and associations gathering round the husband and the father. When he was no longer regarded as "a fool," "an Indian booby," and the like, his manhood developed, and he became a respectable citizen; but the process of transformation was slow and painful.

A curious fact in this case was that the poor Indian captive seemed not to have much affection for his real mother. He never made a secret of the fact that he loved his "Indian mother" the best. He declared that the moment in which she tore herself from him was the most sorrowful moment of his life, and her tears, sobs, and wild shrieks, as she ran away, were the very sorest of his remembrances. Such is habit, such education, such the impressions of childhood. How perfectly imbedded in the human heart is the image of that being whose watchful care and sympathies are associated with our earliest recollections, although it be the image of a wild savage woman!

Dan M'Allum is not the hero of our story, but a specimen of a class, the whole of which constitute a series of illustrations of the principles of savage life, and specimens of human nature in its vast generalization. The more particular relations of his Indian life we simply recollect were curious and interesting, but the details are not now sufficiently clear in our mind for record, and, with the brief notice of his case which we have taken, we shall dismiss it, and proceed to another case characterized by a different class of circumstances and a different sequel.

Among the enterprising emigrants from the east to the famous Valley of Wyoming was a member of the society of Friends by the name of Jonathan Slocum. The place of his previous residence was Warwick, Rhode Island. He emigrated in 1777, with his wife and nine children. The road through the swamp had now been so far improved as to allow, although with great difficulty, wagons to pass. Mr. Slocum removed with his family and effects in a large covered wagon. He located himself near the fort, on lands a portion of which is now in possession of the family, within the present borough of Wilkesbarre, near the public square. Mr. Slocum, being from principle a noncombatant, considered himself and his family comparatively free from danger from the attacks of the savages. His son Giles, not practicing upon the principles in which he had been trained at home, took up arms with the settlers in defense of their hearths and homes against the anticipated attacks of the Indians and Tories. He was in the famous Indian battle in 1778, and it is supposed that this circumstance was the occasion of the terrible vengeance taken upon the family. The battle had taken place in July, and thenceforward, until the conclusion of peace with England, parties of Indians continued to visit the Valley to steal, make prisoners, kill, and scalp, as opportunity offered.

On the second day of November of this year, a party of Delaware Indians visited Wyoming, and directed their way to Mr. Slocum's residence. Nathan Kingsley had been made prisoner by the Indians, and his wife and two sons were taken in by Mr. Slocum, and afforded the protection and comforts of a home. When the Indians came near, they saw the two Kingsley boys grinding a knife before the door. The elder of the lads was dressed in a soldier's coat, which, it is presumed, was the special reason of his being marked as a victim. One of the savages took deadly aim at this young man, and he fell. The discharge of the gun alarmed Mrs. Slocum, and she ran to the door, when she saw the Indian scalping the young man with the knife which he had been grinding. She secreted herself until she saw a stalwart Indian lay hold of her son Ebenezer, a little lad, who, by an injury in one of his feet, had been made lame. The idea that the little fellow would fail to keep up with the party, and would be cruelly butchered, rushed with such force upon the mind of the mother that she forgot all considerations of personal safety, and, running up to the Indian, and pointing at the foot of the boy, she exclaimed, "The child is lame; he can do thee no good." Little Frances, about five years old, had hid, as she supposed, under the stairs, but had been discovered by the Indians. The savage dropped the boy and seized the little girl, and took her up in his arms. All the entreaties of the mother in this case were treated with savage scorn. The oldest daughter ran away with her youngest brother, about two years old, with such speed and in such affright that the savages, after yelling hideously at her, roared out laughing. They took the remaining Kingsley boy and a colored girl, and away they went, little Frances screaming to "mamma" for help, holding the locks of hair from her eyes with one hand, and stretching out the other.

There were three Indians in the gang, and each having a prisoner, they fled to the mountain. An alarm was given at the fort, which was not more than a hundred rods from Mr. Slocum's house, but the wily savages escaped with such celerity, and hid themselves so securely, that no traces of them could be found. That was a gloomy evening in the Slocum family. Mr. Slocum was from home when the descent upon his peaceful dwelling was made by the ruthless savages. He returned to see the gory corpse of young Kingsley, and to find Mrs. Slocum writhing in agony on account of poor little Frances, who was in the hands of a band of Indians, whom her phrensied imagination pictured out as so many demons just let loose from Tophet. Mr. Slocum was petrified with horror; but the deep current of his grief, with characteristic self-control, was not allowed to break over all its natural barriers. Sobs and broken sentences gave character to the scene around that desolate hearth. Sleep fled from that family circle. The last look at the innocent little creature, with outstretched hands, and

THE CAPTURE OF FRANCES SLOCUM.

streaming eyes, and disheveled locks, and her shrieks of "mamma! mamma!" haunted their imaginations like ghosts of darkness. And then the question, which no human reason could solve, was, "What would become of the child?" Would she be cruelly murdered? or would she be worn out with fatigue? or would she suffer a lingering death from want of comfortable food and clothing? Any supposition which was at all probable seemed worse than death. The heart-stricken family passed a little more than a month in sadness and gloom, not then to find relief to their aching hearts, but to feel another blow from savage hands still more terrible.

The venerable historian of Wyoming, Hon. Charles Miner, says: "The cup of vengeance was not yet full. December 16th, Mr. Slocum and Isaac Tripp, Esq., his father-in-law, an aged man, with William Slocum, a youth of nineteen or twenty, were feeding cattle from a stack in the meadow, in sight of the fort, when they were fired upon by Indians. Mr. Slocum was shot dead; Mr. Tripp wounded, speared, and tomahawked; both were scalped. William, wounded by a spent ball in the heel, escaped and gave the alarm, but the alert and wily foe had retreated to his hiding-place in the mountain. This deed, bold as it was cruel, was perpetrated within the town plot, in the centre of which the fortress was located. Thus, in little more than a month, Mrs. Slocum had lost a beloved child, carried into captivity; the doorway had been drenched in blood by the murder of an inmate of the family; two others of the household had been taken away prisoners; and now her husband and father were both stricken down to the grave, murdered and mangled by the merciless Indians. Verily, the annals of Indian atrocities, written in blood, record few instances of desolation and woe to equal this."

The husband and the father were dead, and their ashes reposed beneath the green turf. Time gradually modified the poignancy of the widow's grief, occasioned by the cruel death of her loved husband and venerated father; but Frances, poor child! she knew not where she was. Suspense more terrible than death hung over her fate. The lapse of time only increased the vividness of the traces of memory relating to the minutest circumstances connected, nearly or remotely, with the sad tragedy of her capture. The mother called up all the little griefs and disappointments which family discipline had inflicted upon her dear child. One circumstance distressed her almost incurably. Frances had a pair of new shoes, and, as a matter of economy, she had been required to lay them up for colder weather. She went away with bare feet, and in that condition would doubtless be obliged to travel rough roads, and perhaps through the frost and snow to make long journeys. "Oh! if the poor little creature only had her shoes!" The little shoes were a source of torture to the soul of the bereaved mother for long and weary years.

Time passed, and Mrs. Slocum's sons had become prosperous business men; and peace having been concluded with Great Britain, and every effort made upon the part of Congress to conciliate the Indian tribes, the young men began to meditate serious efforts to recover their sister, or, at least, to ascertain her fate. In 1784, two of the brothers visited Niagara, and made inquiries of the Indians, and offered them liberal rewards if they would give any information concerning their sister. Their mission was without the least shadow of success, no trace of the lost one having been discovered. They returned, after an absence of several weeks, with the impression that Frances was dead. They thought it almost impossible that the secret should be kept if Frances were above ground, especially as a reward had been offered for the information which would be exceedingly tempting to the cupidity of the Indians. They did not consider that, when an Indian undertakes to keep a secret, nothing can break the seal of his lips, nor especially the criminality and disgrace of betraying to white men secrets confided by Indians. Little Frances was extensively known among the Canadian and Western Indians, but she was now a treasure which Indians felt a common interest in concealing.

Four years subsequently the Slocums were on a search among the Western Indians for several months, Indian agents and traders giving them every facility in their researches, and again offering the large reward of *five hundred dollars* for any information with regard to their sister's whereabouts, but all to no purpose.

In 1789, when a large number of Indians assembled at Tioga Point to make a treaty with Colonel Proctor, and a large number of prisoners were brought in to be surrendered to their friends, Mrs. Slocum made a journey, with great labor, to the place, and, after weeks of examination among the prisoners, found no one she could own as Frances.

Still the bereaved mother entertained the idea that her child was alive, and might, after all, be found. The zeal of the brothers in the search did not decline with the lapse of years, and the four brothers undertook another expedition in 1797, and were traveling in the western wilderness, among the Indian settlements, for nearly the whole summer. They conversed with the Indians—offered, as they had done before, the reward of five hundred dollars for any information with regard to their sister: they found captives and examined them, but Frances they neither found nor heard from.

A female captive, hearing of the efforts made by the Slocums to recover their lost one, and hoping that she might be recognized as the real Frances, came to Mrs. Slocum, and told her that she was taken prisoner somewhere on the Susquehanna when a child, and she was anxious to find her friends. She knew not the name of her father, she knew not her own name, but she had come to see if she, Mrs. Slocum, was not her real mother. Mrs. Slocum saw at once that it was not Frances, but bade her welcome. "Stay with me," said Mrs. Slocum, "as long as thee pleases; perhaps some one else may extend the like kindness to my dear Frances." The poor stranger, after a few months, finding herself regarded as a mere object of charity, without the sympathies and attachments of natural relationship, left, and the Slocums heard no more of her.

Mrs. Slocum went down to the grave without finding the least trace of her lost one, but left with her sons a charge never to give up the search so long as the possibility remained of their recovering their sister, or their learning the circumstances of her story or her fate. Mrs. Slocum's death occurred in 1807.

When the mission among the Wyandots became a matter of public interest, and the chiefs Between-the-Logs and Menuncu were converted, the report that Between-the-Logs had a white woman for his wife, the idea of the possibility of her being the lost Frances Slocum induced Mr. Joseph Slocum, attended by a nephew, to visit the mission. In 1826 they made a weary and expensive journey to Upper Sandusky, and found the woman, but were convinced that she was not Frances. They were treated with great hospitality and kindness, and received strong impressions with regard to the influence of Christianity upon the moral character and social condition of the Wyandot Indians.

Hope had been fondly cherished in the mind of the Slocums of some light upon the history or fate of Frances for many long years, but all efforts to gain information with regard to her having utterly failed, they began to despair. They had spent time and money; they had performed long and perilous journeys; they had enlisted Indian agents and traders in the object, but not the slightest trace, as yet, had been found of the little captive. The last they knew of her was that she was borne away by a stout Indian, who disappeared among the trees and shrubs, while the shrieks of the child died away in the distance. From that moment an impenetrable cloud of darkness had enshrouded her story, which all efforts had failed to penetrate. The probability of the removal of the veil of mystery from the subject was now becoming so exceedingly faint, if it had not, indeed, wholly passed away, that the search was given over, and the subject ceased to be matter of conversation, excepting as the capture of the child, and the great efforts which had been made for her discovery, were connected with the history of the classic vale. This was the condition of things when a new scene opens to our vision, apparently by accident, but really under the guiding hand of Providence. A train of circumstances brought to light the whereabouts of the long-lost FRANCES SLOCUM.

### THE DISCOVERY OF FRANCES.

Colonel Ewing, a gentleman connected with the public service among the Indians, having acquired the language in use among the Western tribes, and having business with these tribes, made frequent journeys through the wilderness and among the Indian settlements. On one of these journeys he happened to be benighted near what was called "The Deaf Man's Village," on the Missisinewa, a branch of the Wabash. He asked for and received the hospitalities of a respectable Indian dwelling. The mistress of the house was a venerable and respectable-looking Indian woman, to whom great deference was paid by the whole family circle, composed of children and grandchildren. Colonel Ewing was weary and rather indisposed, and, after taking some refreshments, he laid himself down to rest upon some skins in a corner of the room. The family disappeared, with the exception of the venerable head of the circle, and she lingered, being busy with some of her small arrangements for the night. The colonel's attention was attracted by the color of her skin and hair, and, shrewdly suspecting that she was a white woman, he commenced conversation with her. She said she was a white woman, and was carried into captivity by the Indians when a child, and her father's name was SLOCUM. She had never revealed her history before, for fear that her white relations might come and take her away. But she was now old, and should not stay much longer; and she was willing, if any of them were alive, that they should know where she was.

The colonel, presuming that the information which had been communicated to him might be of great importance to persons still living, concluded to take measures to make the matter public. He accordingly addressed the following letter to the postmaster of the city of Lancaster, Pennsylvania:

"Logansport, Indiana, January 20, 1835.

"DEAR SIR,—In the hope that some good may result from it, I have taken this means of giving to your fellow-citizens—say the descendants of the early settlers of the Susquehanna—the following information; and if there be any now living whose name is Slocum, to them, I hope, the following may be communicated through the public prints of your place.

"There is now living near this place, among the Miami tribe of Indians, an aged white woman, who a few days ago told me, while I lodged in the camp one night, that she was taken away from her father's house, on or near the Susquehanna River, when she was very young—say from five to eight years old, as she thinks—by the Delaware Indians, who were then hostile toward the whites. She says her father's name was Slocum; that he was a Quaker, rather small in stature, and wore a large-brimmed hat; was of sandy hair and light complexion, and much freckled; that he lived about half a mile from a town where there was a fort; that they lived in a wooden house of two stories high, and had a spring near the house. She says three Delawares came to the house in the daytime, when all were absent but herself, and perhaps two other children: her father and brothers were absent making hay. The Indians carried her off, and she was adopted into a family of Delawares, who raised her and treated her as their own child. They died about forty years ago, somewhere in Ohio. She was then married to a Miami, by whom she had four children; two of them are now living—they are both daughters—and she lives with them. Her husband is dead; she is old and feeble, and thinks she will not live long.

"These considerations induced her to give the present history of herself, which she would never do before, fearing that her kindred would come and force her away. She has lived long and happy as an Indian, and, but for her color, would not be suspected of being any thing else than such. She is very respectable and wealthy, sober and honest. Her name is without reproach. She says her father had a large family, say eight children in all—six older than herself, one younger, as well as she can recollect; and she doubts not there are yet living many of their descendants, but seems to think that all her brothers and sisters must be dead, as she is very old herself, not far from the age of eighty. She thinks she was taken prisoner before the two last wars, which must mean the Revolutionary war, as Wayne's war and the late war have been since that one. She has entirely lost her mother tongue, and speaks only in Indian, which I also understand, and she gave me a full history of herself.

"Her own Christian name she has forgotten, but says her father's name was Slocum, and he was a Quaker. She also recollects that it was upon the Susquehanna River that they lived, but don't recollect the name of the town near which they lived. I have thought that from this letter you might cause something to be inserted in the newspapers of your country that might possibly catch the eye of some of the descendants of the Slocum family, who have knowledge of a girl having been carried off by the Indians some seventy years ago. This they might know from family tradition. If so, and they will come here, I will carry them where they may see the object of my letter alive and happy, though old and far advanced in life.

"I can form no idea whereabout upon the Susquehanna River this family could have lived at that early period, namely, about the time of the Revolutionary war, but perhaps you can ascertain more about it. If so, I hope you will interest yourself, and, if possible, let her brothers and sisters, if any be alive—if not, their children—know where they may once more see a relative whose fate has been wrapped in mystery for seventy years, and for whom her bereaved and afflicted parents doubtless shed many a bitter tear. They have long since found their graves, though their lost child they never found. I have been much affected with the disclosure, and hope the surviving friends may obtain, through your goodness, the information I desire for them. If I can be of any service to them, they may command me. In the mean time, I hope you will excuse me for the freedom I have taken with you, a total stranger, and believe me to be, sir, with much respect, your obedient servant,

"Geo. W. Ewing."

The letter reached its destination, but the postmaster, considering it a hoax, flung it by, and for two years it lay among a quantity of old letters and papers in the office which were deemed worthless. There was a providence in the discovery of the lost one, and will that providence, which was concerned in the first development, allow the light to die out, and the whole matter to be hid from the vision of those so deeply interested in the revelation? We shall see. The postmaster died, and, for some reason—possibly mere curiosity—his wife overhauled the mass of old papers belonging to the office, among which she found and read Colonel Ewing's letter. She was more confiding than her husband in the truthfulness of the tale, and she sent the letter to the editor of the *Intelligencer*, by whom it was published. Here providence seems to have again interfered, and saved the letter from final oblivion. Another interesting fact worthy of special attention is, that the letter came to hand just in time to make its appearance in an extra number containing some temperance documents, and these were sent to the clergymen generally through that part of the state. One of these fell into the hands of the Rev. Samuel Bowman, a native of Wilkesbarre, and intimately acquainted with the Slocum family. He had from his childhood been accustomed to hear the melancholy story of the captivity of little Frances Slocum, and well knew the efforts which the brothers had made to find her. He immediately mailed one of these papers to her brother, who lived in Wilkesbarre, and the wonderful development which the letter contained flung the whole community into a state of excitement. There was no father or mother living to say "Frances is yet alive, and I will go and see her before I die," but there were brothers, a sister, and a large circle of nephews and nieces, whose hearts leaped for joy at the prospect of at least learning the veritable history of Frances, who had been for *sixty years* in savage life, but utterly lost to her kindred and friends.

A correspondence ensued between Jonathan J. Slocum, Esq., son of Mr. Joseph Slocum, and Colonel Ewing, which speaks for itself, and here follows:

"Wilkesbarre, Penn., August 8, 1837.

"GEORGE W. EWING, Esq.:

"DEAR SIR,—At the suggestion of my father and other relations, I have taken the liberty to write to you, although an entire stranger.

"We have received, but a few days since, a letter written by you to a gentleman in Lancaster, of this state, upon a subject of deep and intense interest to our family. How the matter should have lain so long wrapped in obscurity we can not conceive. An aunt of mine—sister of my father—was taken away when five years old by the Indians, and since then we have only had vague and indistinct rumors upon the subject. Your letter we deem to have entirely revealed the whole matter, and set every thing at rest. The description is so perfect, and the incidents (with the exception of her age) so correct, that we feel confident.

"Steps will be taken immediately to investigate the matter, and we will endeavor to do all in our power to restore a lost relative who has been sixty years in Indian bondage.

"Your friend and obedient servant,
"JON. J. SLOCUM."

"Logansport, Indiana, August 26, 1837.

"JON. J. SLOCUM, Esq., Wilkesbarre:

"DEAR SIR,—I have the pleasure of acknowledging the receipt of your letter of the 8th instant, and in answer can add, that the female I spoke of in January, 1835, is still alive; nor can I for a moment doubt but that she is the identical relative that has been so long lost to your family.

"I feel much gratified to think that I have been thus instrumental in disclosing to yourself and friends such facts in relation to her as will enable you to visit her and satisfy yourselves more fully. She recovered from the temporary illness by which she was afflicted about the time I spent the night with her in January, 1835, and which was, no doubt, the cause that induced her to speak so freely of her early captivity.

"Although she is now, by long habit, an Indian, and her manners and customs precisely theirs, yet she will doubtless be happy to see any of you, and I myself will take great pleasure in accompanying you to the house. Should you come out for that purpose, I advise you to repair directly to this place; and should it so happen that I should be absent at the time, you will find others who can take you to her. Bring with you this letter; show it to James T. Miller, of Peru, Ind., a small town not far from this place. He knows her well. He is a young man whom we have raised. He speaks the Miami tongue, and will accompany you if I should not be at home. Inquire for the old white woman, mother-in-law to Brouriette, living on the Missisinewa River, about ten miles above its mouth. *There you will find the long-lost sister of your father*, and, as I before stated, you will not have to blush on her account. She is highly respectable, and her name as an Indian is without reproach. Her daughter, too, and her son-in-law, Brouriette, who is also a half-blood, being part French, are both very respectable and interesting people—none in the nation are more so. As Indians they live well, and will be pleased to see you. Should you visit here this fall, I may be absent, as I purpose starting for New York in a few days, and shall not be back till some time in October. But this need not stop you; for, although I should be gratified to see you, yet it will be sufficient to learn that I have furthered your wishes in this truly interesting matter.

"The very kind manner in which you have been pleased to speak of me shall be fully appreciated.

"There perhaps are men who could have heard her story unmoved, but for me, I could not; and when I reflected that there was, perhaps, still lingering on this side of the grave some brother or sister of that ill-fated woman, to whom such information would be deeply interesting, I resolved on the course which I adopted, and entertained the fond hope that my letter, if ever it should go before the public, would attract the attention of some one interested. In this it seems, at last, I have not been disappointed, although I had long since supposed it had failed to effect the object for which I wrote it. Like you, I regret that it should have been delayed so long, nor can I conceive how any one should neglect to publish such a letter.

"As to the age of this female, I think she herself is mistaken, and that she is not so old as she imagines herself to be. Indeed, I entertain no doubt but that she is the same person that your family have mourned after for more than half a century past.

"Your obedient humble servant,
"GEORGE W. EWING."

The way was now plain, and there was no delay in taking measures to visit the locality where, it was now nearly reduced to a certainty, the Slocums would find their long-lost sister. Mr. Isaac Slocum and Mrs. Mary Town resided in Ohio, but not in the same neighborhood. It was arranged by correspondence that Mr. Joseph Slocum should visit Ohio by private conveyance, take Mrs. Town in his carriage, and that they should meet their brother Isaac somewhere near the "Deaf Man's Village," perhaps in the nearest white settlement. Isaac pushed on by public conveyance, and, accompanied by Mr. Miller, the interpreter, went directly to the residence of the old woman described by Colonel Ewing. He found her, to all appearance, a perfect Indian. He had fixed in his mind an infallible mark of distinction. Before she was carried off, her brother Ebenezer had struck her fore-finger on the left hand with a hammer, in the blacksmith's shop, and so injured the bone that the nail was permanently destroyed, and the finger otherwise disfigured. Mr. Slocum accordingly took hold of her hand, and brought her to the light, and saw the mark still remaining, with very little variation from the changes of time. "How came that finger jammed?" asked he, through the interpreter. "My brother struck it with a hammer in the shop, a long time ago, before I was carried away," was the answer.

She, however, said but little; she was coy and suspicious, and manifested no confidence in the claims of the stranger to be her brother. Mr. Slocum was satisfied beyond a doubt that he had found the real Frances Slocum, for whom he and his brothers had so long and so often been employed in ineffectual searches. He now returned to a small village nine miles distant, called Peru, and anxiously waited the arrival of his brother Joseph and sister Town. Here he spent several weary days in great anxiety and suspense.

At length, after hard toiling most of the way over horrible roads through a new country, the brother and sister arrived. For persons in advanced life they had almost performed miracles of endurance; they were much fatigued, but they did not delay long until they were on the line of march for the house of Frances. On their way they paid their respects to Godfrey, the second chief of the Miamis, who was an exceedingly large man, of fine proportions and noble bearing. The chief received them with great courtesy, and promised them his good offices in the matter of their visit, should they be needed.

The party left the chief and hastened on to the point of interest. They entered the decent Indian cabin—constructed of logs, and quite roomy—and found the mistress of the house sitting in her chair. Still she was not disposed to converse freely. She gave a brief account of her family and the circumstances of her capture, but seemed utterly unmoved, and not free from suspicion that there was some plan in operation to take her away or to get her land. The brothers walked the floor with emotions too deep and overwhelming for utterance—the sister wept. Could it be possible that this Indian woman was the dear little Frances, whose sweet smiles lingered in their memory, and which they could scarcely do any other than identify with her still? Has she—dear Frances—been metamorphosed into this stoical, iron-hearted Indian woman—old, wrinkled, and cold as an iceberg? But there could be no mistake about it. She said her father's name was Slocum; he was a Quaker, and wore a broad-brimmed hat; he lived near a fort by a great river; she had seven brothers and two sisters; her brother hammered off her finger nail; she was taken from under the staircase; three Indians took her, with a boy and a black girl, a great many winters ago, when she was a little child. The question was settled; this was Frances.

She was now a widow. Her husband was a chief.

She had two daughters: the younger of the two had lost her husband; the husband of the elder was a half-breed—his father a Frenchman—and his name was Brouriette, who managed the out-door affairs of the family, subject always to the views and feelings of the queen mother-in-law. The family circle scrupulously followed the lead of the venerated head of the household, making no advances, exhibiting no emotion. On this occasion only one tender chord was touched. The long-lost sister had forgotten her own name. She was asked if she thought she could remember it if she should hear it mentioned. Her answer was, "It is a long time; I do not know." "Was it Frances?" Something like emotion instantly agitated her iron-cast features, and, with a smile, she answered in the affirmative, "Francà, Francà."

Things changed a little, but by very slow degrees. The hospitalities of the house were never denied to respectable strangers, and, of course, would be offered to the Slocums. When the conversation was concluded, the Indian queen went about her business, apparently with as much indifference as though nothing of interest had happened. The party surveyed the premises, and were pleased to find every thing in excellent order for an Indian residence. Returning from a stroll, they observed the sister seated on the floor, at work at a deerskin, which was nearly ready for use. She was scraping the rough places with a knife, and reducing its rigidity by friction. She paid little attention to the strangers, only answering when addressed through the interpreter. The daughters evidently observed the strangers with interest, but, Indian-like, only cast at them side-glances when they thought they were not observed.

The company proposed to the sister to accompany them, with her son-in-law and daughters, to Peru. She could not fully pledge herself to comply with this request until she had consulted Godfrey, the chief. He advised her to comply with the request, assuring her that she would be in no danger from the respectable strangers; that, being her relations, they had certainly visited her with none other than the most friendly intentions. The arrangement was completed, and the party returned.

On the Sabbath, the sister, her son-in-law, and two daughters came on horseback, in single file, and presented themselves before the door of the new hotel of the little town, the queen before, the daughters next, and Captain Brouriette bringing up the rear. They were met by the brothers with great cordiality, and requested to alight, and were conducted into the house. Before any intimacy could be entered upon, the strangers must receive a present. The eldest daughter brought something in a clean white cloth and laid it upon the table, which, upon examination, was found to be the hind-quarter of a deer. After a brief explanation through the interpreter, Mrs. Town advanced and took possession of the present, which was the proffered token of friendship, when confidence was established.

There was now only one drawback to the circumstances of the meeting, and that was the fact that it was the *Sabbath*. And was it possible that Frances had lost the idea of the sacredness of the Sabbath? that "she did not know when Sunday came?" Here was an evidence, among many, that Frances Slocum had become an Indian in every thing excepting her parentage, and that she was, in fact, a *heathen*. Nothing else could have been expected, and yet the fact seemed surprising, as it was afflicting, to the Slocums.

The best provisions were now made for the entertainment of the Indian party, and Frances was somewhat more free. She listened with interest to a history of the Slocum family, a part of which was the cruel murder of her father soon after her capture, and the deep anxiety of their mother, while she lived, to find her lost child. They assured her that Mrs. Town was the sister who ran away to the fort with her little brother in her arms, and that Mr. Joseph Slocum was that very little brother. In due time preparations were made to take down in writing her Indian history. To this she seemed to have some aversion until the reasons for it were explained by the interpreter. She then proceeded with a brief account of her captivity, and her Indian life down to the present time, which, as it was more fully recited on the occasion of a subsequent visit, we shall reserve for record in connection with that visit.

This was a most extraordinary meeting, and excited no little interest in the community. People gathered in and around the house, gaping and listening with amazement. They crowded the doors and windows, and so interrupted the free circulation of the air, that the Indian party, so accustomed to the free air of the woods and the prairies, were almost suffocated. The food, too, seasoned with salt and pepper, was not only unpalatable, but was scarcely endurable. The circumstances, altogether, had an injurious influence upon the health of Frances, and she sought relief in accordance with the habits of savage life. She quietly slipped away, and in five minutes was found with her blanket pulled over her head, lying on the floor of the stoop, fast asleep. The two parties remained at Peru three days. They had frequent conferences, during which the following questions and answers are reported:

"Were you ever tired of living with the Indians?"

"No; I always had enough to live on, and have lived well. The Indians always used me kindly."

"Did you know that you had white relations who were seeking you for so many years?"

"No; no one told me, and I never heard of it. I never thought any thing about my white relations unless it was a little while after I was taken."

"We live where our father and mother used to live, on the banks of the beautiful Susquehanna, and we want you to return with us; we will give you of our property, and you shall be one of us, and share all that we have. You shall have a good house, and every thing you desire. Oh, do go back with us!"

"No, I can not. I have always lived with the Indians; they have always used me very kindly; I am used to them. The Great Spirit has always allowed me to live with them, and I wish to live and die with them. Your *Wah-puh-mone* (looking-glass) may be larger than mine, but this is my home. I do not wish to live any better, or any where else, and I think the Great Spirit has permitted me to live so long because I have always lived with the Indians. I should have died sooner if I had left them. My husband and my boys are buried here, and I can not leave them. On his dying-day my husband charged me not to leave the Indians. I have a house and large lands, two daughters, a son-in-law, three grandchildren, and every thing to make me comfortable: why should I go, and be like a fish out of the water?"

Brouriette spoke and said:

"And I know all about it. I was born at Fort Harrison, about two miles from Terre Haute. When I was ten years old I went to Detroit. I was married to this woman about thirteen years ago. The people about here and at Logansport and at Miamisport have known me ever since the country was settled by the whites. They know me to be industrious, to manage well, and to maintain my family respectably. My mother-in-law's sons are dead, and I stand in their place to her. I mean to maintain her well as long as she lives, for the truth of which you may depend on the word of Captain Brouriette."

"What Captain Brouriette says," added the old lady, "is true. He has always treated me kindly, and I am satisfied with him—perfectly satisfied; and I hope my connections will not feel any uneasiness about me. The Indians are my people. I do no work. I sit in the house with these my two daughters, who do the work, and I sit with them."

"But will you at least go and make a visit to your early home, and when you have seen us, return again to your children?"

"I can not. I can not. I am an old tree. I can not move about. I was a sapling when they took me away. It is all gone past. I am afraid I should die and never come back. I am happy here. I shall die here and lie in that grave-yard, and they will raise the pole at my grave with the white flag on it, and the Great Spirit will know where to find me. I should not be happy with my white relatives. I am glad enough to see them, but I can not go. I can not go. I have done."

"When the whites take a squaw," said Brouriette, with much animation, as if delighted with the decision of the old lady, "they make her work like a slave. It was never so with this woman. If I had been a drunken, worthless fellow, this woman could not have lived to this age. But I have always treated her well. The village is called Deaf Man's Village, after her husband. I have done."

The eldest daughter, whose name is *Kick-ke-se-qua*, or "*cut-finger*," assented to all that had been said, and added that "the deer can not live out of the forest."

The youngest daughter, *O-show-se-quah*, or "*yellow leaves*," confirmed all, and thought that her mother could not go even on a visit, "because," said she, "the fish dies quickly out of the water."

The talk closed. The Indian sister was weary and sick, and anxious to return to her wilds, so congenial to her feelings, and so endeared to her heart by many tender associations. There was her home, and there were the graves of her husband and her sons, and there she could enjoy the mode of life which, by long and invincible habit, had become her element, and was necessary to her being.

The brothers and sister returned to their homes with mingled emotions of pleasure and pain. They had found their long-lost sister Frances, but they had found and left her an Indian, with almost every trace of Christian civilization erased, both from her soul, body, and being. She looked like an Indian, talked like an Indian, lived like an Indian, seated herself like an Indian, ate like an Indian, lay down to sleep like an Indian, thought, felt, and reasoned like an Indian; she had no longings for her original home, or the society of her kindred; she eschewed the trammels of civilized life, and could only breathe freely in the great unfenced out-doors which God gave to the Red Man.

There was, however, this to comfort the Slocums: their sister was not degraded in her habits or her character; there was a moral dignity in her manners entirely above ordinary savage life; her Anglo-Saxon blood had not been tainted by savage touch, but bore itself gloriously amid the long series of trials through which it had passed. She was the widow of a deceased chief; she was rich; all that abundance and respectability could do for a woman in savage life was hers. Such was the former Frances Slocum, of Wyoming, now Ma-con-a-qua, the Indian queen of the Miamis. The problem was settled—the veil of sixty years cast over the history and fate of a captive child was now finally removed.

On Mr. Joseph Slocum's return to his family in Wilkesbarre, his relations were listened to with the most intense interest. Every body had a long catalogue of questions to ask about Frances, which he was always ready to answer. He seemed never weary of conversing upon the subject of the captivity—the mysterious history—the visit. But Mr. Slocum was not quite satisfied with that visit; he consequently resolved upon another, and this time he took with him his eldest and youngest daughters.

Mr. Slocum and his two daughters—Mrs. Bennet and Harriet, now Mrs. Drake—left home upon this interesting trip September 10th, 1839. Their route was through Montrose, Owego, Ithaca, the Cayuga Lake, and by the Erie Canal to Niagara Falls. Mr. Slocum's memorandum of the journey contains many interesting entries, besides an account of his expenses; Mrs. Bennet kept a regular journal. Both of these are before us, and, so far as facts are concerned, will be strictly followed.

After a thorough examination of that great natural curiosity, the Falls, the party took the cars for Buffalo, and thence came, by steam-boat, to Sandusky City. After a short visit at Mr. Isaac Slocum's, who resided a few miles back in the country, they took another steam-boat for Maumee. Thence they came by stage, *via* Fort Defiance, to Fort Wayne, through the rain, over horrible roads, heavily loaded: nothing is noted very favorable to the stages or drivers. Here they took passage on a canal packet to Logansport, and thence to Peru, where they arrived September 28th, having been *eighteen days* on their journey. Mrs. Bennet says, "We found comfortable lodgings at Mr. Burnett's, a temperance house. This place has only been settled four years; the country is rich, but unhealthy." Mr. Miller, the interpreter, called upon them; they spent the Sabbath here. On Monday morning they chartered a wagon, and proceeded to "the Deaf Man's Village." The company consisted of Mr. Slocum, his two daughters, Mr. Miller, and two gentlemen—Mr. Taylor and Mr. Fullweller. "Our charioteer likes a dram: to be sure of a supply, he carried a bottle in his pocket; if he had spent the money in getting his harness mended it would have been better for us:" so says Mrs. Bennet. Mr. Slocum says, "Had some trouble with breaking our harness; got up there about half past twelve o'clock."

Having received intelligence of the coming of the party, Brouriette, according to the custom of the Miamis when visited by distinguished guests, came well mounted to meet them. He dismounted and shook hands with them all, and bid them welcome. He then mounted his horse, and galloped off through the woods with great speed to apprise the family of the approach of the company. He spoke broken English, and Mrs. Drake says, "He is a very fine, tall Indian; his head was covered with a handkerchief something like a turban, with nearly a yard of red calico hanging down behind." As he ran his horse through the woods, with his red streamer flying after him, "he made," as she says, "a grotesque appearance."

The Slocums and their friends arrived at the residence of Frances September 30. Captain Brouriette met them at the door and brought them into the house. Mrs. Drake says, "We found our aunt seated in a chair, looking very much as represented in the water-colored portrait now in possession of Judge Bennet, with her two daughters standing by her."

Mr. Slocum, after the accustomed salutations, told his sister that he had brought his eldest and youngest children to see her. The coldness and reserve of the former visit were now entirely gone, and Frances expressed great joy upon the occasion of again seeing her brother, and particularly that he had brought his daughters so far to see her. The mother and daughters immediately commenced an animated conversation upon the subject of the family resemblances which were observable. The old lady, looking at the ladies earnestly, passed her hand down her cheeks, stopping the motion at the posterior point of her lower jaw. There is an unusual fullness and prominence at that point of the Slocum face.

The preparations for dinner were soon commenced. They spread the table with a white cotton cloth, and wiped the dishes, as they took them from the cupboard, with a clean cloth. They prepared an excellent dinner of fried venison, potatoes, shortcake, and coffee. Their cups and saucers were small, and they put

MA-CON-A-QUA.

three or four table-spoonfuls of maple sugar in a cup. They were told by their white visitors, "Our way is not so much sugar." They seemed very anxious to please, and would often ask, "Is that right?" The eldest daughter waited on the table, while her mother sat at the table and ate with her white relations. After dinner they washed the dishes, and replaced them upon the shelves, and then swept the floor. The ladies were surprised at these evidences of civilization, and upon asking their aunt why they did these things, she made answer that her mother used to do so, and she had always done it, and learned it to her daughters. It was, therefore, a uniform rule in her house to wipe the dust from the dishes when they were put upon the table, and when the meal was concluded to wash them and return them to the cupboard, and then to sweep the room.

In the afternoon all left but Mr. Slocum, his daughters, and Mr. Miller; the last remained till near night, when he returned. They strolled over the premises, and visited the burying-ground. They raise a pole over the grave fifteen or twenty feet high, with a white cloth at the top, which remains until destroyed by time. The premises showed great skill and industry for savage life, and no little order and attention to comfort in its arrangements. The house was "a double hut." A neighboring squaw came in to help do the work, and the Indian daughters kept close to their white cousins, and talked with them incessantly. They supposed candles would be wanted, and, to meet the emergency, the squaw melted some tallow, twisted wicking on a stick, and with a spoon poured the tallow down the wicks until "quite a respectable candle" was produced.

For supper they had the breast of a wild turkey stewed with onions—"quite a delicate dish." When they came to retire, "*the pillow*," all there was in the house, was assigned to Mr. Slocum by the Indian sister. "They pay great respect to age. They had six beds, principally composed of blankets and other goods folded together," says Mrs. Bennet. "They were made of almost every thing," says Mrs. Drake. The visitors slept sweetly, and, after taking "a comfortable breakfast," they commenced their arrangements to return to Peru.

After breakfast a white man came to purchase a steer, and brought with him a colored man as an interpreter. He could not trade for the want of the money, as "he might move away," and that would be the last of it. No business transaction takes place in the family without the consent of Frances. She usually makes the bargains herself.

The colored man served so well in the capacity of an interpreter that he was retained by Mr. Slocum for the purpose. Frances was more free in her communications through him than she had been through Mr. Miller, and gave many circumstances in her history and recollections which she had not previously given.

They seemed anxious to tell their white relatives as much as possible about themselves, and to make as favorable an impression as possible. They had made in the spring "eleven barrels of sugar." "She says she could have a better house, but fears to do it on account of the jealousy of the Indians. She has money; some that has been saved since the treaty of St. Mary's, eighteen years ago. They had cloths and calicoes enough to fill a country store. They have a looking-glass—several splint-bottomed chairs—a great many trinkets hung about the house—beads and chains of silver and polished steel. Some of their dresses are richly ornamented with silver brooches, seven or eight rows of them as close as they can be put together—many silver ear-rings: my aunt had seven pairs in her ears; her daughters perhaps a dozen a piece. They have saddles and bridles of the most costly kind—six men's saddles and one side-saddle. They have between fifty and sixty horses, one hundred hogs, and seventeen head of cattle. They have geese and chickens. Their house is inclosed with a common worm fence, with some outhouses, principally built of logs. A never-failing spring of excellent water is near the door, with a house over it." This is Mrs. Bennet's description, with some items added by Mrs. Drake. From the same sources I give the following description of the family.

"My aunt is of small stature, not very much bent; her hair clubbed behind in calico, tied with worsted ferret; her dress a blue calico short-gown, a white Mackinaw blanket, a fold of blue broadcloth around her, red cloth leggins, and buckskin moccasins. Her hair is somewhat gray, her eyes a bright chestnut, clear and sprightly for one of her age, her face very much wrinkled and weather-beaten. She has a scar on her left cheek, which she received at an Indian dance. Her skin is not so dark as would be expected from her age and constant exposure. Her teeth are remarkably good."

This extraordinary family had not been without their griefs. The first husband of the youngest daughter had died, and the second had been killed in a fight. The only child of the eldest had been poisoned by a desperate lover, son of Godfrey the chief, because her family would not consent to her marrying him on account of his intemperance and idleness. These sad events had left traces behind them which death alone would efface.

At the time the whole family gave themselves up to inconsolable grief.

"*Lady Cap.* Alack the day! she's dead, she's dead, she's
    dead.
  *Cap.* Ha! let me see her. Out, alas! she's cold;
Her blood is settled, and her joints are stiff;
Death lies on her, like an untimely frost
Upon the sweetest flower of all the field.
Accursed time! unfortunate old man!
  *Nurse.* O, lamentable day!
  *Lady Cap.*                O, woeful time!
  *Cap.* Death, that hath ta'en her hence to make me wail,
Ties up my tongue, and will not let me speak.
  *Lady Cap.* Accurs'd, unhappy, wretched, hateful day!
Most miserable hour that e'er time saw
In lasting labor of his pilgrimage!
But one, poor one, one poor and loving child,
But one thing to rejoice and solace in,
And cruel death hath catch'd it from my sight."
                    SHAKSPEARE—*Romeo and Juliet.*

The following is from Mrs. Bennet's journal: "The eldest daughter is large and fleshy—I should think would weigh near two hundred pounds. She is active, observing, and intelligent, thirty-four years of age. The youngest is smaller—is quiet and very retiring—is twenty-four years of age. The mother's name is Ma-con-a-qua, *a young bear.* The eldest daughter's name is Kich-ke-ne-che-qua, *cut-finger.* The youngest is O-saw-she-quah, *yellow leaf.* The grandchildren's names are Kip-pe-no-quah, *corn-tassel,* Wap-pa-na-se-a, *a blue corn,* Kim-on-sack-quah, *young panther.*"

As to the religious notions of Frances, Mrs. Bennet says, "She is well apprised of a heaven and hell, and the necessity of living a sober, honest, and quiet life, and if she does she thinks she will be happy when she dies, having been taught these things by her adopted parents." The heathenism of the Delawares, into whose hands she fell, had been much modified by Christian influences and instructions, through the agency of the

Moravian missionaries. It is not at all unlikely that the Christian ideas of a state of future rewards and punishments had made a deep impression upon the general mind of that tribe far beyond what was developed in the form of a profession of Christianity. These ideas, being in harmony with the childish impressions and early instructions of Frances, would be likely to take a deeper hold upon her heart and life than upon those of native Indians. There was a high moral bearing in this adopted Indian mind that well accords with this theory; and how far the Holy Spirit may have wrought these principles into the texture of her soul, and, through them, finally sanctified that soul, is not for us to know. But it would scarcely border upon presumption to entertain a hope of the final happiness of Frances Slocum.

To proceed with the visit. It had been arranged that Frances, her eldest daughter, and Captain Brouriette should accompany the visitors to Peru, in the way of an interchange of hospitalities. After breakfast Captain Brouriette left upon some business, promising to meet the company at Peru at three o'clock P.M. The arrangements for proceeding on horseback were nearly completed. Frances had but one side-saddle, and she went to the brink of the river, and took off her moccasins and leggins, waded the river, and went a mile and borrowed another side-saddle, that both of her fair nieces might be accommodated. As for herself, like the Indian women generally, she rode a man's saddle.

About noon the horses were all rigged and at the door. When the company were all seated in their saddles, Frances started off, followed by her eldest daughter. Mr. Slocum rode on next, followed by his two daughters, "all in Indian file." They forded the Missisinewa twice and the Wabash once. Just before they arrived at Peru, Frances and her daughter fell behind, wishing her white relatives to take the lead as they entered the village. They arrived a little before three, and, punctual to the minute, Captain Brouriette rode up at three. They were now all seated in the parlor, with Mr. Miller, the interpreter, and visiting proceeded briskly. The Indian portion of the party were now more observing than ever, and did not try to conceal their preferences for many of the usages of the whites. They would neither eat nor do scarcely any thing else until they saw how their white friends did it. They spoke of many things they saw upon the table, and said they must get some like them. Harriet had knitting, and the Indian daughter would scarcely allow her to lay it down until she had learned "the stitch." She said she would knit herself a pair of stockings, "they were so comfortable." At night the ladies all retired to the same room. Here Frances and her daughter closely observed the garments of the ladies, and, so far as was physically practicable, tried them on. The bulky young Indian woman, by shrewd signs, intimated that if she had *stays* to wear she would be small too. When their curiosity was gratified, the queen Ma-con-a-qua and her daughter lay down upon the floor, not listening for a moment to the solicitations of the ladies to take a bed, and in a few minutes were sound asleep.

We will now proceed to give the history of Frances as she gave it, piecemeal, during the two visits.

She said that before her father removed to Wyoming they lived by a great water. They had a large house, and she thought her father had sold it, as she saw a great heap of paper money counted out on the table. In a few days there was a large new wagon brought up, and they were all put into it like a flock of quails or chickens. The wagon had a sail or tent over it. They used to peep out sometimes, and her brother, who rode on one of the horses, would strike at them with his great whip. He called her "red-head," and told her to keep her head in, or it would get knocked off against the trees. She said, they would take us out and feed us, and then put us back again under the tent. She remembered her mother—remembers seeing her spin: she was a large woman, and she would make her mind, and make her work. She tells this to her girls: when she was small, her mother would make her wash up the dishes as soon as they had done eating, and she taught them the same thing. When they came to Wyoming they lived by a long river near a fort. On being asked if they had any black people in the family, she said they had, and the Indians took a black girl before they took her.

### THE CAPTIVITY.

We will now proceed to the story of the captivity of Frances Slocum as related by herself. "Three Delaware Indians came suddenly to our house. They killed and scalped a man near the door. A boy ran into the house, and he and I hid under the staircase. The Indians came into the house and went up stairs. They took some loaf-sugar and some bundles of other things. They carried us through the bushes. I looked back, but saw no one except my mother. They carried us over the mountains—it seemed to me a long way—to a cave where they had left their blankets and some other things. There was a bed of leaves, and here we staid all night. We reached this place while it was yet light. I was very tired, and I lay down on the ground, and cried until I fell asleep.

"The next morning we set off early, and we traveled many days in the woods before we came to an Indian village. When we stopped at night, the Indians would make a bed of hemlock boughs, and make up a great fire at their feet which would last all night. They roasted their meat by sticking a stick into it, and holding it to the fire. They drank at the brooks and springs, and made me a little cup of birch bark to drink out of. The Indians were very kind to me; when they had any thing to eat, I always had the best; when I was tired, they carried me in their arms; and in a short time I began to feel better, and stopped crying. I do not know where the Indian village was which we first stopped at; we only staid there a few days." It was probably Sheshequin.

"Very early one morning two of the same Indians took a horse, and set the boy and me on it, and set off upon a journey. One Indian went before, and the other behind, driving the horse. We traveled a long way, when we came to the village where these Indians belonged. I now found that one of them was an Indian chief whom they called *Tack-horse*. I do not know what that name means." The name, it is probable, has allusion to some fact in the chief's history while he mingled with the whites, for we shall subsequently see that he had quite a sprinkling of civilization in his character. Her story proceeds: "Early one morning Tack-horse took me and dressed my hair in the Indian fashion, and painted my face. He then dressed me up, and put on me beautiful wampum beads, and made me look very fine. I was much pleased with the wampum.

"We then lived on a hill not far from a river"—probably the Genesee River. "I was now adopted by Tack-horse and his wife in the place of one they had lost a short time before, and they gave me her name. When the Indians lose a child, they often adopt some one in its place, and treat that one in all respects as their own. This is the reason why they so often carry off the children of white people.

"It was now the fall of the year, for chestnuts had come. There were a great many Indians here, and here we remained all winter. The Indians were furnished with ammunition and provisions by the British. In the spring we went to Sandusky, and staid there through the summer, but in the fall we came back, and we lived one year at Niagara. I recollect that the Indians were afraid to cross above the Falls on account of the rapidity of the water. I also recollect that they had a machine by which they raised goods from below the Falls, and let things down." This was, no doubt, a tackle erected by the English.

"We went from Niagara near Detroit, where we lived three years. My adopted father made chairs, which he sold; he also played on the fiddle, and frequently went into the white settlements and played, and received pay for it. My adopted mother made baskets and brooms, which she sold. The British made them presents of ammunition and food, which they had to go after in the night.

"In the spring we went down to a large river—Detroit River—where the Indians built a great many bark canoes. When they were finished we went up Detroit River, where we remained three years.

"There had been war between the British and Americans, and the American army had driven the

Indians around the fort where I was adopted. In their fights, the Indians used to bring home scalps. I do not know how many. When peace was made between the British and Americans, we lived by hunting, fishing, and raising corn. The reason why we staid here so long was that we heard the Americans had destroyed all our villages and corn-fields."

Frances had now been among the Indians eight years, and was thirteen years of age. She had been tenderly treated, and taught that the white people were enemies to the Indians. She had adopted the Indians for her people, and had a dread of being recaptured and taken back among the whites. She was taught the use of the bow and arrow, and became expert in all the wild sports and athletic exercises of the squaws. She was a successful hunter. She would mount an Indian pony, and gallop through the woods with almost the speed of the wild deer, and with the spirit of the most romantic princess of the Western forests.

> "Soft was the light that filled her eye,
> And grace was in her every motion;
> Her tone was touching, like the sigh
> When young love first becomes devotion.
> Among a savage people, still
> She kept from savage moods apart,
> And thought of crime and dream of ill
> Had never swayed her maiden heart."
> *Pocahontas*, by W. G. SIMMS.

> "She'd often wander in the wood, or roam
> The wilderness in quest of curious flowers,
> Or nest of bird unknown, till eve approach'd,
> And hemm'd her in the shade."
> LOGAN.

But let us proceed with our story.

### REMOVES TO FORT WAYNE.

"After three years, my family and another Delaware family removed to Fort Wayne, after Wayne's victory. I do not know where the other Indians went. This was now our home, and I suppose we lived there thirty years. We lived on Eel River, three miles from Fort Wayne. I was there at the time of Harmer's defeat. At the time when this battle was fought, the women and children were all made to run north. I do not know whether the Indians took any prisoners, or brought home any scalps at this time. After the battle they all scattered and returned to their homes. I then returned to Fort Wayne again. The Indians who returned from this battle were Delawares, Potawatomies, Shawnees, and Miamis."

> "There stood the Indian hamlet, there the lake
>   Spread its blue sheet that flashed with many an oar;
> Where the brown otter plunged him from the brake,
>   And the deer drank: as the light gale flew o'er,
> The twinkling maize-field wrestled on the shore.
>   And while that spot, so wild, and lone, and fair,
>   A look of glad and innocent beauty wore,
>   And peace was in the earth and in the air,
> The warrior lit the pile, and bound his captive there.
>
> "Not unavenged, the foeman from the wood
>   Beheld the deed; and when the midnight shade
> Was stillest, gorged his battle-axe with blood;
>   All died: the wailing babe, the shrieking maid;
>   And in the flood of fire that scathed the glade,
>   The roofs went down; but deep the silence grew,
> When on the dewy woods the day-beam played;
>   No more the cabin smokes rose wreathed and blue,
> And ever by their lake lay moored the light canoe."
>
> BRYANT.

"I was always treated kindly by the Delawares;

and while I lived with them I was married to a Delaware by the name of Little Turtle. He afterward left me and went west of the Mississippi. I would not go with him. My old mother staid here, and I chose to stay with her. My adopted father could talk English, and so could I while he lived. It has now been a long time since I forgot it all.

"The Delawares and Miamis were then living together as one people. I was afterward married to a Miami, a chief, whom the white people called 'The Deaf Man.' His Indian name was She-poe-ken-ah. We came to this reserve about twenty-four years ago. I had no children by my first husband, but by the last one I had four—two boys and two girls. My boys died while they were young; my girls are still living, and are here with me." At the period of the last visit her husband had been dead six years. As to the Indian wars, she says:

"I can not tell much about the Indian wars with the whites, which were so common and so bloody. I well remember a battle and a defeat of the Americans at Fort Washington, which is now Cincinnati. I remember how Wayne and 'Mad Anthony' drove the Indians away, and built the fort. The Indians then scattered all over the country, and lived upon game, which was very plenty. After this they encamped on Red River. After peace was made we all returned to Fort Wayne, and received provisions from the Americans, and there I lived a long time. I had removed with my family to the Missisinewa River some time before the battle of Tippecanoe. The Indians who fought in that battle were Kickapoos, Potawatomies, and Shawnees. The Miamis were not there. I heard of the battle on the Missisinewa; but my husband could not hear, and never went into the wars, and I did not know much about it."

The day after their arrival at Peru, Frances was prevailed upon to have her likeness taken. An artist was sent for from Logansport, but, for some reason, he did not arrive as was expected, and the consequence was that the adieu was not so formal as it would have been. Frances went home with Brouriette and her daughter, expecting to return, and, after having her portrait taken, to bid the visitors a formal farewell. After waiting two or three days, the party became weary and set off for home. Arrangements were, however, made for the portrait, and the painting was executed. Subsequently another was taken, and both are in the possession of her friends in Wilkesbarre.

Before leaving, Frances made a serious effort to prevail upon her brother to come and live with her. Not to be outdone by her brothers, who had made her such liberal offers if she would come and live with them, she told Mr. Slocum that, if he would come to her village and live, she would give him *half of her land*, and this would have been no mean present. Her sincerity and earnestness in this proposition were affecting. No arrangement could be made by which the brother and sister—so long separated, and to each other as dead, and now so mysteriously brought together and united in affection—could spend their remnant of life in the same neighborhood. They both bowed submissively to what was evidently the order of Providence, and tried to adjust their feelings to the separation.

The Indian daughter took a fancy to Harriet Slocum, dressed her in beads and wampum, and said she looked like her daughter, who had been cruelly poisoned. "Would I not make a nice squaw?" asked Harriet. "Yes, beautiful squaw; will you be in the place of my daughter, and live with me?" On being told that her friends could not spare her, she was satisfied. She seemed sensible that she was asking too much; but, could the boon have been granted, it would have been most grateful to her heart.

Frances, Brouriette, and his wife finally gave their white relatives the parting hand, expressing their high gratification with the visit and the affection which they had manifested for them in coming so far to see them.

But, before the final adieu, Captain Brouriette gave Mr. Slocum the most ample assurances that he would take good care of his mother-in-law while she lived. He said he had never left her but once, and that was because of a disagreement with his brother-in-law, who was a drunken, lazy Indian, and would do nothing for himself or any one else. He was now dead, and they lived in the utmost harmony.

They shook hands and parted, expecting to meet in a day or two; but this was the final adieu. Mr. Slocum and his daughters returned from this most interesting visit *via* Indianapolis, Cincinnati, and Pittsburg. They brought home many little remembrances of their Indian relatives.

### ACT OF CONGRESS IN FAVOR OF FRANCES.

When arrangements were being made by the government to settle the Indians of Indiana west of the Mississippi, Mr. Slocum did not forget his sister. He petitioned Congress in her behalf, and succeeded in enlisting powerful support. Hon. B. A. Bidlack took charge of the bill, and John Quincy Adams made one of his strong speeches in its support, and it became a law. The bill provided that one mile square of the reserve, embracing the house and improvements of Frances Slocum, should be granted in fee to her and her heirs forever. She remembered the kindness, and went down to the grave, in a goodly old age, with the gratitude of a warm heart, and wishing many blessings upon her good brother.

### LAST DAYS OF FRANCES SLOCUM.

The Miamis had removed West, in accordance with the policy of the government. Frances Slocum was surrounded by white settlers, of whom she naturally entertained suspicions which were not calculated to promote the comfort and quiet of her latter days. She was, in fact, suspicious that she and her family might at last be robbed of the home to which the government had given them a title. She sent word to her brother Joseph to come and protect her from the frauds which she apprehended were likely to be practiced upon her. As the best that could be done for her, a son of Isaac Slocum took charge of her business. But all her old associates were gone, and a new order of things was established around her. Despairing of the return of the scenes of the past, she sighed for release from the associations and vices of civilization. Contrasting the freedom and the romance of savage life with the thirst of gain and the overreaching policy of a white frontier settlement, she thought she had truly fallen upon evil times, and was really weary of life. The prestige of her character and her name had departed with her tribe, and she was looked upon simply as a favored old Indian woman, whose claims to equal rights with her white neighbors were entitled to very little respect.

During her last sickness, which was brief, Frances Slocum refused all medical aid, declaring that, as her people were gone, and she was surrounded by strangers, she wished to live no longer. She departed this life March 9th, 1847. She had Christian burial, a prayer being made at her house, and her remains conducted to the grave by a clergyman. Her daughter, the wife of Captain Brouriette, overcome with toil and grief, followed her mother to the Spirit-land four days subsequently.

Frances Slocum sleeps upon a beautiful knoll near the confluence of the Missisinewa and the Wabash, by the side of her chief and her children, where her ashes will rest in peace until the morning of the resurrection. The tenacity with which she clung to that spot, and her obstinate refusal to leave it for the association of civil society, is one of the prominent facts in her wonderful story.

## IX.

### QUEEN ESTHER'S ROCK.

This celebrated rock is situated east of a direct line between the monument and the site of Fort Wintermoot, on the brow of the high, steep bank which is supposed to have been the ancient bank of the river.

The rock is a boulder, and is a sort of conglomerate, principally composed of quartz. It rises about eighteen inches above the surface of the ground. A portion of this rock is of a reddish color, which some have been credulous enough to believe to be a blood-stain; hence the name of "Bloody Rock," by which it is known in the neighborhood. This stain—like that, with equal credulity, which is supposed to have been made by the blood of Rizzio upon the floor of Holyrood Palace—is believed to be judicially and miraculously indelible. We need not say that this is a mere fancy, while it is an undoubted historical fact that blood was spilled upon this rock.

Perhaps the night after the battle, sixteen prisoners were arranged in a circle around the rock in question, to be sacrificed by Queen Esther to the manes of a son who had been killed by a scouting-party before the battle. According to a usage of savage warfare, it was the right, if not, indeed, the duty of the old queen to take sweet vengeance upon the prisoners which had fallen into her hands for the loss of her son. Armed with a death-mall and hatchet, she now assumes the office of executioner, according to the most approved Indian forms. The prisoners, one after another, were seated upon the rock, held by two strong Indians, while the priestess of the bloody rites which were performed upon that fatal altar chanted a savage dirge or Indian war-song, and raising the death-mall with both hands, dashed out the brains of the helpless victim, or with one hand buried her hatchet in his skull.

This was a terrible tragedy, but we are happy to know that there was one relieving circumstance connected with it. There were two men in that devoted circle possessed of strong will, iron nerve, and almost lightning agility. Lebbeus Hammond and Joseph Elliott were near each other, and their turn was about to come. Eleven had been sacrificed, and Hammond's brother was seated upon the rock, and the ceremony was proceeding: Hammond's soul was stirred to the very bottom. As all eyes were fixed upon the bloody tragedy, Hammond, in a low tone, muttered, "Let's try." In an instant they were both free: they had taken their keepers by surprise. With a sudden jerk and spring the bloodhounds that held them were shaken off, and, like two wild deer, they bounded down the bank. They expected to be shot dead, but such was the confusion of the moment that the Indians simply trusted to their legs. Elliott, in relating the story to a friend who related it to us, said he was surprised that they were not fired upon. Their line of flight diverged, a circumstance which the Indians did not observe. Hammond steered up the river, and, glancing his eye over his shoulder, he discovered that the Indians were shaping their course with the expectation of intercepting the fugitives in the direction of Forty Fort. He then turned still more directly up stream. He had, however, not proceeded far before a root caught his toe, and he was plunged headlong down the bank under a tree-top with thick foliage, where he immediately judged that he was more secure than he would be upon the run.

When the Indians returned from the pursuit of Elliott, they scoured the hill side in search of Hammond. As they were peeping here and there among the brush and old logs, he tried to hold his breath and to keep his heart still, but in spite of him his breathing seemed to amount to a roar, and the beating of his heart to be like the pounding of a beetle. Once he thought they saw him, and for a moment his heart sunk. He was soon measurably relieved by observing that the Indians seemed to give up the pursuit as hopeless, and directed their course toward the fatal rock.

Hammond remained in his concealment until all was still, and then swam the river, crossing Monocasy Island, and found his way to the fort at Wilkesbarre. There he found his friend Elliott, who had swum the river to the bar on the lower point of Monocasy Island, as he thought, all the distance under water. When rising above the water, he received a shot in his shoulder which seriously disabled him. On reaching the opposite side of the river he providentially found a horse, which he managed to ride, using the bark of a hickory sapling for a bridle. Here Dr. Smith dressed his wound, and the next morning he went down the river, with his wife and child, in a canoe managed by a lad, and found sympathy among kind friends at Catawissa. These two brave fellows lived long to enjoy their well-earned reputation for good conduct under the most appalling circumstances.

It has been made a question whether indeed Queen Esther was the savage executioner of the prisoners at "Bloody Rock," and there are some circumstances which would really seem to militate against such a supposition. Her strong expressions in favor of peace to Esquire Sutton and Colonel Jenkins, and the deep sympathies for the settlers which she manifested when visited at her camp by Mrs. Bennet but a short time before seem to indicate a degree of civilization and a spirit of humanity which would render improbable the part attributed to her in the awful tragedy at Bloody Rock. In addition to all this, Colonel Stone considers "the statement improbable" upon more general grounds. He says, "Catharine Montour, sometimes called Queen Esther, was a half-breed, who had been well educated in Canada. Her reputed father was one of the French governors of that province when appertaining to the crown of France, and she herself was a lady of comparative refinement. She was much caressed in Philadelphia, and mingled in the best society; hence the remotest belief can not be entertained that she was the Hecate of that fell night."

All this seems very fair, but it is not only against the best established traditions of the times, but the clearest testimony of contemporaries. Colonels Denison and Franklin and Mrs. Myers agree in sanctioning "the statement." Mr. Miner represents Queen Esther as entering Forty Fort at the head of the Indian warriors. She here met Colonel Denison, and, drawling out his name, she insultingly said, "Colonel. Denison, you told me to bring more Indians; see here, I have brought you all these." "Be silent," said Colonel Butler; "women should be seen, but not heard."

The historian of Tryon County, Hon. William W. Campbell, says, "Catrina Montour, who might well be termed a fury, acted a conspicuous part in this tragedy. She followed in the train of the victorious army, ransacking the heaps of the slain, and, with her arms covered with gore, barbarously murdering the wounded, who in vain supplicated for their lives."—See *Border Warfare of New York*, p. 305.

Another illustration is given by Mr. Campbell of the character of this woman. One of her sons made Mr. Cannon a prisoner on the destruction of Cherry Valley. He was an old man, and was severely wounded with a musket ball. When Kate Montour saw him she fell into a rage, and reproached her son for his humanity. "Why," said she, "did you bring that old man a prisoner? Why did you not kill him when you first took him?"—*Ibid.*, p. 219.

Elliott and Hammond lived long after the conclusion of the war. They received a pension from the government, and were universally considered men of honor and veracity. These men, who so narrowly escaped the death-mall or the hatchet—who witnessed a portion of the bloody ceremonies which Queen Esther is charged in the popular belief of the times with having performed with her own hands, give their sanction to the common opinion. These facts are not easily disposed of. The name of the supposed "Hecate of that fell night" being " Catharine Montour"—her being "a half-breed"—her having been "educated in Canada"—her "refinement"—her having been "caressed in Philadelphia," and "mingling in the best society" there in 1744, may have furnished ground of doubt with regard to the truth of the story of "Bloody Rock" to the mind of Colonel Stone, but to minds less predisposed to vindicate the Indian character from the charge of inhuman cruelties, will do but little toward unsettling the best established traditionary belief and the positive statements of contemporaries, and even of eye-witnesses.

The history of "Kate Montour," as a whole, furnishes no evidence of the improbability of the story of "Bloody Rock." Indeed, her savage nature exhibited itself on other occasions in a manner which proves but too clearly that it had not all been eradicated by the refined education which she received "in Canada." —See *Lossing's Field-Book of the Revolution*, vol. i., p. 358.

The horror in which this same "Catharine Montour" was held is seen in the treatment which she received from Colonels Hartley and Butler, and General Sullivan. In October, after the Wyoming massacre, Colonel Hartley, of the Pennsylvania line, joined Colonel Z. Butler, and they proceeded with 130 men to Sheshequin, where they met the Indians in a battle, burned the Indian settlement, and destroyed Queen Esther's palace, and laid waste her plantation. And when General Sullivan proceeded to the Lake country, the first town he ordered destroyed was Catharine, at the head of the Seneca Lake, the town which was named in honor of Catharine Montour, and in which she resided. These proceedings seem consonant with the idea that Catharine Montour deserved special chastisement.

It is not doubted but that this "half-breed" woman, uninfluenced by the war spirit, had amiable qualities, and a certain polish in her manners. But the sound of the battle and the sight of human gore aroused the demon within her. She who "shed tears" at the prospect of war, when it began to rage entered into its spirit. She had lost a son in the expedition, and she must avenge his death, or, in the estimation of her people, be "no good squaw." Her feelings of resentment and her reputation with the Indians united to urge her on, if, indeed, she needed any urging, to acts of savage barbarity. Then, if she had not been predisposed to take a part in the murder and plunder of the settlers, why was she on hand at all? Her age, if no other reason—for she must have been near eighty—would have justified her remaining at home, instead of following Butler and his Indians and Tories in a murderous onslaught upon a defenseless settlement.

Upon the whole, we see no good reason for doubting the part attributed to Catharine Montour, or Queen Esther, in the affair of Bloody Rock, in the popular traditions of Wyoming. A little examination into her character will explain the mystery of her being, under some circumstances, almost a saint, and under others a very fiend.

## X.

### CAPTIVITY AND ESCAPE OF THOMAS AND ANDREW BENNET AND LEBBEUS HAMMOND.

"Near where Meshoppen meets our river,
    When in the quiet night
Through trees we saw the star-beams quiver,
    We nerved us for the fight.
Where stood the arms we quickly drew,
    No gentle blows to strike or die;
Two wounded fled, the rest we slew,
    In ghastly death we saw them lie:
E'en now I see them glare, as in cold death they lie."
        *Susquehanna, an unpublished Poem.*

IN 1779 General Sullivan had pursued the Indians with the scourge of war, and driven them west of the Genesee River. Colonel John Butler and Brant had been worsted at every point, and had fled to Niagara. It was obvious enough to the fierce braves that it was in vain to attempt to meet the Americans in force in the open field, but they shrewdly concluded to take vengeance upon them by visiting their settlements in small parties, and by stealthy approaches to take property and prisoners, or murder and scalp, as the case might be. They consequently, in small gangs, followed down General Sullivan upon the very heels of his army, and he had no sooner disposed the garrison at Wilkesbarre, and crossed the mountain with his army, than the work of plunder and murder was resumed on the north and the west branches of the Susquehanna and on the Delaware. In some instances these parties were fearfully successful, and in others they met with a terrible retribution.

The following is a true account, communicated by the parties engaged, of one of these savage expeditions, and the tragedy with which it wound up.

On the 27th of March, 1780, Thomas Bennet, with his son Andrew, a lad of thirteen or fourteen years of age, commenced plowing on the flats on land now owned by Elijah Shoemaker, of Kingston. They took their guns with them, and tried to shoot some ducks in the river. Hiding their guns, they commenced their work. Their team consisted of a yoke of oxen and a horse, the boy riding the horse. They had been watched by four Indians, who stole up to the place where the guns were concealed and broke them. They then sprang upon Mr. Bennet and his son, and hurried them away.

On the same morning, Lebbeus Hammond had left Wilkesbarre in pursuit of a fine horse, which he found on a place he had occupied a few miles up the river, on the west side. He made a bridle of hickory withes, and was proceeding homeward, when he saw moccasin tracks. He was much alarmed, and expected every minute to be fired upon. All at once two Indians leaped from the bushes, and one seized his horse, while the other pulled him off. After a brief consultation in Indian, which Hammond did not understand, they led him a short distance into the woods and pinioned his arms, and then tied him to a tree. In this situation they left him for about an hour, when they returned with four others, having Bennet and his son as prisoners. Their greetings were such as might have been expected. Hammond had made an almost miraculous escape from "Bloody Rock," and Bennet was a notorious patriot, and their prospects now were any thing but agreeable.

An Indian mounted Hammond's horse, but when they came to the marsh, which lies between the river and the mountain, he ran the horse into the mire and left him there. The Indians hurried on with their prisoners over the mountain, and lodged that night near the foot of "Cummings's Pond," in what is now Northmoreland. The Indians evidently did not know the prisoners, for they left them unbound; and Bennet was for attempting to escape, but Hammond thought it not possible to succeed, and the idea was given up. The next day they proceeded on to Bowman's Creek, and when they came into "the green woods" they found the snow "waistband deep." Of course it was laborious traveling, especially for a man of years like Mr. Bennet. But the party pushed on, and made what progress they could. Occasionally one of the Indians would yell horribly, as though he wished to attract the attention of another party. At length they met a party of about forty Indians, commanded by a white man—a *Tory*, of course. An old Indian belonging to the party sung out, "Ah! old Bennet; I'd rather see your scalp."

Some of the Indians fell back and held a council, while the Tory asked Bennet many questions with regard to the situation of the fort, the number of fighting men, the number of inhabitants in the settlement, and the like. He was told that there were three hundred fighting men in the fort, that they were well armed and provisioned, and that they had cannon, and that the settlers had all taken refuge there. They then concluded to strike the river below the fort. They divided their company into three parties, and committed various outrages, some of which will be noticed in another connection. Before the two parties separated, an Indian went up to a burnt stump and blackened his face, and coming up to Mr. Bennet, he directed his attention to his face, with the significant sentence, "Ho! Bennet." The movement was well understood. One of the party of Indians which they met joined their party, which made seven.

That night the prisoners were *pappoosed*, that is, fastened down with poles laid across them, with an Indian on each end of the poles. The prisoners had as yet little or nothing to eat, and were heavily burdened with the luggage belonging to the Indians. Of course, they were worn down, and nearly ready to give up and die. The next day—the third day of their captivity—Mr. Bennet accidentally pulled a button from his coat, and put it in his pocket. They were now searched, and the button being found, Bennet asked for it, saying he wished to put it on again. The Indian flung it away, saying, "Fool, Bennet; only one day more. You die at Wyallusing." That day the Indians hunted for deer, and starting one, left the prisoners a few rods behind, and gave them an opportunity to consult. Bennet said to Hammond, "We must rise upon them to-night." "It will be a great undertaking," said Hammond, "but it may be our last chance." "They will kill me," answered Bennet, "and I know not with what cruel tortures. It may be we shall succeed, and if we do we will again return to our families; but if I am to die, I will sell my life as dearly as possible." In the consultation the boy said little, but thought much. In his heart he said with Percy,

"I tender you my service,
Such as it is, being tender, raw, and young,
Which elder days shall ripen and confirm
To more approved service and desert."

How he acted his part will appear as the story proceeds. The arrangement was made by the time the deer was taken, and the party proceeded to cross the river. They came up to the Meshappen, which was much swollen by the melted snow, and before they could venture to wade the stream they went up two or three miles.

Having crossed the creek, and descended to the place of encampment near the Susquehanna, they built a fire under a shelving rock. While the Indians were seated around the fire, roasting and eating the meat of the deer, the leader of the party entered into conversation with Mr. Hammond. He spoke tolerable English, and seemed particularly free and communicative. He said he had expected to meet a large company of Indians at that place, but he supposed they had encamped farther up the river. He then asked him various questions about the war. Would there be peace? Did the white men wish to make peace with the red men? He had been told so. Did he know Lieutenant Boyd? Hammond said he was intimately acquainted with him. In September Boyd had been sent out with a reconnoitring party by General Sullivan, in Genesee, and had been surrounded by a superior force, taken, and most barbarously tortured. The Indian said he led the party that took Boyd, and he further said, "Boyd brave man—as good a soldier as ever fought against the red man." He said they tortured Boyd, cut off his fingers and toes, plucked out his eyes, etc., "still brave Boyd neither asked for mercy nor uttered a complaint." Ah! "brave Boyd" knew very well the character of the Indians.

"You may as well go stand upon the beach,
And bid the main flood bate his usual height;

> You may as well use question with a wolf,
> Why he hath made the ewe bleat for the lamb;
> You may as well forbid the mountain pines
> To wag their high tops, and to make no noise
> When they are fretted with the gusts of heaven;
> You may as well do any thing most hard,
> As seek to soften that—than which what's harder?
> His [Indian] heart."
> SHAKSPEARE.

He then brought a sword and said, "There Boyd's sword." Hammond took the sword, and discovered the initials of Boyd's name stamped on the blade near the hilt. To the whole tale Hammond listened without expressing the slightest emotion, well knowing the consequences of the least manifestation of the indignation which he felt burning in his bosom.

When the Indians were ready to lie down, they *pappoosed* the prisoners as on the preceding night; then they drew their blankets over their heads and fell into a sound sleep. One only seemed to be on the watch. About midnight Bennet manifested great uneasiness, and asked to get up. He received for answer, "Most day—lie down, dog." He insisted that he was sick, and *must* get up. About one o'clock the Indians all got up and relieved the prisoners, allowing them to get up and walk about. Bennet brought wood and flung it on the fire. In about two hours all the Indians were snoring again except the old watchman, and he commenced roasting the deer's head, first sticking it in the fire, and then scraping off the meat with his knife and eating it. Finally the old fellow began to nod over his early breakfast. Hammond placed himself by an Indian axe, and Andrew Bennet, the boy, stood by the guns, which were stacked. Both watched the movements of Mr. Bennet, who was poking up the brands. He had on a long great-coat, and, as he came

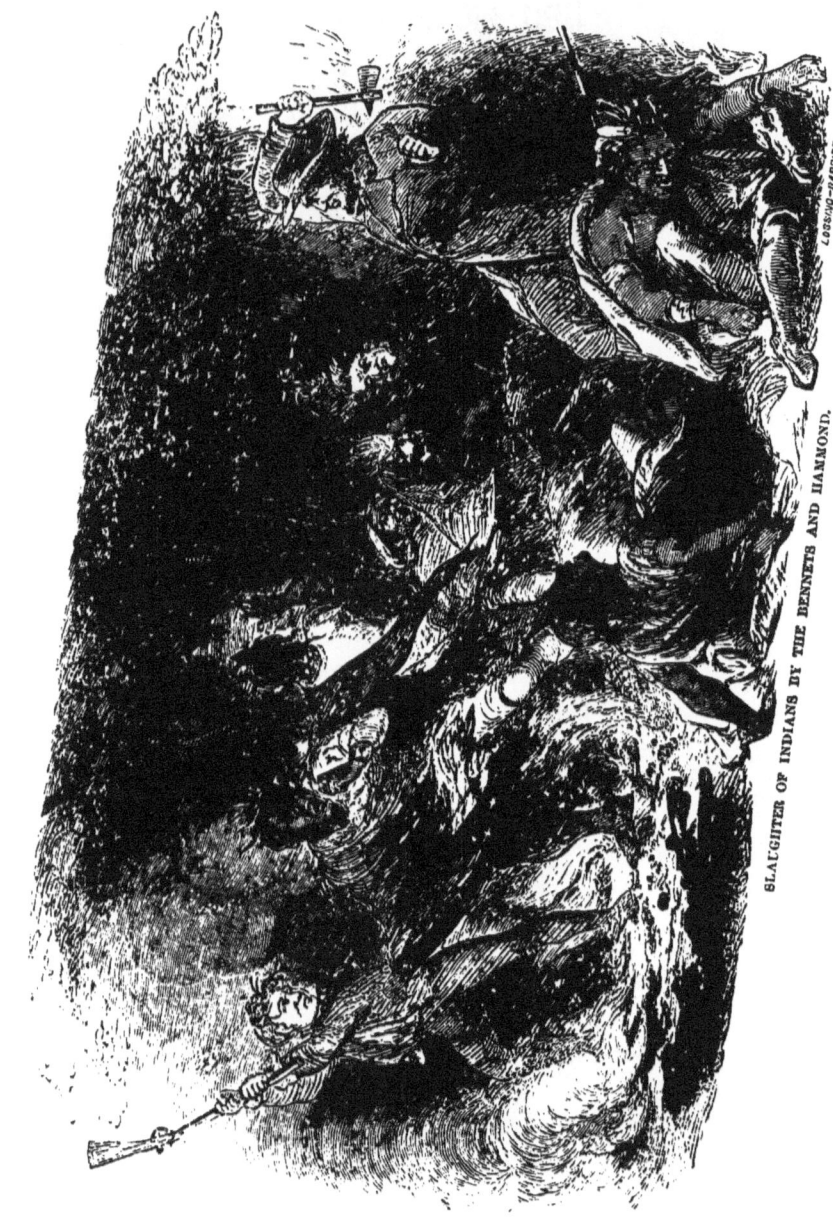

SLAUGHTER OF INDIANS BY THE BENNETS AND HAMMOND.

round near the Indian, he cautiously took hold of a spontoon, or war-spear, which lay by his side, and stepped back with the instrument covered by his coat, holding it in a perpendicular position behind him. When he had reached the right point behind the Indian he plunged it through him. He gave a tremendous jump and a hideous yell, and fell upon the fire.

> "If death so terrible appear, die thou.
> With cruel spear he lanced his naked side,
> Warm streams of blood his arms o'erflow :
> His panting bosom heaves with dying sighs,
> Hard lab'ring to retain departing breath ;
> At length he yields ; black darkness veils his eyes,
> Sealed in eternal sleep of iron death."
>
> SAMUEL WESLEY—*Battle of the Frogs and Mice.*

The spontoon was so firmly fixed in the body of the Indian that Bennet was obliged to abandon it, and to use a gun and a tomahawk during the rest of the fight. Hammond used the axe, dashing it into the head which was first lifted. The old Indian who had given the account of Boyd's massacre was the first to take the alarm. He yelled out "*Chee-woo! chee-woo!*" when Hammond buried the head of the axe in his brains, and he fell headlong into the fire. The next blow took an Indian on the side of the neck, just below the ear, and he fell upon the fire. The boy snapped three guns, not one of which happened to be loaded, but his operations made the Indians dodge and jump straight under Hammond's axe, or the breech of a gun which old Mr. Bennet had clubbed, and with which he did terrible execution. A stout Indian undertook to secure a weapon by a rush upon the boy. He sprang upon him with the fury of a demon, his eyes seeming to blaze, when the brave little fellow swung the breech of a gun, and buried the cock in the top of his head.

Just at that moment the only two Indians remaining alive took to their heels, when Mr. Bennet, who could throw a tomahawk with the precision and force of any red-skin on the frontier, picked up a tomahawk and let it slip, and it stuck in the back of one of them. The Indian turned round, being at about the distance of forty feet, and hollowed out "whoo," and his blanket fell from his shoulders, and the hatchet was left with it on the ground, he running off naked.

It was an awful struggle, but it was not long. A minute and a half or two minutes, and the work was done. Five of the savages were piled up on and around the fire, and two had fled badly wounded. There was a great contrast between the present appearance of the Indian camp under the rock, and that same camp the evening before, when the bloodthirsty savage gloried in the barbarous deed of cutting off Boyd's fingers and toes, and pulling out his eyes; and looked forward to, perhaps, the next night, when he would glut his savage vengeance in a similar manner upon the prisoners, who were obliged to listen to the recital without the slightest expression of sympathy for their brave companion and friend. The prisoners were now free, and no time was lost. They supplied themselves with good moccasins from the feet of the dead and dying Indians, and took guns and ammunition for defense, and blankets for their protection from the cold, and fifteen minutes from the moment the last blow was struck they were upon the line of march for their home and friends.

### THE FLIGHT OF HAMMOND AND THE BENNETS.

The wounded Indians took a position on the side of the mountain where they had a fair view of the camp, and watched the movements of the victors. When they had gone, the poor wretches returned to see if any thing remained by which they might be saved from freezing or starvation. Here the miserable savages saw their companions, with whom they had shared common dangers and hardships, all gory and cold in death. They laid them down to sleep the stern, cruel masters of a band of helpless captives; they awoke to see their own weapons in the hands of those captives, and to feel the cold steel which they had often stained with the blood of the white man. Their comrades were dead, and they were naked and helpless. This was a terrible lesson to the infuriated savages, and one they did not forget.

The victors made their calculations to take as straight a course as possible through the woods to the "Capouse Meadows," near where the flourishing town of Scranton is now located, avoiding all Indian trails. They pushed on up the Meshoppen about three miles. The stream was high and the current rapid; but there was no alternative; they must wade it, if possible, at that point. The two men took the boy between them, lest the angry current should sweep him away, and, with tremendous efforts, succeeded in reaching the other shore. The morning was extremely cold, and they had proceeded but a short distance before their clothes were frozen stiff. They had brought away with them no provisions of any kind, and such was the excitement under which they labored that they scarcely felt the need of any. They toiled on, alternately inspired by hope and depressed with fear. The danger was that a fresh party of Indians might get upon their track and overtake them.

They had reason to think that there was a large

party above, and that party might meet the wounded Indians, and learn the story of the slaughter of their fellows, and give the escaped prisoners chase, or they might meet a party crossing over from the Delaware to the Susquehanna, and in either event there would be scarcely a ray of hope of their escaping the most barbarous tortures. The images of their loved ones at home stood before them every moment, and stimulated them to hold on their way. Every step brought them nearer the goal, and enlarged the space between them and the scene of the fearful tragedy at Meshoppen. The excitement of the journey was little inferior to that of the terrible struggle with the savages through which they had just passed. Such fearful tension of the nerves can not long be endured, but for a time will almost perform miracles. They were hungry, but thought not of food; weary, but there was no place of rest short of friends and home. From early dawn till late at night they were on full stretch, heeding nothing which they passed, and taking no note of time, simply marking the ranges of the hills which bordered the large streams which empty into the Susquehanna from the east. When they saw the last range peering up in the distance, they, like Paul when he saw "the Three Taverns," "thanked God and took courage."

### SAFE AT HOME AGAIN.

Mr. Bennet was an old hunter and understood the ground. They kept their course, crossing the high ridges and deep valleys which lay across their path, generally being able to walk on the frozen crust, until, on the second day, they reached the south side of the mountain range northwest of the Lackawanna valley. Here they found bare ground, and now they paused occasionally for a few minutes and picked wintergreen to eat. They pursued their journey down the side of the mountain to the mouth of the Lackawanna, and so found their way to the fort at Wilkesbarre after an absence of six days. The appearance of the Bennets and Hammond at the fort was an occasion of great joy, as they had been given up for lost. When the excitement passed off, there was little of life left in the returned captives. Nursing and rest finally brought up their emaciated forms and their exhausted spirits to their former condition.

Lieutenant Boyd's sword was brought away by Hammond, and was afterward presented to his brother, Colonel John Boyd.

As to the two Indians who escaped, one died in the woods from his wounds and subsequent exposure, and the one tomahawked by Mr. Bennet was taken up in a state of insensibility by a party of Indians coming over from the Delaware. After they had restored him to consciousness, he gave an account of the slaughter of the Indians by Hammond and the Bennets, which was communicated to Mr. Bennet in a letter from Esquire Consollus, who was a prisoner in the party, and listened to the Indian's story.

Seven years after the terrible scene which we have described, at an Indian treaty held at Newtown, Hammond saw the old Indian who had been wounded by the tomahawk, considerably disfigured, walking with his head bowed. Hammond was not altogether certain that he was the same Indian, and requested a friend to ask him what was the cause of his stooping. When the question was asked, the Indian promptly replied, "A —— Yankee tomahawk me at Wyoming." The poor fellow lingered out a wretched existence for several years, and then was drowned in crossing the Canisteo, falling from a foot-bridge.

## XI.

### THE CAPTURE AND ESCAPE OF JONAH ROGERS, MOSES VAN CAMPEN, PETER PENCE, AND ABRAM PIKE.

> "To *kill man-killer*, man has lawful power,
> But not the extended license to devour."
> — DRYDEN.

IN the account given in the preceding section of the capture of the Bennets and Hammond, it is stated that they met a large party of Indians, led by a Tory, on their way to Wyoming. This company divided into three parties, and made their descent upon the settlers at the foot of the valley, and on the west branch. The information which they received from Mr. Bennet induced them to keep clear of the neighborhood of the fort, which was what he designed to accomplish by his strong representation of the strength of the garrison and the security of the settlers.

On the 29th of March, ten of these Indians in a gang, at daybreak, surprised Upson and Rogers, who were camped out, making sugar, on what was called "Stuart's Flats," at the lower extremity of Wyoming Valley. Upson was killed and scalped. Mrs. Myers says the Indians poured boiling sap down his throat as he lay on his back asleep, with his mouth open. This account was extensively circulated and believed, but Rogers says he was shot. Rogers was thirteen years of age, and has left a written statement of his captivity and deliverance, which is now before us. He was taken prisoner, and told that he "must go to Niagara." They put a blanket around him, and he submitted with apparent cheerfulness, saying, "I will go and be an Indian too." They left the river, and went through the woods to "Big Fishing Creek." Here they surprised another encampment, where Mr. Van Campen, his two sons, and Peter Pence were making sugar. This was on the morning of the 30th of March. Mr. Van Campen was shot and speared, and one of his sons tomahawked and flung into the fire, while the eldest son and Pence were made prisoners. The savages hastened on to another "sugar camp," where they found another Van Campen and two sons, brother to the one previously killed. They murdered Mr. Van Campen and his youngest son, and took the other, a lad twelve years of age, and took the back track. On the road from Shickshinny to Huntington, the Indians saw "signs of Yankoos." Six of the Indians took the road, and surprised four men. Shots were exchanged, and Parks and Ransom were wounded; but, taking refuge in a house near by, the Indians left them. The two fractions of the company were united the next morning in Dallas. They started early, and soon saw fresh shoe-tracks. The leader, who spoke good English, said to Van Campen, "Call." On his doing so, some one answered, and soon Abram Pike came in sight, and nine Indians seized him. He fell on his knees, and cried "Quarter! quarter!" His wife and a child were with him in a sugar camp, and the Indians painted her, and told her to go home. The leader of the party said, "Joggo-squaw, tell Captain Butler me captain too."

This gang were now well freighted with prisoners. Besides the boys and young Pence, they had two military characters of considerable importance. Van Campen had been lieutenant in a company of volunteers, and quarter-master under General Sullivan during his expedition against the Indians, and Pike was a British deserter. Pike had been in the Continental army under General Washington; came into the Valley before the Indian battle; had his thigh broken in the battle, and escaped down the river before the capitulation. He had on a coat of the Continental uniform, which marked him in the eye of the Indians as a considerable prize. They knew not his former relations to the English army, but from the buttons on his coat they concluded he was an American officer, and they called him, by way of eminence, "Congless."

Pike was an Irishman, strongly marked with the peculiarities of his race. He was witty and roguish, presuming and adventurous. It used to be told of him that, when in Washington's army on the Hudson, he and three other fellows stole by the sentry in the night, crossed the river, and broke into a store near the enemy's lines. His comrades were shot, and he narrowly escaped. He was reported in the morning, and, on being brought before the general, he said, "Plase your excellency, I went over with three boys to make a prisoner of the English officer, but we had bad luck." The general, turning to his staff and smiling, said, "Did you ever see such a set of foolhardy fellows? Four of them went to capture the British general! Pike, go to your duty."

Pike was always poor, but always preserved an air of independence. He used to say, "The world owed him a living, and he was determined not to be chated out of it." He sometimes committed petty thefts, and always avoided the penalties of the law, either from the kind consideration of the party injured, or by some stroke of Irish wit. He was once brought before a magistrate charged with having stolen a silver spoon. The evidence was circumstantial, and not very conclusive. Pike solemnly denied the charge, and appealed to all the saints for the truth of the denial. "Well," said the squire, "I will swear you, Pike." "Jist as your honor plases about that," was the reply. Pike kissed the Bible, and still positively denied any knowledge of the spoon. The complainant, being shrewd, and knowing the soldier well, then said, "Now, Pike, if you will lift up your hand, and swear by the honor of a soldier that you did not take the spoon, I will let you off." The court said, "Pike, lift up your hand." Pike looked wise, and, shrugging up his shoulders and shaking his head, said, "The de'il a bit;" and, thrusting his hand into his bosom, he drew out the spoon and dashed it upon the table, exclaiming, "Troth, an' I'll not violate the honor of a soldier for all the spoons in America." The owner took his spoon, and the squire laughed heartily. Pike was finally discharged with a reprimand.

The company now commenced their march for the north. They encamped before they reached Bauman's Creek. Early the next morning they set off, and that day came to their canoes, in which they crossed the Susquehanna above Tunkhannock, and then set them afloat. That night they encamped on the Meshappen, but how they passed without observing the scene of Bennets' and Hammond's slaughter of the Indians, which had occurred but two days before, directly in their path, it is difficult to say. There was no doubt a providence in this, for the discovery would have provoked them to put their prisoners to torture without delay, or would at least have put them upon their guard.

On the next day, April 1st, Mr. Rogers says, "There was some talk of trying to make our escape, as we came across flocks of deer, which gave the prisoners an opportunity of being by themselves. Pike, upon inquiry, found out who was the commanding officer at Niagara, and said he knew him as well as he did his father. He swore that he would that night be a *free* man or a *dead* man. He well knew his fate should he reach Niagara."

Van Campen says, "It came into my mind that sometimes individuals performed wonderful actions, and surmounted the greatest dangers; I then thought that these fellows must die, as well as of the plan to dispatch them." Their views were compared and their plans matured. That night was the time, for later than that time they might be in the hands of a large body of Indians, who would certainly put to torture the first prisoners they should secure after the ravages of the American army in their country. Such was the reasoning of the prisoners, and such their conclusions.

The spirit of liberty struggled in the bosom of these brave fellows: to them the hazards of an unequal fight were preferable to the exigencies of captivity among the savages. With the poet they said:

> "Thy spirit, Independence, let me share,
> Lord of the lion-heart and eagle-eye:
> Thy steps I follow with my bosom bare,
> Nor heed the storm that howls along the sky."
> 
> SMOLLETT.

That night they encamped near the river, about fifteen miles below Tioga Point, not far from the mouth of the Wysox. The prisoners brought wood and made up a good fire. How they were to get loose from their pinions was a question. As the boy Rogers had not been pinioned, it was presumed he would still be left free, and he could help them to the "wood-hatchets" and a knife. The prisoners were pinioned and laid down, each one between two Indians. When all were sound asleep, Rogers arose, and secured a knife and gave it to Pike, and at the same time put an axe in the way of Van Campen, and returned to his place. "Pike cut himself loose, and then cut the other prisoners loose." So says Mr. Rogers, albeit Mr. Van Campen says, "I slipped to Pence, who rose; I cut him loose, and handed him the knife; he did the same for me. I, in turn, took the knife and cut Pike loose; in a moment's time we disarmed them." Pike's account agrees with that of Rogers, that *he cut the prisoners loose.* And, according to him, while he took away the guns, Van Campen and Pence, each with an axe in his hand, resumed their position, with the understanding that, should the Indians take the alarm before the guns were removed, they should each dispatch the two Indians which lay by their side. The guns were all removed, and set up by a tree at a short distance. All, so far, seems probable and well planned; but after this, Pike's story and Van Campen's differ widely. According to Pike, he next proceeded to take the blankets from the Indians, that they might freeze if they should escape. He pulled off their blankets, and they shrugged their shoulders and shivered, but slept on until he had uncovered the last one, when, in stepping over him, he hit him with his toe, upon which he lifted up his head and exclaimed "Woo!" Then the slaughter began. Rogers says, "An Indian awaked and began to jabber." Van Campen and Rogers agree in saying that Pence fired upon them; he, of course, must have sprung to the guns during the first onslaught. Several—it is not certain how many—were slaughtered at the first onset, and the remainder fled a few paces to the woods; but, finding themselves naked and defenseless, they made a rush upon the prisoners, when nearly all shared the same fate. Pence fired; Pike dealt out heavy blows with his axe, first using the head and then the edge, as Rogers reports, while Van Campen had a grapple with a stout fellow whom he had wounded, which is thus graphically described by himself: "There was one—his name was Mohawk—a stout, bold, daring fellow. In the alarm he jumped off about three rods from the fire; he saw that it was the prisoners that made the attack, and, giving the war-whoop, he darted to take possession of the guns; I was as quick to prevent him; the contest was then between him and myself. As I raised my tomahawk, he turned to jump from me; I followed him and struck at him, but missed his head: my tomahawk struck his shoulder, or, rather, the back of his neck; he pitched forward and fell; at the same time, my foot slipped, and I fell by his side; we clinched; his arm was naked; he caught me around the neck; at the same time, I caught him with my left arm around the body, and gave him a close hug, feeling for his knife, but could not reach it. In our scuffle my tomahawk dropped out; my head was under the wounded shoulder, and I was almost suffocated with the blood. I made a violent spring, and broke his hold; we both arose at the same time, and he ran. It took me some time to clear the blood from my eyes; my tomahawk got covered up, and I could not find it in time to overtake him. He was the only one of the party that escaped."

> "Now cuffing close, now chasing to and fro,
> Now hurtling round advantage for to take,

> As two wild boares together grappling go,
> Chaufing and foaming choler each against his foe.
> At last they have all overthrown to ground
> Quite topside turvey, and the pagan hound
> Amongst the iron hooks and grapples run,
> Torn all to rags, and rent with many a wound."
>
> SPENSER.

The bloody tragedy closed, and Rogers began to jump up and down. Pike, frantic with joy, gave him a blow on the side of the head which felled him to the ground. They remained in the camp until morning; Van Campen, recovering the scalps of his father and other relatives, and scalping the Indians, strung the scalps on his belt. Early in the morning the victors gathered up the plunder and proceeded to the river. They constructed a raft, which proved insufficient; it sunk under them, and they lost nearly all their plunder. They traveled down as far as "the Narrows," where they saw a smoke, and had no doubt an Indian's camp was there. After a little reconnoitring, they discovered that the Indians had left, probably upon a hunting expedition. They found a new raft, which they immediately took possession of, and paddled off with all their might. Just as they were out of danger, the Indians made their appearance on the shore and fired upon them, but without effect. They landed on an island, and made themselves as comfortable as possible for the night.

Van Campen tells a ludicrous story of Pike, of what he says occurred that night. They heard a noise, and Pike, supposing it to be the tread of an Indian, was much alarmed. He, Van Campen, "kept watch, and soon a noble raccoon came under the light." He shot the raccoon, "when Pike jumped up and called out, 'Quarter, gentlemen—quarter, gentlemen.'" He took the raccoon by the leg, and threw it down by the fire, saying, "Here, you cowardly rascal, skin that, and give us a roast for supper." This story is wholly incredible upon any other supposition than that Pike was merely exhibiting a little of his Irish humor; more, it is wholly inconsistent with Mr. Rogers's account of the facts of this famous retreat.

According to Mr. Rogers, they left the scene of conflict, and landed on the island on the 2d of April. He says, "April 3d, early, crossed on to the west side, and traveled with nothing to eat. We have now been two days without any thing to eat." Where was that "noble raccoon" which the "cowardly rascal" Pike was ordered to dress and prepare "a roast for supper?"

"April 4, traveled all day; nothing to eat but a small piece of dead deer we found." The deer had died of wounds which it had received, and had began to decay. The flesh was a sorry morsel for any but starving men. At this point the boy Rogers became overcome with fatigue, and besought his friends to let him lie down and die. Pike took him upon his back, and encouraged him to keep heart. He said to his companions, "I'll tak' the boy to his mother, or I'll die in the struggle." After a little rest on the back of the old Irish soldier, the lad plucked up courage and went on.

"April 5, traveled all day; nothing to eat. April 6, came to the river not far from Esquire Sutton's, in Exeter. About the middle of the afternoon we killed a deer. I ran, and before it was dead I had a piece in my mouth." He paid but little attention to the "hair and skin," but forced the quivering flesh between his teeth, as he says, "until the blood dropped from my mouth. It was the sweetest morsel I ever tasted." The same day, at nine o'clock, they arrived at Wilkesbarre. The journal concludes:

"Friday, April 7, I went from Wilkesbarre to Plymouth, to my parents, who received me as one from the dead."

This wonderful tale we have drawn up partly from Mr. Van Campen's narrative, found in his memorial to Congress asking for a pension, partly from a brief narrative written by Mr. Rogers, which has been in the hands of John Bennet, Esq., of Kingston, since 1830, and which he has kindly allowed us to use, and partly from our own recollection of a verbal relation of the circumstances by Abram Pike in 1818. There is some clashing between Van Campen's story and Pike's. Each makes himself the great hero of the tragedy, and makes the other a "coward." In this they were both influenced by prejudice, and are both wrong. Colonel Stone, in the second edition of his history of Wyoming, fully credits Van Campen, and brands Pike with cowardice. The colonel was misled by Van Campen's memorial. Pike was a regularly disciplined soldier; was in the Indian battle, and escaped by swimming down the river a mile or more with his thigh broken. "Sergeant Pike, the Indian Killer," as he was often familiarly called, was no coward; nor were either of his comrades in that heroic exploit "at the mouth of the Wysox" cowards. The testimony of Jonah Rogers, which we now have in writing from under his own hand, is entirely reliable, and he gives the two contestants for the honor about an equal measure of credit.

The account which Pike gives us of his pulling off the blankets from the Indians is scarcely credible;

and a portion of the story of Van Campen's grapple with "Mohawk," while Pike and Pence were on hand, is doubtful. It is hardly likely that they would stand by and see their comrade so near being killed by a wounded Indian, and finally let him escape, when all the company excepting him were dead or dying. The main facts are indisputably true; as to some of the particulars, it is not strange that there should be some diversity, and even contradictions in the different relations. Van Campen's story was published after Pike and Rogers were both dead, and, so far as it is unnaturally in his own favor, and against one of his companions in captivity and danger, it is to be taken with a large discount.

The stories of Pike and Rogers were as familiar in the country as household words for many years, while they were both living in the same neighborhood, and they were always understood to agree in all essential particulars. When Pike related the tale to us, it was in the presence and at the instance of old Mrs. Reynolds, of Truxville, who had heard it so often that she understood it perfectly, and would have marked the slightest variation from the known truth of the history. We have made these remarks from a regard to historical truth, and without the slightest prejudice against or in favor of either of the parties.

## XII.

### THE CAPTIVITY AND ESCAPE OF GEORGE P. RANSOM AND OTHERS.

GEORGE P. RANSOM was the son of Captain Samuel Ransom, who was one of the three men who arrived just in time to engage in the battle and fall upon the field of gore and slaughter.—See Mrs. Myers's account of the battle, p. 158.

The subject of this sketch entered the army at the commencement of the Revolutionary war, at the age of fourteen. He served for two years as his father's waiter. When Wyoming was threatened with an invasion from the Indians and Tories, two companies which had been raised in Wyoming, under the command of Captains Ransom and Durkee, were consolidated into one, and sent on under the command of Captain Simon Spaulding. This company was encamped at Merwin's, thirty-three miles from the Valley, on the night of the battle.* On the following day, a scout was sent on in advance to learn the position of affairs. The scout met the fugitives, who gave them the sad intelligence of the defeat and slaughter of the little patriot army, and that the settlement was in the possession of the Indians and Tories. Upon their return, Captain Spaulding proceeded with his men to Stroudsburg.

After a delay there of several weeks, Spaulding's

---

\* So say the historians; but Colonel Hollenback is represented as locating Spaulding's company on that night at Bear Creek, twenty-four miles nearer Wyoming.

company, together with some of the settlers under the leadership of Colonel Butler, proceeded to the Valley, and buried the dead who lay upon the battle-field. Young Ransom was in the company, and, after diligent search among the slain, was finally enabled to identify the body of his father from his shoe and knee buckles. His head was severed from his body, and the body was much burned. Another son of Captain Ransom who was in the battle had his arm broken by a ball, and escaped by swimming the river and diving when the savages shot at him from the shore.

George P. Ransom joined Sullivan's army, was in the battle at Newtown, and shared in all the dangers and hardships of the expedition into the Indian country. He related with much interest the circumstance of Luke Swetland's meeting the army. Swetland had been taken prisoner by the Indians in August, 1778, and had managed to make his escape. When he met the army, supposing he had fallen in with Butler's Tories, he asked if they had heard any thing of "the rebel army," when, taking him for a stray Tory, the soldiers commenced abusing him with kicks and cuffs. Fortunately, young Ransom happened to be near him, and sung out, "Is that you, Swetland?" "Good God!" exclaimed Swetland, "is there any one here that knows me?" The course of treatment was now suddenly changed from abuse to hearty congratulations, and the supposed Tory was taken into the arms of his Yankee brothers, and, with them, returned to his beloved Wyoming after more than a year's absence.

Upon the return of the army to the Valley Mr. Ransom obtained a furlough, and visited his friends at Plymouth. On one Sunday evening in December,

1780, young Ransom, with two other young men, paid a visit to a house where were three young ladies, for the purpose of whiling away an hour or two in pleasant chat. When they had become agreeably engaged in soft nonsense and relating yarns, three heavy raps fell upon the door. The party knew well the signal, and looked around for some way of escape. Upon looking out of the windows they found them guarded, and, turning to the door, in rushed a band of Indians and Tories, and made captives of the whole company. The lovers were now, in sorry plight, hurried up the mountain, and at a suitable distance from the settlement the Indians and Tories prepared to encamp. Before they had concluded their arrangements for the night they let the girls go. Two of them—Lucy Harvey and Rachel Bullock—took a bee-line to the fort at Wilkesbarre.

The venerable Charles Harris, now eighty-nine years of age, was on duty as a sentinel that night. He was then a lad, and wide awake for Indians. He says, "I saw something black, and I thought it moved. I was first at a loss to know what to do; I thought it might be an Indian stealing up to shoot me; but, as it might be a friend, I concluded to call out. 'Who is there?' I demanded. A female voice answered, 'A friend.' Then advance, said I, and up came the two girls, and told me the story of their capture and release, and said that the Indians and Tories had the three young men, and were going off with them to Niagara. I awoke Colonel Butler, and he ordered the alarm-gun fired. When it was fired it created terrible confusion; an Irishman jumped out of his bed and ran to the door roaring, and appeared to be half scared to death."

The prisoners on the mountain heard the alarm-gun, and from that concluded that their lady-loves had safely reached the garrison. The prisoners were tied, and the Indians and Tories lay down in a ring around them. Before they laid themselves down, one of the Tories told the prisoners, with great emphasis, that if either of them escaped, the Indians would kill the others. When all were asleep, Ransom thought of making his escape, and succeeded in untying the rope which confined his arms. They were situated on the brow of a hill, and he had no doubt but he could dash down the hill among the bushes, and escape without harm. But then he thought of his companions in captivity. From the manner in which the Tory had premonished them of the consequences of the escape of any one of them, he had no reason to doubt but the threat would be executed, and that, too, under circumstances of savage barbarity. Upon reflection, he tied the rope as it was before. He could not sleep; his thoughts were busy. What would become of him? He wore the uniform of Sullivan's army; he remembered the fate of "brave Boyd;" and, almost without willing it, the rope was again slipped. He looked upon the darkness down the hill side; he was upon the point of leaping over the ring of Indians and Tories; he held himself down; he did the deed in imagination over and over. But ah! his two companions in captivity — their fate brought him up again. He could have no hope of releasing them. One might escape, loose as he then was, but to liberate the other two, and for all to run away, would be beyond the bounds of all rational probability. Here he paused, and finally drew the knot up again, and waited for daylight, resolving to share a common fate with his companions in captivity.

When the day broke the company made preparations to move on. They loaded the prisoners with heavy packs, and moved up the river. It was in the month of December, and they suffered much from fatigue and cold, besides being nearly starved. At Tioga Point they killed a horse, and kept in tolerable case while their horse-beef lasted. Ransom was known from his dress to have been in the army which had devastated the Indian country, and of course was singled out as a special object of vengeance. Before they reached Niagara they fell in with a large body of Indian families, and now it was time to proceed with some ceremony of savage cruelty, in which all who had suffered from the invasion of the "rebel army" might have a taste of sweet vengeance on their enemies. The method resorted to was one of the milder sort in use among the Indians.

Ransom was seated on a log, and was told by the Tories that the Indians were about to whip him. The law which governed this ceremony was that the whole body of Indians, squaws, and pappooses would pass by him in single file, and each one would give him a blow: he might dodge, but must not leave the log; if he did, he would be killed. The procession was formed, every one having in hand some weapon, generally being armed with sticks or whips. The old chief came up at the head of the procession, and, taking him by the hand, muttered out something in his own language, and gave him a blow. Then came the queen squaw and did the same. Then followed about forty Indians, then about as many squaws. Last of all came on the young brood, and they struck their blow, some of them showing the venom of young vipers. The victim of this savage cruelty dodged the blows so adroitly that he was not much injured excepting in one instance: a young Indian, with murderous intent, flung a tomahawk at his head, which would have cloven his skull had he not dropped his head down as quick as lightning. The deadly weapon passed over his head, but struck his back near the lower extremity of the spine, and inflicted an injury, the effects of which he felt, at times, through the rest of his life.

The prisoners were ten or twelve days in reaching Niagara. They were soon removed to what was called "Prisoners' Island," in the St. Lawrence, forty-five miles above Montreal, where there were one hundred and sixty-six American prisoners. The following account of the treatment which the prisoners received there is from Mr. Ransom's own hand, and is taken from Miner's History. He says, "We were guarded by Refugees, or what was called Tories, that belonged to Sir John Johnson's second regiment. The commanding officer of the guard on the island was a young Scotchman by the name of M'Alpin, about eighteen years of age. The winter was very severe, and a great snow-storm came and drifted before the door of the guard, who sent for some of the American prisoners to come and shovel it away. They refused, saying they were prisoners of war, and he had no right to set them at work for his pleasure. Enraged at this, the officer ordered them into irons, and directed others to take the shovels and go to work: these also refused and were ironed. So he went on commanding and meeting with resolute disobedience to what they considered a tyrannical order. They had taken up arms and periled their lives to resist British tyranny, and would not now, though prisoners, submit to it. Some were ironed two together, some to a bar four together; but he kept putting on irons as long as he had handcuffs left. Among the last who refused were myself and one William Palmeters. We were then put into an open house without floor or windows, and directions given that we should have neither victuals, brandy, nor tobacco; but our faithful friends contrived to evade the guard, and we were furnished with all. There we remained all night, suffering extremely from the cold. The next morning M'Alpin came, thinking our spirits were broken, and demanded if we would not shovel now. All answered in a word, 'Not for a Tory.' He then took us out of that place and put us into a hut just finished, with a good floor, and we sent for a black man, a good fiddler, for we had two on the island. We then opened our ball, dancing, to keep ourselves warm, jigs, hornpipes, four and six-handed reels. Where four were ironed to one bar, they could dance the cross-handed, or what we called the York reel. We continued in this merry mood until our Scotch gentleman found the place was too good for us. He then took us out and put us into a loft of one of the huts, which stood so low that a man could stand up only under the centre of the ridge. There we were kept in extreme suffering two days and nights. In the mean time, M'Alpin sent for Charles Grandison, our fiddler, and ordered him to play for his pleasure. The black went, but firmly declared that he would not play while his fellow-prisoners were in irons. The officer then ordered a sort of court-martial, composed of Tories, who, of course, brought in the poor negro guilty. The sentence of the court was that he should be stripped, tied up, and receive ten lashes on his naked back, which was done. While smarting with the lash, the officer asked if he would fiddle as he was ordered. 'No;

not while my fellow-prisoners are in irons,' was his answer. Again he was tied up and ten lashes laid on; but his firmness was not to be shaken, and the officer sent him to his hut.

"M'Alpin then sent a party of soldiers to bring up some of the prisoners, several of whom were flogged severely; and one, against whom the Tories had a particular spite, was tied neck and heels, a rope put around his neck, and he was thus drawn up to the chamber floor and kept until he was almost dead, let down and then drawn up again. One John Albright, a young Continental soldier, was flogged almost to death for speaking his mind freely. But not one American was found to shovel snow."

On the opening of spring, Ransom and his two fellow-prisoners, James Butterfield and John Brown, were permitted to make gardens for themselves. They planned their beds with some taste. They now conceived the project of making a raft and escaping on it. They laid out their work and proceeded, one keeping watch while the other two worked. They put together old sticks, and whatever they could procure that could be used, and bound them together, and, as fast as they proceeded, they contrived to bury their work under the sand, leaving the surface in the form of a bed, the outer rails of their raft seeming to be designed to keep the earth from washing away.

There is some truth as well as poetry in the lines of Dryden:

> "For there's the folly that's still mixed with fear,
> Cowards more blows than any heroes bear;
> Of fighting sparks some may their pleasures say,
> But 'tis a bolder thing to run away."

They provided themselves with some bread, pork,

and salt, and on the 9th of June, just after sundown, they dug out the raft and committed themselves to the treacherous current. Their paddles were round sticks flattened at the end with a pocket-knife. They pulled out with might and main, and had but just got under way before the alarm-gun bellowed and reverberated like terrible thunder. The thick darkness now covered the fugitives, and they were borne down the current on their crazy raft, to what haven they knew not. Their raft being constructed of old materials, it absorbed the water until it ran so deep that the adventurous passengers sat in the water some eighteen inches. That was an anxious night, and as perilous as anxious. The doubt which harassed their minds was whether they would not be wrecked and drowned, or be obliged to land where they would be an easy prey to the British soldiers or the Indians.

At daybreak they landed on the Canada side, and when they attempted to raise themselves to their feet they found it impossible. Their lower limbs were stiff, being benumbed with their long continuing motionless under water. They succeeded in pulling themselves to land by some bushes, and then commenced rubbing their legs and whipping them with switches. Finally they could walk, and they moved on down the river, and concealed themselves for the day under the trees in a windfall. When night came they started on, looking out for some sort of craft in which they could find their way across to the American side. They saw a bark canoe, but were kept at bay by two savage dogs, which it was not possible for them to pacify. Soon after this they found two bark canoes lying near each other. They took possession of these light vessels, and soon found the American shore. They now directed their course toward the head of Lake Champlain.

Their bread was wet and spoiled; they saved their meat and salt. In a written account of this wonderful escape, which we have received from Mr. Samuel Ransom, son of Colonel George P. Ransom, it is said that their meat lasted them seven days, and then they were left without food. They concealed themselves in the daytime for six days, and traveled by night. Their way lay through a fearful swamp, where for more than a week they could find no water fit to drink. They traveled with forked sticks, and with these they captured snakes and frogs, upon which they lived for more than a week.

They all became exceedingly weak, and one of the company came to the conclusion that he must lie down and die. The other two stimulated him on by telling him that if he died they would fill their packs with his flesh and eat it. This terrible threat drove him on for a while, but he became feverish, and evidently could go no farther. Providentially they came to a beautiful spring of water. He drank, and lay down by the side of it. He insisted upon being left, as it was better for him to die alone than for the whole company to perish, and no one be left to tell their story. Upon the whole, it was concluded to make the best provision for the poor fellow they could, and then go on. They accordingly gathered a pile of wood, caught a quantity of frogs and snakes, and built a brush booth over him, and bade him farewell.

Now Mr. Ransom and one of his companions proceeded, but with feeble and faltering steps, being nearly exhausted. On the fourteenth day of their adventurous journey they found two old horses. Their first idea was to kill one of them and fill their packs. The next thought was the wisest one—that was, to mount the horses, and let them go where they would, presuming they would take them to some habitation of man. This plan succeeded. The horses brought them to a house where there was a kind-hearted old lady. She saw their condition, and gave them half a pint of milk each, mixed with about as much water, and a little bread. They took their scanty ration, and lay down upon the floor. They reached this hospitable hut just before night. They slept until about twelve o'clock, and then awoke with such a voracious appetite that they could almost bite the flesh out of each other, or devour their own fingers. They called to their benefactress, who arose and gave them the same allowance as before. They then lay down and slept until morning. They remained here three or four days, and became so recruited that they proceeded with good heart upon their journey.

They came to the lake, and three days after reached Hubbertston, Vermont; the next day they reached a fort at Castleton; then they came to Poultney, where Mr. Ransom found a home for the time being with an uncle. Some three weeks after their arrival at Poultney, who should make his appearance but the poor fellow they had left to die by the spring! Rest under his booth, the frogs, broiled by the fire, seasoned with a little salt his companions had left him, and the pure cold water, sustained nature until she had rallied; the fever left him, and he set off upon the track of his comrades, and came through in safety.

Colonel Ransom says, "My companions went on to Albany, and there proclaimed the cruelty of the Scotch officer: it was published in the papers. A flag was dispatched to remonstrate against such abuse of our men; and we had the pleasure to hear, not long after, that M'Alpin was tried and broke, the prisoners being called to witness against him."

Some of the Wyoming prisoners had the pleasure of seeing M'Alpin drummed out of the camp. About this time a prisoner brought in a report that Cornwallis was taken at Yorktown, and the American prisoners, after due consultation, concluded to give vent to their feelings upon the occasion. Accordingly, on a signal being given, at dead of night, the very ground was made to tremble with three cheers for General Washington. The officers sprang from their beds, and the sentinels almost jumped out of their boots; but, upon examination, all was order and quiet among the prisoners. The iron rule had ended. The time had now come to begin to arrange for the exchange of prisoners, instead of tying Yankees neck and heels, and hanging them up. Henceforth law and decency obtained on "Prisoner's Island."

After becoming sufficiently recruited, Mr. Ransom visited his friends in Canaan, Connecticut, and then, after a short stay in Wyoming, returned to the army at West Point, where he remained until the conclusion of the war, when he was honorably discharged.

Mr. Ransom married and settled upon lands which his father had occupied before the war in Plymouth. Like nearly every body else in Wyoming, the young couple had hard work to live until they could raise what was necessary for their comfort from the rich flats which they commenced tilling. The greatest difficulty was to obtain materials for clothing. Mr. Ransom sowed flaxseed in the spring, but it would not grow in a day. Before his flax had come to maturity he found on the flats a luxuriant growth of nettles; these he mowed, and rotted by sinking them in a pond of warm water, and then drying them in the sun, and of the fibres Mrs. Ransom made coarse cloth for pants for her husband. They were neither elegant nor durable, but they held out until the flax came to maturity. Such was now the pressure of Mr. Ransom's necessities that the flax was pulled, rotted, dressed, spun, woven, and a shirt and pants made in *eight days!* The ninth day after the flax was pulled the enterprising young farmer was dressed in the fabric which was manufactured out of it. The thing seems scarcely possible, but such, we are assured, was the fact.

Mr. Ransom graduated in regular course to the office of colonel of the regiment, and spent a long life on the place upon which he first commenced housekeeping. He lived much respected, and departed this life in September, 1850, in the ninetieth year of his age.

Colonel Ransom was a man of high spirits, and was an uncompromising patriot. We are indebted to his son Samuel for the following anecdote, illustrative of the permanence and strength of his feelings as a Revolutionary soldier. While in one of the old taverns in Wilkesbarre, when quite advanced in years, he heard a windy young man speak very disrespectfully of General Washington. The general, he said, was not a great man nor a great soldier, but had taken advantage of fortunate circumstances to palm himself off upon the world as such. This was more than the old soldier could well bear, and he lifted his cane and felled the impudent young sprig to the floor. The whipped puppy prosecuted the colonel for assault and battery. When the case came on, Colonel Ransom appeared in court without an advocate, and simply pleaded guilty, and flung himself on the mercy of the court. Hon. David Scott was presiding judge; his associates were the venerable Matthias Hollenback and Jesse Fell. Judge Scott remarked, This is a case which I choose to leave to my associates, as they are old soldiers, and can fully appreciate the circumstances of the case, and then left his seat. Judge Hollenback asked Colonel Ransom where he was at such a date. The answer was, "In my father's company, in Washington's army." "And where on the 3d of July, 1778?" Answer, "With Captain Spaulding, on my way to Wyoming." "And where the following summer?" Answer, "With General Sullivan in the Lake country, flogging the Indians." "And where the next fall and winter?" Answer, "A prisoner on the St. Lawrence." "Ah!" said the judge, "all that is true enough, Colonel Ransom. And did you knock the fellow down, colonel?" "I did so, and would do it again under like provocation," was the answer. "What was the provocation?" asked the judge. "The rascal abused the name of General Washington," was the answer. The judge coolly said, "Colonel Ransom, the judgment of the court is that you pay a fine of one cent, and the prosecutor pay the cost." A roar of applause succeeded, during which the prosecutor fled from the court-house in great consternation, and immediately left the place for parts unknown.

During this singular trial the colonel stood in the calm dignity of a soldier of the old school, with his son standing by his side, indulging no little anxiety with regard to the event. When the affair had terminated, the boy walked out of the court-house with his father, proud of his courage and of his noble bearing before the court, and abundantly flattered with the public demonstrations of approbation of an act which, whatever might have been the result of it under other circumstances, he considered both lawful and expedient.

We give this anecdote as we received it, for the purpose of illustrating the spirit of the parties concerned, judging comments entirely unnecessary.

## XIII.

#### BENJAMIN BIDLACK—CAPTURE BY THE PENNAMITES AND SINGULAR ESCAPE.

> "Therewith, in all this world, no nightingale
> Ne coude by an hundred thousand dell
> Singen so wonder merrily and well."
>
> "Full faire was *Mirthe*, full long and high,
> A fairer man I never sigh;
> As round as apple was his face,
> Full roddie and white in every place."
> WICLIF.

Mr. Bidlack came to Wyoming at an early period with his father, mother, and several brothers. He served his country under General Washington through nearly the entire period of the Revolutionary war. He was at Boston when Washington took charge of the patriot army to oppose General Gage. He was at Trenton on the taking of the Hessians. He was at Yorktown on the occasion of the surrender of Cornwallis; and was in Washington's camp, at Newburg, when the army was disbanded.

One of Mr. Bidlack's brothers was captain of a company of volunteers in the Indian battle, and fell at the head of his men. The year after, his father was taken prisoner by the Indians from Plymouth. After his father's imprisonment, his mother earnestly requested that her son Benjamin might be permitted to return home on furlough, to assist her in her lonely and helpless condition; but such were the necessities of the country that it was thought the example would be dangerous, and her prayer was not granted.

When peace was concluded, Captain Bidlack was released from his captivity; and when the army was discharged, his son Benjamin returned home; and now those who remained of the family were once more together. They were a family of patriots—were all tall, large-boned, powerful men, and good soldiers. Mr. Bidlack passed through the perils of the war without seeming to realize his exposure to death, until, about the time of its close, he came near being killed by the accidental explosion of a bomb-shell, which ignited on being flung from a wagon. The fragments flew, apparently, within a hair's-breadth of him on every side, and yet he escaped without harm. The event led to much serious reflection, which he never forgot.

He assisted in building "the Temple of Liberty," and in constructing a causeway across the marsh which lay between the two lines of the encampment at Newburg. The "temple" lingered in his memory as a great institution; he almost seemed to regard it with superstitious veneration. There they had religious worship, and the "splendid singing," in which he took a prominent part, was with him the *beau ideal* of harmony. "I never," said he to us, "heard such singing in my life. Some of the officers from New England were trained singers, and many of the men could sing well, and they made the temple ring with sweet and powerful melody."

> "For the armony
> And sweet accord was so good musike,
> That the voice to angels most was like."
> CHAUCER.

> "She said, In air the trembling music floats,
> And on the winds triumphant swell the notes;
> So soft, though high—so loud, and yet so clear,
> Ev'n listening angels lean from heaven to hear."—POPE.

He here witnessed the debates of the officers upon the subject of disbanding the army. They spoke in their uniform, with their swords by their sides. On one occasion, one of them, laying his hand upon the hilt of his sword, demanded, with great vehemence, "Gentlemen, are you prepared to give up these swords, which have procured freedom for the country, and for yourselves glory and renown? Can you retire to your farms or shops, and ingloriously abandon the profession of arms? Will you not rather spill your hearts' blood in defense of rights which have been so dearly bought in the camp and upon the field of battle?"

Here "the Armstrong Letters" originated, and here the feelings of General Washington were sorely tried. We once took a stroll over the ground of the old encampment, saw the rude masonry and portions of the foundations of the huts, and some vestiges of "the Temple of Liberty," and here the whole story, so eloquently told by "Father Bidlack," as he was then called, before his intellect had begun to fail, was revived in our recollection. We imagined we saw him before us, describing the scenes which took place during that interesting and critical period of our national history, shaking his venerable head, and remarking, with deep gravity and with great earnestness, "Ah! that was a trying time; but the wisdom, firmness, and patriotism of General Washington were equal to the emergency. He might have kept the army together and have been *king* of the country, but he preferred to be the farmer of Mount Vernon under a republican government."

Some time before the conclusion of the last Pennamite and Yankee war, young Bidlack undertook some sort of a commercial expedition down the river in a boat. At Sunbury he was made a prisoner by the

BIVOUAC AT BUCKRIHNNY.

Pennsylvanians, and confined in a place which they called a jail. He was a splendid singer and a merry fellow. Like many of the old soldiers, he was "addicted to strong drink," and on evenings, when jolly circles love to assemble to while away an hour, to shake off the burdens of business, or to stimulate their exhausted nerves by the exhilarating draught, a company were accustomed to gather upon the stoop and hear Bidlack sing songs, of course affording him a sufficiency of the desired stimulant. The numbers of those evening gatherings increased from evening to evening, and the songs, the romantic stories, and the jokes of the soldier became increasingly interesting, until he had become an object of more absorbing interest in the little town of Sunbury than a company of minstrels is now in one of our large cities.

The company were finally not quite satisfied with seeing the face of their interesting prisoner through the grates of the prison, but wished to view him at full length as he poured out his harmonious and powerful numbers. The door was accordingly opened, and he stood upon the threshold; but here he was too much cramped, and his gestures were evidently impeded by his position. "What's the use?" said one; "let him have room." And he was then allowed to come out and give himself free scope in gesticulation. He was a tall, straight, majestic figure. The more room he had, the more fully did his sallies, cuts, and thrusts illustrate and enforce the sentiment—either sense or nonsense—of the poetry, and the higher was the excitement and the louder the bursts of laughter among the merry companions of the gathering.

Evening after evening passed away in these exercises without the least abatement of the interest, when, at a late hour, the gallant hero of the farce would throw himself upon his pallet of straw, and sleep away the excitement of the maddening bowl. As Bidlack seemed to enjoy the company of his new associates, they began to regard him as a sort of fixture of the place, and to suppose that perhaps to be lionized would be thought a fair compensation for the loss of his liberty; but they did not know the man. He was always ready to make the best shift possible when under pressure. He would be merry in prison if in prison he must be, but it was not a place to his taste at all. Liberty had cost him too much to be bartered away for a mess of pottage.

Understanding perfectly his position, and noticing that the sympathies of his nightly visitors and the confidence he had inspired in their minds had completely put them off their guard, he began to meditate turning the advantages of these circumstances to his account. He studied the matter thoroughly, and arranged his plans.

> "Now, since I have performed every part
>   Of thy command as near as tongue can tell,
> Content thee yet, before my sense depart,
>   To take this sonnet for my last farewell."
>
> GASCOYNE.

He finally came out with a new song, entitled "The old Swaggering Man." "That's the song for me," said one. "The best one yet," said another. "Let's have that over again," roared a third. "Well," said the performer, "let me rest a little, and take a good drink." "Yes, yes," all responded. After a few minutes' intermission, and the "drink," of course, "Now," says the actor, "if you want a rouser, I must have a cane, and room to act it out. I want the whole length

BIDLACE'S ESCAPE.

of the stoop." "Bring on the cane! clear the way! clear the way!" bawled a dozen. He sung one stanza, and then came on the chorus, "Here goes the old swaggering man." He brandished his cane, and staggered, and plunged from end to end of the stoop. A roar of merriment and shouts of applause resounded through the whole neighborhood. He now faced about, breathed hard, took another drink, and this time his movement was in the direction of Wyoming. He sang another verse, and then he roared out the chorus, "Here goes the old swaggering man," and in a trice sprang from the stoop, leaped the six-foot rail-fence which surrounded the premises, and was out of sight.

Some were petrified with astonishment, others cursed and swore, while others laughed immoderately. "After him! after him!" cried the jailer. Half a dozen ran a few rods in the dark, and then, pausing to listen, heard his heavy, hurried tread dying away in the distance. "There's no use," said they; "he can outrun a deer." They returned to have a hearty laugh over the romantic adventure of the jolly Yankee prisoner. They separated, more regretting the loss of the amusement which Bidlack had afforded them while detained as a prisoner, than the success of the ruse he had practiced upon them.

As may well be supposed, the fugitive made great progress during the night. He had fifty miles to travel, and the dawn of day found him on the homeward half of his journey. He often laughed to himself at the mere fun and romance of his escape so loud as to scare the night-birds of the mountains and glens. He repeated over with great glee the talismanic chorus, "Here goes the old swaggering man," and then he would skip and bound like the buck which had swum the river, reached the shore, and left the hounds on the other side. As he hies along the bank of the river, over the flats and through the narrows, we may imagine him singing Hudibras, slightly altered, to suit the occasion.

> He that sings and runs away,
> May live to sing another day;
> But he that doth in jail remain,
> May never sing at home again.
> *Chorus.* Here goes the old swaggering man.

The next day our hero safely arrived at his father's house in Plymouth. It was soon noised abroad that "Ben Bidlack had sung himself out of jail, and was at home safe and sound."

Young Bidlack married an Alden, a descendant of a family by that name which came to this country in the *May-Flower*. He struggled hard with poverty, and still harder with his army habits, but made no progress, and there seemed no human probability of his improving either his character or his fortune. At length he became awakened through the instrumentality of the pioneers of Methodism, and finally became a Methodist preacher. He sustained this character to the termination of a protracted life. He had great power in the pulpit, and was as great a singer of the songs of Zion as he had been of the old patriotic ballads. He was for many years a most laborious and successful minister of the Gospel. He lost his wife while engaged in the active duties of the ministry, and was united in marriage to the widow of Lawrence Myers, Esq., of Kingston. He lived for many years in that place, a superannuated minister, much respected and beloved by all his neighbors. He finally died from a cancer on his nose.

In the year 1825, we think, the citizens of Wilkesbarre called upon the venerable man for a Fourth of July oration. The surviving soldiers of the Revolution were invited in from all the region round about, and they constituted quite a respectable company. Each had a sprig of laurel attached to the left breast of his coat. The orator was then as straight as an arrow, and marched to the music like any trained soldier, keeping the step while the band poured out the old national air, Yankee Doodle, in the very best style. The oration consisted principally of a narrative of the events of the Revolutionary war as they came under his own observation. His text or motto was, "For consider how great things the Lord hath done for you." His doctrine was that the hand of God was evidently concerned in the events of the Revolution.

He kept General Washington constantly before the audience. "When the Hessians were captured," said he, "the general rode round among the men, who were falling upon the spoils, and said, 'My brave fellows, don't drink and become intoxicated. God has given us the victory, but the enemy, in large force, is just at hand, and, should they find any of you lying upon the ground, which they will be sure to visit in a few hours, you will lose your lives.' He rode from company to company, repeating the same caution with the greatest earnestness."

His description of the cannonading of the British works at Yorktown was most thrilling. "For fourteen days and nights," said the orator, "there was one continual thunder and blaze. At night it was so light that you could see to pick up a pin. A white flag was raised from the British breastworks, and the firing ceased. It seemed as though the wheels of nature stood still; the silence was really distressing. Cornwallis proposed to leave the ground with the honors of war, with colors flying, and to embark his army on the English ships in the nearest harbor. 'No,' was the answer, and the parley closed. 'Now,' said Washington, 'give it to them hotter than ever.' And, sure enough, the storm of the battle raged more terribly than ever. They soon came to terms, and the **heart of the war was broken.**"

The illustration is a truthful representation of the Rev. Benjamin Bidlack in his preaching attitude in a private house, behind an old-fashioned chair. The sketch was executed by the Rev. Marmaduke Pearce, it is supposed, after hearing the old patriarch preach a funeral sermon in his own neighborhood.

## XIV.

A VIEW FROM CAMPBELL'S LEDGE, CONTRIBUTED BY REV. L. W. PECK.

At the head of Wyoming Valley is Campbell's Ledge. The Susquehanna comes in from the northwest, and the Lackawanna winds around the base of the mountain from the northeast to mingle with the larger and bolder river. The mountain whose base they thus lave, and separate from the valley, is crowned by Campbell's Ledge. Having a few hours at Pittston, I cast my eye wishfully over at the mountain, a distance of about two miles, and resolved to make the ascent. I was alone. My way led over the canal bridge, over the viaduct, and across the meadows to the mountain. I had just entered the wood and begun the ascent when a beautiful pheasant started out near my feet, and ran some distance through the leaves, and then flew into the deep forest. I pursued my way, following an old mountain road, or making a path for myself through the underbrush. At length I came out upon a plateau of ground gently sloping to the north; but the thick foliage would permit no view of the valley, which I was looking for as one looks for the genial face of an old friend. Still I wandered on, seeking the higher ground, but no ledge was visible. A pile of rocks, crowned with a scraggy oak, now and then appeared, but nothing was to be seen that answered the description I had received. I began to reproach myself for coming without a guide, and wondered whether I should know Campbell's Ledge if I should happen

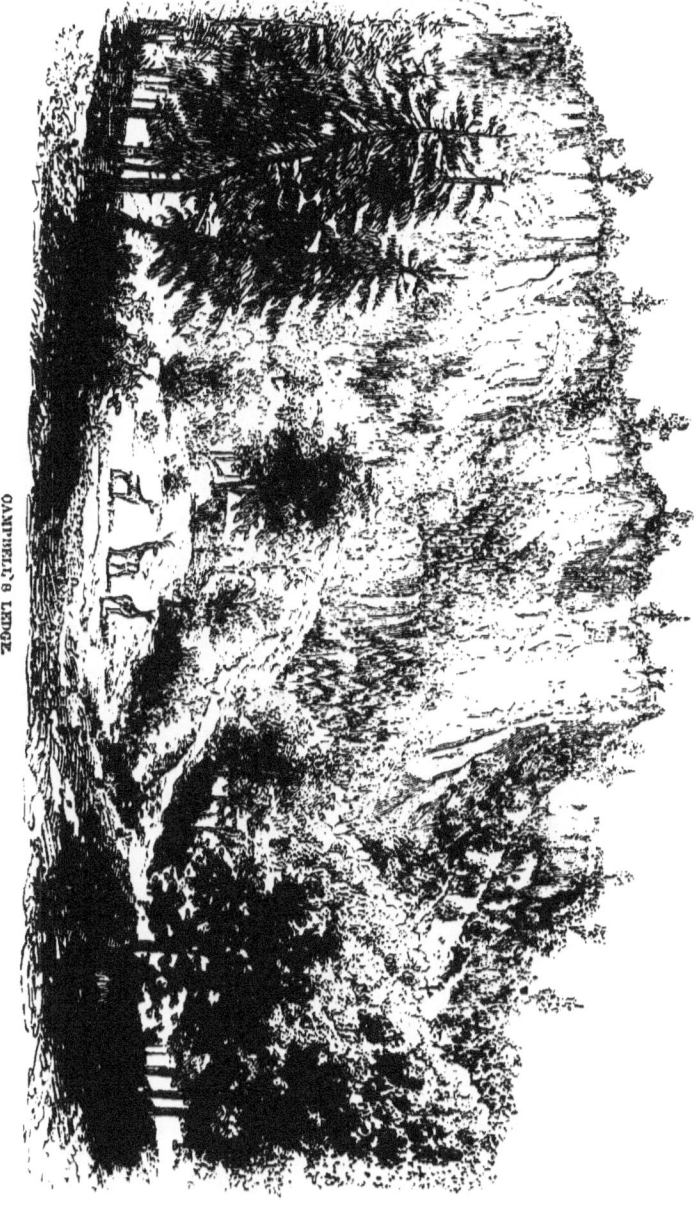

CAMPBELL'S LEDGE

to come in sight of it. The woods at last became more open, and I saw the mountains at the west nearer. I turned at once toward them, when I found myself just ready to step off from the abrupt brow of a frightful precipice. I seized hold of a tree and hung upon the verge, and gazed down with awe upon the calm river, the green fields, and the grazing flocks hundreds of feet below. This, said I, in a subdued breath, is Campbell's Ledge.

I sank back upon the grass, and looked down upon Wyoming cradled between the mountains. The view of the Valley here presented differs from every other. The hilly portions are more prominent, and undulate far away southward till they terminate in the mountains. The river, like a broken belt of steel, is seen here and there glittering in the sun. I have often wandered in Wyoming, admiring her beauty, but Campbell's Ledge inspired me with a new emotion, that of overpowering sublimity. This view reminds me of the Hudson and the Catskills, but the precipice is more stupendous than that on which stands the Mountain House. Ye grand old mountains, which laugh in the sunshine and reverberate in the storm, "ye are wondrous strong, yet lovely in your strength." I have been carrying in my mind, amid these scenes, the stirring words of Ruskin:

"Mountains are to the rest of the earth what muscular action is to the body of man. The muscles and tendons of its anatomy are, in the mountains, brought out with force and convulsive energy, full of expression, passion, and strength; the plains and lower hills are the repose and the effortless motion of the frame, when its muscles lie dormant and concealed beneath the lines of its beauty, yet ruling those lines in their every undulation. This, then, is the first grand principle of the truth of the earth. The spirit of the hills is action, that of the lowlands repose; and between these there is to be found every variety of motion and of rest, from the inactive plain, sleeping like the firmament, with cities for stars, to the fiery peaks, which, with heaving bosoms and exulting limbs, with the clouds drifting like hair from their bright foreheads, lift up their Titan hands to heaven, saying, 'I live forever.'"

There is a wild legend which has given the name to this ledge. A man named Campbell was pursued by the Indians. He had taken refuge in the ravines of this mountain, where are many fine living springs, and where the thick foliage afforded a safe shelter. But the fierce Red Men are on his track. He is an old enemy, and is singled out for special torture. He knows his fate if taken. He tries every path that winds out into the deeper forest, but without success. He is hemmed in like the roe by the relentless wolves. But he does not hesitate; he springs forward to the verge of the hanging rock. One glance behind him shows him that escape is utterly hopeless. The shouts of the savages are heard as they rush upon their prey. With a scream of defiance, he leaps into the friendly arms of death.

The solemn traditions of the olden time were stealing around me like an enchanter's spell as I gazed down upon the plain and the river where once my kindred struggled with the dusky foe. A loud yell, as if a thousand Indian warriors were in the wood, started me to my feet; it was the whistle of the locomotive, which told of civilization bursting through the ancient gloom.

THE NEW YORK
PUBLIC LIBRARY

ASTOR, LENOX AND
TILDEN FOUNDATIONS.

THE FALLING SPRING.

## XV.

### AN INTERVIEW WITH RICHARD GARDNER.

"So must thou live till, like ripe fruit, thou drop
  Into thy mother's lap, or be with ease
  Gather'd, not harshly pluck'd, for death mature:
  This is old age." MILTON.

WE had been told that "old Mr. Gardner, of Exeter," was "almost a hundred years old," and that he could give a great amount of information in relation to Revolutionary times; that he had been a prisoner among the Indians for a long time, and had suffered untold miseries in cruel captivity. We resolved upon an early visit to the residence of the centenarian. On a beautiful morning early in June, 1857, we took the cars for Pittston, where we procured a horse and buggy, and proceeded through the long narrows on the east side of the Susquehanna. Passing the bold front of Campbell's Ledge, we wound our way along on the North Branch Canal, which is protected on the river-side by a sea-wall. A short distance above Campbell's Ledge a beautiful cascade comes rushing from the height, called Falling Spring. Upon the top of the mountain is a small spruce swamp, formed by never-failing springs. From this swamp issues the rill which falls over the precipice, and presents the beautiful object copied in the accompanying picture. On the road-side a perpendicular wall is built to the level of the road, but there is no barrier whatever to prevent the traveler from being precipitated into the canal in case a horse should be frightened and become unmanageable.

The road is narrow, in general not affording room for two carriages to pass. The almost perpendicular ledge of rocks has been blasted out to make room for the canal and the road. The rocky steep above frowns down upon the passenger in awful majesty. Now you find the broken fragments of trees which have been precipitated from the lofty height above, and then vast masses of rock which have been rent from their ancient beds by the frost, tumbled down the steep, and have filled up the narrow pass, a portion of them having been removed, leaving space barely sufficient for the passage of a carriage. Often the awful visage of the mountain height seems to assume an air of pensiveness, and weeps streams and gushing rivulets, as though in grief for the wounds and fractures inflicted upon her slopes and precipices, and her separation from immediate communion with her ancient friend and companion, the great and noble Susquehanna. Such havoc do modern improvements make of the sublime beauties of nature that the very rocks and hills are convulsed with agony.

We have often passed these terrible narrows, but never without a sort of terror. We can never help asking ourselves, What if some of the huge masses of rock, which seem just ready to topple from their foundation, should take a leap just as we are passing? In a moment we should be ground to powder. A mere pebble falling down the precipice might at any time frighten the horse of the traveler, and occasion an unlucky leap into the canal. Either of these events are possible, and more or less probable, at any moment; the providence of God, however, preserved us, and we made the trip in safety.

In due time we reached "Gardner's Ferry," six miles

above the mouth of the Lackawanna. Coming up to an ancient dwelling—one with which we were familiar near forty years ago—upon the stoop we saw a venerable man, much bent down, leaning upon a cane. We asked him if his name was Gardner. "Yes; but you have the advantage of me: I don't know you," was the response. After being informed of the object of our visit, he commenced conversation standing. His position seemed so uneasy that we were pained, and we suggested that perhaps he had better be seated. We were then invited into the house, and shown to a chair. Several respectable-looking females were present, who looked inquisitively as we, without farther ceremony, entered into conversation.

Mr. Gardner had never been a prisoner among the Indians. His father was made a prisoner when the Hardings were killed, as he was in the field at work with them at the time, on the west side of the river. He never returned, but, as they learned, was cruelly tortured by the savages, being burned alive.

Mrs. Alexander, from whom we received much information in relation to Colonel Hollenback, has furnished us with the following painful tale of the last interview between Mr. Gardner and his afflicted companion. She says:

"I will relate a fact which was told to my mother and myself by Mrs. Jenkins, the wife of Lieutenant Jenkins. She, with a Mrs. Gardner, was at Fort Jenkins after its capitulation. The husband of Mrs. Gardner was a prisoner in the hands of the Tories and Indians, and she wished much to see him once more, and asked Mrs. Jenkins to accompany her. Having consented and obtained leave, they went, under escort of young Wintermoot, who was a Tory, and offered to go with them upon the condition that they would manifest no surprise or sorrow at the sight they might see, telling them, at the time, that they would behold many strange and heart-rending ones.

"They therefore schooled themselves to appear indifferent, and entered the camp as coolly as possible. Mrs. Gardner obtained an interview with her husband, who told her that he was well aware they would never meet again. He was lame, and knowing that if unable to keep pace with his captors when on the march they would kill him, he advised her to take their two little boys and go to Connecticut, and remain with her friends until, the troubles being over in Wyoming, it would be safe to return and live upon the farm he had purchased her, bidding her a lasting farewell. During all the time she had such possession of herself as to exhibit no outward sign of sorrow. Mrs. Jenkins also told us that the Indians were at that time busily engaged in burning their victims. They had thrown down an old dry pine fence, and piled upon it the dead, wounded, and some unhurt white men, added more combustible matter, and set it on fire; and that the whole line of the fence was filled with the charred bones and flesh of the poor creatures, and men still burning: an awful sight, and I do not doubt her statement of the facts."

Mr. Miner gives the following account of Mr. Gardner's captivity and death: "One taken at Exeter the first of July, when the Hardings and Hadsels were massacred, deserves our special notice. Mr. John Gardner was a husband and a father, a highly respectable man, against whom some unappeasable spirit of enmity is supposed to have existed. On the morning of the fourth, his wife and child were permitted to see and take leave of him. Elisha Harding, Esq., then a boy, was present, and represents the scene as extremely affecting. When the last adieu was exchanged, an Indian placed a grievous load on his shoulders which he could scarcely raise, then put a halter round his neck, and led him off as he would a beast. The farewell expressed the sentiment, 'I go to return no more.' Exhausted with fatigue before he arrived at his captor's home, he fell, crushed by the weight of his load, when he was handed over to the squaws, who tortured him to death by fire. Daniel Carr, a fellow-prisoner, saw the remains the following day, and represented it as a sight to awaken the deepest pity."

At the time of the Indian battle Mr. Gardner was eleven years of age, and was with his mother in a fort on the west side of the river, immediately opposite the place where Pittston now stands; he knew not by what name the fort was called. The fort consisted of a house built of hewed logs, and surrounded by a stockade: it was Fort Jenkins.

They heard the firing plainly on the day of the battle, and on the day following learned that "our army was cut off." On that day Butler sent in a flag, and demanded the surrender of the fort.* There was nobody there to defend the fort but women and children, and a few old men. The gate was opened, and the Indians and Tories came in. They ordered all the things taken out of the house and spread upon the ground. They then set fire to the house, and, after taking what they wanted of the goods which lay upon the ground, they went away, and no more was seen of them.

* The articles of capitulation are signed July 1, 1778, but it probably was not thought necessary to enter it, as it was a small, helpless concern.

"Several of the Tories who were with the Indians," said Mr. Gardner, "had often been at my father's house, and been kindly treated there. One by the name of Vanderlip, and another by the name of Showers, I distinctly recollect. I saw upon the Indians clothes taken from the bodies of our men covered with blood." This is the amount of Mr. Gardner's personal knowledge of the wars of Wyoming. The first Pennamite and Yankee war had subsided when his father came into the country, and the last was concluded before he returned finally to remain.

The old men, with the women and children who were in the fort, left the country and returned to Connecticut. Mr. Gardner's mother had a young child, which she nursed and carried in her arms. The feeble and defenseless little company traveled through the swamp on foot. There was no road but a mere footpath, and no bridges across the streams. They suffered indescribably from hunger and weakness, but, by the most indomitable perseverance, they finally reached the settled country, where they received aid and comfort from the people.

What fearful times were these! The strength of the settlement was gone. The husbands, sons, and brothers, who were expected to clear the farms and raise the bread, had perished upon the field of battle, or been led away into hopeless bondage. A few old men leaning upon their staves, mothers with infants at their breasts, and boys and girls of tender age, were left in a country overrun by murderous savages, without food, and often stripped of their clothing, until not enough was left to screen their bodies from the extremities of the weather, and in this condition obliged to undertake a long journey through the wilderness on foot. The fathers and mothers had lost the support of their age, and the wives and the children their natural protectors and their only earthly source of dependence. One old gentleman lost three sons in the battle, and thus, in an hour, was left with three widows and twelve helpless, fatherless children upon his hands to provide for! What were the sufferings of the bereaved fathers, mothers, wives, and children on that memorable occasion, it is impossible to tell or even to conceive. Look for a moment at the mother of Mr. Gardner—made a widow under the most heart-rending circumstances, with a child hanging to her breast, and a little boy scarcely able to take care of himself, on so long and laborious a journey. Why did she not faint, or give herself up to inconsolable grief or to utter despair? Ah! the women of those times were made of stern stuff. How nobly they bore themselves when the storm beat furiously upon them, when the iron entered into their souls. There was a religious element in their character, which came to their relief in that terrible day of need. When they could truly say, "All thy waves and thy billows are gone over me," they could also add, "Yet the Lord will command his loving kindness in the daytime, and in the night his song shall be with me, and my prayer unto the God of my life."

At the age of twenty-one Mr. Gardner married and returned to Wyoming. He settled upon land which his father had occupied, and there he has lived from that day to the present. He established a ferry, and often was subjected to great labor, and exposed to great danger on the river. He is now a most remarkable man. He was *ninety* years of age the eighth day of last February. He has suffered from several casualties, but still his constitution remains unbroken, and his intellect is sound.

Soon after he settled in the country he received an injury in one of his elbows, which has ever since been to him a source of trouble, although it did not make him a cripple. In a bear-hunt, one of his companions, not perceiving that Mr. Gardner was nearly in range between him and a ferocious old dam with two cubs, drew up his piece and fired just as his friend was in the same act. Unfortunately, the ball struck his elbow. "I've hit her," exclaimed the delighted hunter. "You've hit me," answered Mr. Gardner. The blood streamed from the arm of the wounded man, while the bear escaped unhurt. They were in the woods some miles east of the settlement. One of Mr. Gardner's companions accompanied him home, while the other took a straight course through the woods to Lackawanna to procure the services of Dr. Hooker Smith. It was two days after the wound was inflicted before Dr. Smith could be on hand. When he came the arm was much inflamed and swollen, and the probing, cutting, and picking out splinters of bone was a most terrible operation, but it had to be endured. The wound was some time in healing, and the injury of the joint was such that the consequences were permanently troublesome.

Two years since, Mr. Gardner received an injury to his spine by a fall in the barn. This much increased his stooping position, and considerably diminished his power of locomotion. He assured us that, before he received the last-mentioned injury, he could walk to Wilkesbarre, the distance of fourteen miles, and back again the same day; indeed, he affirmed he could do so now if his back had not been injured. Summer before last, he said, he laid up thirty rods of stone fence, and he should do a good business in that line this season, if his son could find time to draw the stone. On the day before our visit he had crossed the river, walked three miles, helped his son-in-law plant his potatoes, and returned before sundown. If he stood erect, he would appear to be about seventy years of age—perhaps not so old. He is one of that small class of human beings who seem to defy the laws of natural decay.

Mr. Gardner had been twice married, and been blessed with thirteen children, two of whom died in childhood, while the remaining eleven lived to mature years. Two of the number have been cripples from early youth. A son had his lower limbs paralyzed when a child, and they have ever since been almost incapable of locomotion. He hitches about on his hands and hips, but is cheerful, and converses sensibly and with animation. He is sixty-one years of age. A daughter walks upon crutches in consequence of having lost the use of one of her limbs by a fever-sore.

Before we left dinner was announced, and we were invited to "sit by" and share in the repast, which we did with a relish. The table was well supplied, and the cookery done up in comfortable country style. When all were seated, the old gentleman craved a blessing, somewhat in the ancient Puritanic style as to length and particularity. We found he had long been a member of the Baptist Church, and should judge him a truly religious man. We asked him how he enjoyed life; his answer was, "Oh, very well. I have always enjoyed very good health — have never been sick much, and have no reason to complain."

Mr. Gardner said that when he first came into the

country, and for a long time afterward, game was abundant every where in the woods, and the waters furnished plenty of the finest fish. In the spring the shad were abundant in the river, and in the little stream not far from his house, called Gardner's Creek, a mess of the finest trout could be caught at almost any time except in winter.

Many years since, a company of Indians passed down the river on their way to Philadelphia, to conclude a treaty with the government. There seemed to be two parties, one taking the east and the other the west side of the river. Several of them lodged in an old, deserted house near by. He visited them, and one of them spoke good English. The Indian asked him if he ever saw an Indian before. "Yes," said he, "at the time of the Wyoming massacre." "Ah! you live there?" responded the Indian. "Yes," was the answer. From that moment the Indian seemed shy. He finally said his tribe, the Oneidas, were not here on that occasion, but some of the other company were here, and he and his friends would not go in their company, for they expected every one of them would be killed. "How many Indians do you think were in the battle?" asked the Indian. "I do not know; I have heard about a thousand," answered Mr. Gardner. "Oh no," responded the Indian, "not near so many."

We take the following account of this visit of the Indians to Wyoming from Mr. Miner: "Fifteen years after the battle, a number of Indians, among whom were several chiefs of distinction, passed through Wyoming on their way to Philadelphia, on business with the government. Apprehending danger, they sent word to Wilkesbarre, and an escort of respectable citizens turned out to accompany them into the town.

In the evening a council was held in the court-room, where mutually pacific assurances were given. It is not surprising, considering their cruel conduct during the war, that the Indians entertained fears for their safety. On their return, passing on the opposite side of the river from the battle-ground, the old braves showed much excitement, talking and gesticulating with great emphasis and spirit, as they seemed to be pointing out to the younger savages the position and incidents of the conflict. I met Red Jacket at Washington in 1827 or '8, and strove to lead him to talk of Wyoming, but on that subject his lips were hermetically sealed."

From this time, we believe, no Indians visited Wyoming until the summer of 1852, when a company of performers made their appearance in Wilkesbarre. They rode through the town in single file in native costume, and whooped, and yelled, and performed many curious feats. At night they had a war-dance on the bank of the river, on the ground of the old fort. Few of the people who had been raised in the Valley ever saw an Indian before, and, of course, they were objects of great curiosity.

Mr. Gardner's conversation is all in a plain, straightforward style, without a particle of enthusiasm, and exhibits evidence of an unimpaired intellect. We left him, and returned right well satisfied with our trip through the Narrows. We had learned some things, and among them was the fact that there were some other things not to be learned.

Q

## XVI.

### PROVIDENTIAL DELIVERANCE OF RUFUS BENNET ON THE FATAL 3D OF JULY.

> "Woe to the vanquish'd! was stern Runo's word
> When sunk proud Rome beneath the Gallic sword;
> Woe to the vanquish'd! when his massy blade
> Bore down the scale against her ransom weigh'd;
> And on the field of foughten battle still,
> War knows no limit save the victor's will."
> 
> *The Gailliard.*

> "Slaughter grows murther when it goes too far,
> And makes a massacre what was a war."
> 
> DRYDEN.

THE retreat of the patriot army on the fatal 3d of July became a flight and a massacre. Each man shifted for himself as best he could, and the more swift on foot took the lead. The Indians, frantic with the war spirit and thirsty for blood, shot down, scalped, and tomahawked those they overtook. More than two hundred of the New England people fell in that ill-judged and disastrous encounter. A portion of these were first captured, and then massacred in cold blood. Very few—it is thought only two—of those who were captured upon the field of battle escaped torture. Of Butler's Loyalists and Indians from fifty to eighty are supposed to have fallen, but no reliable report of the number has ever been made. It is reported that all the "shovels and picks" which could be raised were put into requisition the next morning. This certainly was not for the purpose of burying our people, for they were all left above ground. The facts will probably never be revealed until the morning of the resurrection, when it is probable that "the marsh" will yield up some scores of the Red Men who fell upon that memorable day.*

In the flight and chase down the plains, there were hair-breadth and providential escapes as well as diabolical deeds of cruelty. Among the strange escapes we would notice that of Rufus Bennet, a young man of seventeen years of age. He was tall and slender, but resolute and quick of foot. He was hotly pursued by two stalwart Indians, one of them close behind him. Colonel Butler, who was almost the last to leave the ground, galloped his horse close by Bennet. Quick as lightning he seized the long switch tail of the colonel's horse. He now made long strides, and hoped to out-distance his pursuers. They, however, presuming upon the fact that he would not be able long to keep his hold, kept on at the top of their speed, although for a few moments they fell in the rear.

Bennet broke his hold, and his spirit sunk. He and

---

* Since writing the above, we have learned from John Bennet, Esq., of Kingston, that when his uncle Solomon was in Wyoming last—in 1820—he went with him upon the battle-ground, and showed him where he stood when the battle began, and how far they pushed John Butler's men. He also pointed out the spot where the British and Indians who were killed were buried. It was on what was called "the Island," in the marsh, under some large yellow pines which were then standing. There sixty were consigned to their long resting-place by their fellow-royalists—British, Tories, and Indians. The number of the slain and the place of burial were communicated to Mr. Solomon Bennet by the Wintermoots and Secords in Canada in 1812. Mr. Bennet was in Canada upon a visit to a daughter when the late war broke out, and there was obliged to remain for about two years, and during this period he had frequent interviews with his old Tory acquaintances above named, who were perfectly frank in their communications.

the Indians had severally discharged their guns and could not take time to reload, and there was no hope for the poor fellow but in a deadly close encounter against great odds. The foremost of the two, tomahawk in hand, now rapidly gained upon his supposed victim, and, with a yell which echoed from mountain to mountain, bounded forward like the bloodthirsty wolf in pursuit of the exhausted fawn. A few more leaps, and his prey would be secure.

On the march of the little army up the plains, Richard Inman had fallen back from the ranks, and lay down in a wheat-field just above Tuttle's Creek. It is said that he had "taken a little too much," and requiring a nap, he flung himself upon the ground and fell asleep. By the time the fugitives came rushing down from the battle-field Inman had come to himself, and when he heard the heavy tread of Colonel Butler's horse he began to rub open his eyes. The colonel saw him lift his head and lay his chin in his hand, his elbow resting on the ground. Throwing the point of his sword back, Colonel Butler roared out, "Inman, shoot that Indian!"

Inman was a dead shot, and the order was no sooner given than it was obeyed. Crack went Inman's rifle, and down fell the Indian brave. He fell within a few feet of the exhausted fugitive, and his companion was not far behind him.

The next moment, and Bennet would have spent the last remnant of vital power, fallen prostrate upon the ground, and been scalped and tomahawked. He was a young man of nerve; he neither fell into a swoon nor forgot that another foe was upon his track. Gathering up his energies, he was now ready, supported by his friend, to give battle hand to hand to the remaining savage; he, however, came to a sudden

THE NEW YORK
PUBLIC LIBRARY

ASTOR, LENOX AND
TILDEN FOUNDATIONS.

ESCAPE OF RUFUS BENNET.

pause, turned about, and took to his heels. The crack of Inman's rifle and the fall of the Indian warrior had measurably restored the equilibrium of Bennet's system, and, after a few long breaths, he and his companion were on their way to the fort, where they arrived without farther molestation.*

Rufus Bennet married Martha Bennet, a young woman of the same name, but not immediately related to him, and settled in Hanover, where he raised a large family, and lived to advanced years. His wife outlived him, and after long having been called "Aunt Martha," was by every body called "Grandmother." She died one mile below Wilkesbarre in the year 1853. We visited her upon her dying-bed, and, although in the very jaws of death, she entertained us for an hour or more with accounts of "the battle" and the flight "through the swamp."

The company she was in "went through Capouse on to Shehola, and across Jersey." They were in constant excitement from fear of Indians. At Capouse they found one of the settlers—if we recollect right, a Mr. St. John—lying dead in the road, who had the same day been shot and scalped.†

* The Inman family were great patriots, and suffered severely from the Indians. Three of Richard's brothers fell victims to their barbarous cruelty. Richard lived to old age, and, after the termination of the wars, became a religious man. Colonel Edward Inman, his brother, was also, to the day of his death, a man of influence and respectability. Both these veteran pioneers had a high reputation for hospitality, and were gratefully remembered by the early itinerant ministers.

† Mr. Miner gives the following account of the Capouse murders. "News came down from Lackawanna that Mr. Hickman, his wife and child, were murdered at Capouse. The very next day, two men, by the name of Leach and St. John, who were removing with their families, were shot six miles up the Lackawanna. One of them had a child in his arms, which, with strange inconsistency, the Indian

It is not wonderful that impressions made upon the minds of children by these bloody scenes should be durable. Seventy-five years had elapsed, and Mrs. Bennet was all but in her death-struggle, and yet she seemed to have a passion for thinking and conversing of those awful scenes. True enough, "The ruling passion strong in death." The day following she breathed her last.

We offered her the consolations of religion, and commended her soul to God, but have one thing to regret. We made no memorandum of the particular facts which she communicated, and which are now beyond recovery. Thus are the materials of history constantly perishing through the mere thoughtlessness of those whose duty it is to give them permanence. Our acquaintance with Rufus and Martha Bennet was long and somewhat intimate, and we have general impressions of the stories which we heard from their lips of the troublous days of Wyoming, but the particulars, except in a few instances, are indistinctly marked upon the tablet of our memory. The same remark we may make in relation to a score or more of those who were sharers and actors in the same scenes which are presented in this volume, who were active members of society when we first entered the Valley. Diligence in committing to writing what we then heard from the early settlers would have furnished us with a magazine of facts which, at this time, we should prize above silver or gold. Most of these opportunities are now gone beyond the possibility of recovery. All we can now do is to use what has escaped the ruins of a past generation.

<small>took up and handed to the mother, all covered with the father's blood. Leaving the women in the wagon unhurt, they took the scalps of their husbands and departed."</small>

## XVII.

### NOAH HOPKINS—HIS LIFE SAVED BY A SPIDER.

"To turn purveyor to an overgorged
And bloated spider, till the pampered beast
Is made familiar, watches his approach,
Comes at his call, and serves him for a friend."—*Task*.

"It is not, I say, merely in a pious manner of expression that the Scripture thus ascribeth every event to the providence of God, but it is strictly and philosophically true in nature and reason that there is no such thing as chance or accident."—Dr. S. CLARKE.

THE following singular and providential escape we copy from the second edition of Colonel Stone's History of Wyoming.

"Among the individual incidents marking this singular tragedy was the following: Some of the fugitives were pursued for a time by a portion of the Indians, and among them was a settler named Noah Hopkins—a wealthy man, from the county of Dutchess, in the State of New York, bordering upon Connecticut. He had disposed of a handsome landed patrimony in his native town, Amenia, and invested the proceeds as a shareholder of the Susquehanna Company, and in making preparations for removing to the new colony. Finding, by the sounds, that the Indians were upon his trail, after running a long distance he fortunately discovered the trunk of a large hollow tree upon the ground, into which he crept. After lying there several hours, his apprehensions of danger were greatly quickened by the tread of footsteps. They approached, and in a few moments two or three savages were actually seated upon the log in consultation. He heard the bullets rattle loosely in their pouches. They actually looked into the hollow trunk, suspecting that he might be there; but the examination must have been slight, as they discovered no traces of his presence. The object of their search, however, in after-life attributed his escape to the labors of a busy spider, which, after he crawled into the log, had been industriously engaged in weaving a web over the entrance. Perceiving this, the Indians supposed, as a matter of course, that the fugitive could not have entered there. After remaining in his place of concealment as long as nature could endure the confinement, Hopkins crept forth, wandering in the wilderness without food until he was on the point of famishing. In this situation, knowing that he could but die, he cautiously stole down into the Valley again, whence five days before he had fled. All was desolation there. The crops were destroyed, the cattle gone, and the smouldering brands and embers were all that remained of the houses. The Indians had retired, and the stillness of death prevailed. He roamed about for hours in search of something to satisfy the cravings of nature, fording or swimming the river twice in his search. At length he discerned the carcass of a wild turkey, shot on the morning of the massacre, but which had been left in the flight. He quickly stripped the bird of his feathers, although it had become somewhat offensive by lying in the sun, dressed it and washed it in the river, and the first meal he made therefrom was ever afterward pronounced the sweetest of his life. Upon the strength of this turkey, with such roots and herbs as he could gather in the way, he traveled until, after incredible hardships he was obliged to encounter—his clothes being torn from his limbs in the thickets, and his body badly lacerated—he once more found himself among the dwellings of civilized men."

## XVIII.

### THE FRATRICIDE.

THE story of a Tory shooting his brother on Monocasy Island on the day of the battle, which we have told from the historians, we believe has never been questioned. Such an astonishing instance of depravity would be past belief if it were not well authenticated; but, giving it due credit upon the credibility of the witnesses, we naturally desire to know something of the subsequent history of the perpetrator of so unnatural and barbarous a deed. We have obtained some reliable information upon this subject, which we will now proceed to give.

The name of the brothers was Pencil. The Christian name of the patriot was Henry, and that of the Tory was John. When John Pencil deliberately shot his brother Henry, the Indians who witnessed the horrible crime seemed shocked, and shook their heads, muttering, "Too bad—too bad; kill his brother."

John Pencil fled to Canada with the other refugees, and settled in a wilderness. He was twice chased by wolves, and each time rescued by the Indians. The savages, however, began to think there was something judicial in the matter, and concluded to leave him to the retributions of Providence. They said, "He too wicked—too wicked; Great Spirit angry; Indian no more help him." It was not long before another pack of the ferocious wild dogs scented the fratricide, and this time they were left to satisfy their thirst for his blood. The miserable wretch was killed and devoured, an end well becoming such a monster.

The death of John Pencil occurred not many years after the perpetration of the crime which has given him eminence among the greatest and vilest of sinners. It is not our object to moralize much upon the circumstances of the death of the fratricide. It is, however, not unworthy of notice, that, as the man's crime was stupendous, his death was marked by extraordinary circumstances, and such as indicate that "there is a God that judgeth in the earth."

The fact of Pencil's death, under the circumstances above described, was communicated to Mrs. Alexander by a gentleman from Canada who professed to know the truth of what he related, and, so far as could be known at the time, was perfectly reliable.

The following lines are by a literary friend:

> The morning sun rose bright and clear,
>    The birds sang blithely on the bough;
> But many an eye held trembling tear,
>    And many a one show'd troubled brow.
>
> \*    \*    \*    \*    \*    \*
>
> And there was one, a tear was in her eye,
>    As silently she gazed upon her Henry dear,
> Which spoke a language that all words defy—
>    That jewel of the heart, a sympathetic tear.
>
> "Oh, Henry, go not out to-day,"
>    His good companion cried;
> "Can fiends snatch thee from me away?"
>    She wept, and sobbed, and sighed.
>
> One moment in each other's arms entwined
>    They stood, as one united strong;
> The next saw Henry tread the wild,
>    Toward the muster, 'gainst the wrong.
>
> At what befell that gallant little band,
>    Mem'ry would shrink in horror to relate;
> How some did fall by cruel savage hand,
>    And some had torturing, lingering fate.

THE NEW YORK
PUBLIC LIBRARY

ASTOR, LENOX AND
TILDEN FOUNDATIONS.

THE FRATRICIDE'S FATE.

## THE FRATRICIDE.

But Henry fled to Susquehanna's isle,
   And sought a covert in Monocasy;
And thought himself secure from Indian wile—
   Equally safe from treacherous Tories' eye.

But hark! he hears a crackle and a tread,
   And, looking up, his Tory brother spies;
Then shrinking back instinctively with dread,
   He finds himself perceived, and upward hies.

"Oh, it is you!" the haughty brother said;
   "You are a d——d rebel, and not fit for life!"
Then raising up his gun, the fatal bullet sped,
   Making children orphans, a widow of his wife.

John Pencil wander'd outcast and alone;
   The Indians shunn'd him—were themselves afraid—
The awful deed soften'd their hearts of stone,
   They thought his company a curse was made.

He tried to flee; Conscience always pursued,
   And found him ev'ry where—asleep, awake;
His brother's blood was in his soul imbued,
   Himself a fiend, and it a burning lake.

The hungry, ravenous wolves pursued him twice;
   As many times the Indian saved his life;
They thought, "Great Spirit angry" at his vice,
   And would not save again: they came on thrice,

And, seizing him, his limbs from limb they tore,
   And cracked his living bones with bloody jaw,
And quench'd their thirst upon his spouting gore,
   And yet alive, his flesh they tear and gnaw.

Some scatter'd bones, uncover'd in the wood,
   Now mark the spot where died the fratricide;
Where he by living inches served for food,
   Because by him his brother Henry died.

Oh, justice! Retribution, it is right
   That thou shouldst fix upon the soul thy doom,
And on the body exercise thy might,
   And stigmatize the name beyond the tomb.

\* \* \*

## XIX.

#### THE MOMUMENT.

Colonel Butler returned to the Valley in August, but no attempt was made to gather up the remains of those who fell upon the battle-field until October. On the 21st of October he issued an order "that there be a party, consisting of a lieutenant, two sergeants, two corporals, and twenty-five men, to parade to-morrow morning, with arms, as a guard to those who will go to bury the remains of the men who were killed at the late battle at and near the place called Wintermoot's Fort." On the day the settlers, who had returned to the Valley, assembled and proceeded, protected by the military escort provided by Colonel Butler, to perform the melancholy duty of interring what remained of their comrades, relations, and neighbors in as decent a manner as possible. The late General William Ross, who was present, informed Professor Silliman, when he was in the Valley in 1829, that, "owing to the intense heat of the weather, and probably the dryness of the air, the bodies were shriveled, dried, and inoffensive, but, with a single exception, their features could not be recognized."

The bodies were taken up with pitchforks and carried upon a cart to the place of sepulture, where they were buried in a common grave.

Strange as it may seem, the grave of the patriots who fell in the fatal "Indian battle" was for years wholly lost. It was known to be located not far from the main road, in a field belonging to Fisher Gay,

Esq. This field had long been cultivated, the plow and the scythe alternately passing over the remains of the relatives and friends of nearly every leading family in the Valley, and yet there was none to rise up and claim for Wyoming's heroes the respect accorded in all civilized countries to the ashes of the common dead. Public sentiment was finally directed to the subject, and there was an awakening of the feelings of virtuous shame for a delinquency so strange and unnatural. A suitable monument over the bones of the patriot band finally came to be talked of as a matter of decency, to say nothing of the gratitude to which their memory was entitled. So early as 1809, Hon. Charles Miner published several essays upon the subject in a Wilkesbarre paper, but it was not until 1832 that any thing like a decided movement was made to carry out the project.

Several leading citizens of the Valley becoming deeply interested in the question of the proposed monument, the first thing which it was thought necessary to settle was the precise spot where the bones of the patriots lay. The ground was originally owned by "the widow Lee," and she subsequently married Philip Jackson, long after her death a resident at Forty Fort. Jackson remembered the mound which indicated the place of interment, and was employed to identify it. But little effort was necessary to effect the object. The common grave, where were mingled together the bones of brothers and neighbors, officers and common soldiers, in close contact, was opened in the presence of several of the citizens residing in the vicinity.

Some of the most interesting specimens of the remains were deposited in a box, and were kept for the examination of curious visitors, until most of them finally disappeared. We saw them before any of them had been conveyed by sacrilegious hands to parts unknown. The skulls exhibited the marks of the tomahawk and scalping-knife. Some of them had been broken in with the head or spike of the tomahawk, and others chipped with the edge by a glancing stroke. One had been broken in with the rim of the pipe of a smoking-tomahawk. We can imagine with what gusto the murderous wretch tasted the fumes of "the weed" taken in from the bowl of his favorite smoking-hatchet while it was yet stained with the blood of his victim. One skull was perforated by a bullet, and a thigh-bone had a bullet hole in the centre, which was made without effecting a lateral fracture, leaving the bone entirely sound with the exception of the smooth perforation.

What awful associations did these memorials of the fatal 3d of July, 1778, bring up! The bones are without sense or motion, but once they were the framework of bodies like our own—bodies which were inhabited by intelligent immortal spirits. They were deprived of their conscious reasoning tenant in a moment, or by slow, lingering agonies. The separation was violent, but, when consummated, the shouts of the victors and the clangor of the battle, which echoed from mountain-top to mountain-top, no more shocked the ear nor quickened the pulsations of the slain. They sleep in death until the morning of the resurrection.

These sacred relics were now objects of universal curiosity and no ordinary veneration, and increased the tendency of the public mind in the direction of the monument which had been commenced. The time for action had come, and "a meeting of a number of the early settlers of Wyoming Valley, who had relatives and acquaintances in the Wyoming massacre, and other citizens of Luzerne County, convened at the house of Major O. Helme, in Kingston, on the 16th day of June, 1832, to take into consideration the subject of erecting a monument to the memory of those who fell in that disastrous conflict. General William Ross was appointed chairman, and Charles D. Shoemaker secretary." After the object of the meeting had been stated by the chair, the following persons were appointed a committee to draft resolutions: John Carey, Colonel Benjamin Dorrance, Rev. Benjamin Bidlack, Colonel George P. Ransom, Calvin Wadhams, John Gore, Sen., Anderson Dana, Sen., Joseph Wright, and Benjamin Reynolds.

The resolutions proposed and passed expressed the deep sympathy of the meeting with the movement, and prescribed preparatory measures for the accomplishment of its object. One resolution was, "That we request the citizens of the Valley to meet at the house of F. Gay, in Kingston, on the 3d day of July next, at ten o'clock, for the purpose of adopting such measures as may be thought necessary to insure the erection of a monument." It was also "Resolved, That we invite our fellow-citizens to unite with us in paying a tribute of respect to the remains of those patriots on that day, it being the anniversary of the day of their massacre, by visiting the spot where rest their ashes."

A committee was then appointed to negotiate for the purchase of "half an acre of ground, including the burial-place of those who fell in the battle of Wyoming." The committee was composed of Benjamin Dorrance, Calvin Wadhams, Anderson Dana, David Scott, and George M. Hollenback.

"A committee of superintendence" was then appointed "to arrange the order of the day, and that they be requested to procure a suitable person to deliver an address on that day." The committee was as follows: John Carey, George P. Ransom, Sharp D. Lewis, Pierce Butler, Charles D. Shoemaker, Fisher Gay, Elisha Harding, Sen., Ebenezer Slocum, Samuel Wadhams, Joseph Jameson, Edward Inman, Benjamin A. Bidlack, Joseph Slocum, William Swetland, Harris Jenkins, William C. Reynolds, William S. Ross, Charles Dorrance, Jonah Rogers, Francis Dana, Hiram Denison, Jonathan Stephens, Asa Stephens, John Bennet, Dr. John Smith, Isaac Harding, John Gore, Jr., Henry Pettibone, Daniel Ross, Avery Gore, and Jeremiah Gore.

The committee immediately arranged the following programme for the proposed meeting:

"The procession will be formed at twelve o'clock, in the following order:

"Those who may be present who were in the battle.

"The soldiers of the Revolution.

"The connections and descendants of those who fell in the battle.

"The orator of the day and the committee of superintendence.

"The early settlers who were not in the battle.

"The citizens.

"The procession will march in silence, or with suitable music, to the place where those who were massacred were interred."

The meeting was one of great public interest, and, as might be expected, a vast concourse of people attended. Rev. James May, now Rev. Dr. May, of the Protestant Episcopal Church, was the orator. Associated with him in the services were Rev. Nicholas Murray, now Rev. Dr. Murray, of the Presbyterian Church, and Rev. Charles Nash, of the Methodist Episcopal Church, then all pastors in the borough of Wilkesbarre. The oration of Mr. May and the remarks of Mr. Murray were published in the papers, and are now before us.

Mr. May's address consists of a brief sketch of the objects of the meeting, the battle, and the consequences which followed. Toward its close we have the following beautiful paragraphs:

"When upward of fifty years have gone, we are in quiet possession of this valley. The sun in his daily journey looks upon few spots on which the Creator has combined more of the materials necessary for earthly happiness. No object of price in general can be gained without painstaking and sacrifice. The independence of our common country was not secured without a long and toilsome struggle. This valley, so rich in soil, so lovely in scenery, could not be possessed securely till the sacrifice was made, and that, too, of blood. The hands that more than half a century ago first struck the axe into the forests that had for ages shadowed these plains, lie mingled with the dust. The troubles of those times, when the Indians descended upon this valley, were borne by heads that are pillowed beneath the soil. See, fellow-citizens, the sacrifice which was made by the first civilized tenants of this valley. The grave containing their bones is uncovered before you. You see for yourselves the marks of the tomahawk and scalping-knife on the heads which are here uncovered, after having rested for more than fifty years. Peace be in this grave—sacred be the memory of them that sleep here.

"A few who were themselves sharers in the toils and difficulties of those times yet survive, and are here this day to bear witness for us. Venerable citizens, we respect you for your years; we honor you for the part you bore in the doings and sufferings of those days; we love and cherish the principles of liberty which animated you; we owe you a debt of gratitude for the happy inheritance which you did your part to preserve unimpaired for your children. You have passed within the lines of the second half century since you opened a grave here for your brothers whom the Indians slaughtered on these plains. This valley, which you saw as it was when but a frontier, you survive to see in the midst of a population of many hundreds of thousands overspreading the country beyond you. But on this day, and where you now are, you can not but think of what you once saw in this place. We would stand aside while you look into this grave, and see the bones of your brothers, which fifty years ago you assisted in sadly laying here. We would not intrude while, as you stand beside these bones, you think how you stood beside your friends when they lived. For your sakes we are glad that this day has come. We rejoice to think that you may see yet a stone raised here, on which the names of those you laid in this spot shall be engraven."

Mr. Murray made a few characteristic and happy remarks, among which were the following:

"You see these bleached heads and bending forms around me. These worthies have come down to us from the last century, and are the companions of the heroes to whose manly frames these mouldering bones belonged. Could the breath of life be breathed into these bones—could they rise in the possession of living energy, they would find, even among this small remnant, a few brothers and sons. As the gentleman on my right was narrating the incidents of the horrible massacre, I saw the tear stealing down the furrowed cheeks of these fathers of our community. That tear told me that they felt—that they deeply felt; and methinks that there is not a heart in this vast concourse that does not sympathize with them. They desire that a monument should be erected over the common grave of their fathers, and brothers, and companions. And do you not sympathize with them? I know you do. I feel persuaded that you are anxious to place a liberal subscription on this paper before you retire from this place. You court the honor of contributing to the erection of the Wyoming Monument. My great fear is that we shall not all have the privilege of giving. I would therefore caution the rich not to indulge their patriotic feelings too freely, lest the poor should be debarred. We all want to have our stone in the Wyoming Monument."

Our friend Murray's fears of being overwhelmed with a deluge of money turned out not to have been very well founded, for the subscription was so inadequate that the enterprise rested for seven years. In 1839, an able committee was sent to Hartford to solicit aid from the Legislature of Connecticut. The claims of the original settlers of Wyoming upon Connecticut were ably advocated, and a report was presented which proposed a grant of three thousand dollars to aid in the erection of the proposed monument, but was not acted upon. In 1841, another petition and another deputation were sent on, and for a time the thing seemed likely to succeed. The Lower House voted the appropriation by a large majority, but the Senate did not concur.

Having failed in their efforts to procure foreign aid, like the wagoner in the fable who prayed to Hercules for help, the people of Wyoming resorted to the better plan of putting their shoulder to the wheel. This time the ladies took the matter in hand, and it was bound to go. They formed what was denominated "The Luzerne Monumental Association." The names of the officers and committee were as follows: Mrs. Chester Butler, *President;* Mrs. G. M. Hollenback and Mrs. E. Carey, *Vice-presidents;* Mrs. Butler, Mrs. Nicholson, Mrs. Hollenback, Mrs. Lewis, Mrs. Ross, Mrs. Cunningham, Mrs. Beaumont, Mrs. Drake, Mrs. Bennet, Mrs. Carey, *Executive Committee;* Miss Emily Cist, *Treasurer;* Miss Gertrude Butler, *Secretary;* Mrs. Donley, Mrs. L. Butler, *Corresponding Committee.*

The ladies solicited donations, held fairs, and, by dint of zeal and perseverance, succeeded in raising the funds for the erection of a monument at once of the patriotic deeds of their fathers and of their own power. The monument is constructed of granite, and is sixty-two and a half feet in height. On three marble slabs are engraved the following inscriptions.

On the front slab, composed by Edward Mallory, Esq., is the following:

Near this spot was fought, on the afternoon of the 3d of July, 1778, the Battle of Wyoming, in which a small band of patriotic Americans, chiefly the undisciplined, the youthful, and the aged, spared by inefficiency from the distant ranks of the Republic, led by Colonel Zebulon Butler and Colonel Nathan Denison, with a courage that deserved success, boldly met and bravely fought a combined British, Tory, and Indian force of thrice their number. Numerical superiority alone gave success to the invader, and widespread havoc, desolation, and ruin marked his savage and bloody footsteps through the Valley.

This monument, commemorative of these events, and in memory of the actors in them, has been erected over the bones of the slain by their descendants and others, who gratefully appreciate the services and sacrifices of their patriotic ancestors.

On the other slabs the following:

Dulce et decorum est pro patria mori.

Slain in the battle: Field-officers: Lieutenant Colonel George Dorrance, Major John Garret. Captains: James Bidlack, Jun., Aholiab Buck, Robert Durkee, Rezin Geer, Joseph Whittlesey, Dethic Hewit, William M'Karaghan, Samuel Ransom, Lazarus Stewart, James Wigton. Lieutenants: A. Atherton, Stoddart Bowen, Aaron Gaylord, Timothy Pierce, Perrin Ross, Elijah Shoemaker, Lazarus Stewart, Jun., Asa Stevens, Flavius Waterman, James Wells. Ensigns: Jeremiah Bigford, Asa Gore, Silas Gore, Titus Hinman, John Otis, William White. Privates: Jabez Atherton, Christopher Avery, —— Acke, A. Benedict, Jabez Beers, Samuel Bigford, Elias Bixby, David Bixby, John Boyd, John Brown, Thomas Brown, William Buck, James Budd, Amos Bullock, Henry Buck, John Caldwell, Isaac Campbell, Josiah Cameron, Joseph Carey, Joel Church, James Coffrin, William Coffrin, Samuel Cole, Robert Comstock, [three] brothers Cook, Christopher Cortright, John Cortright, Anson Coray, Rufus Coray, Jenks Coray, Samuel Crocker, Joseph Crocker, Jabez Darling, D. Denton, Conrad Devenport, Anderson Dana, James Divine, George Downing, Levi Dunn, William Dunn, —— Ducher, Benjamin Finch, John Finch, Daniel Finch, Elisha Fitch, Cornelius Fitchett, Eliphalet Follett, Thomas Faxen, John Franklin, Thomas Fuller, Stephen Fuller, —— Gardner, George Gore, —— Green, Samuel Hutchinson, William Hammond, Silas Harvey, Benjamin Hatch, Cyprian Hebard, Levi Hicks, James Hopkins, Nathaniel Howard, John Hutchins, Israel Inman, Elijah Inman, Joseph Jennings, Samuel Jackson, Robert Jameson, Henry Johnson, —— Lester, Joshua Landon, Daniel Lawrence, William Lawrence, Francis Ledyard, James Lock, Conrad Lowe,

R

Jacob Lowe, Nicholas Manvill, Job Marshall, New Matthewson, C. M'Cartee, A. Mccleman, Robert M'Intire, Andrew Millard, John Murphy, Joseph Ogden, John Pierce, Abel Palmer, Silas Parke, William Packer, Henry Pencil, Noah Pettibone, Jun., Jeremiah Ross, —— Reynolds, Elisha Richards, Elias Roberts, Enos Rockway, Timothy Ross, James Shaw, Constant Searle, Abel Seeley, Joseph Shaw, Abraham Shaw, Darius Spafford, Levi Spencer, Josiah Spencer, Eleazar Sprague, Aaron Stark, Daniel Stark, Joseph Staples, Rufus Stevens, James Stevenson, Naler Sweed, Ichabod Tuttle, John Van Wee, Abraham Vangorder, Elisha Waters, Bartholomew Weeks, Jonathan Weeks, Philip Weeks, Peter Wheeler, Stephen Whiting, Esen Wilcox, John Williams, Elihu Williams, Jun., Rufus Williams, Azibah Williams, John Ward, John Wilson, Parker Wilson, —— Wade, William Woodringer, Ozias Yale.

The plan of the monument has not, as yet, been fully carried out. It has around it no railing of any sort. The ground is not ornamented by trees, shrubs, and flowers. The spot looks neglected; and we are free to confess, mortifying as it is for us to say so, that the Wyoming Monument—a thing that should be the pride of the Valley—is indicative of too great a want of public spirit in our citizens. Where are the ladies of Wyoming? Since the monument has been brought to its present state, the daughters of those who did the work have come upon the stage. Let them arise in their might, and finish the work so well begun by their noble mothers. Let the present generation of Wyoming ladies prove by their works that they are not inferior to the preceding generation in patriotism, energy, taste, and public spirit. A thousand dollars could be well laid out upon the monument and grounds, and ought to be forthcoming. Half that sum would redeem this noble monument of patriotism rarely met with on the pages of the world's history from the disgrace which seems to rest upon it. Happy indeed we are that the Wyoming Monument is a fact, but much more happy should we be to see the original design, so well conceived, fully completed, that visitors from all quarters of the globe might be struck with admiration not only of the bravery of the patriots who fell in the battle, but also of the pious gratitude, the liberality, the love of art, and the elevated taste of their descendants. "The Monument" should be the most beautiful and inviting spot in the Valley. It should be surrounded with an iron railing, and the plot of ground around it should be ornamented with the choicest shrubbery and flowers. The genius of patriotism and of art should preside there. It should be a place where one would love, in solitude, to spend the twilight of evening in holy meditations, and in reminiscences of the olden time. While it points back to a stern, bloody period in our history, it should indicate the fact of progress, and prophesy a glorious future.

## XX.

#### COLONEL JOHN JENKINS.

The sketches of the historic life of Wyoming would be incomplete without Colonel Franklin or Colonel Jenkins. They were the representatives of one of the two classes of opinions which divided the people of Wyoming at an important period of its history. The reader will already have been made acquainted with the fact that, subsequent to the decree of Trenton, the people of Wyoming were divided into two factions: one was for yielding to the jurisdiction of Pennsylvania, and the other was for resistance. A series of irritating causes on both sides served to embitter feelings and provoke violent hostility. Colonel Hollenback may be considered as representing the Pennsylvania side of this great question, and Colonel Jenkins that of Connecticut. The former—after the question of the right of jurisdiction had been legally settled, saying nothing about the justice of the decision—was for giving up the struggle; while the latter, believing the decision unjust to the State of Connecticut, and especially to the Connecticut settlers, and also that Pennsylvania had acted in bad faith, was for defending what he considered the right to the last. The two men are historical characters, and each deserves an impartial representation in these pages. The feud and the embittered feelings which the struggle engendered have long since passed away, and the time has come for the historian to review the whole scene with calmness and impartial justice.

The materials for the following sketch have been derived partly from the contributions of Hon. Steuben Jenkins and John K. Jenkins, Esq., grandsons of Colonel Jenkins; partly from the papers of Colonel Pickering, copies of which have been kindly furnished us by Mr. Hollenback; and partly from Mr. Miner's history. The portion derived from Mr. Miner we have faithfully quoted.

John Jenkins, the elder, was a lineal descendant of Judge Jenkins, who was imprisoned by the Long Parliament, was born in Wales, whence he migrated to this country about the year 1735, landing at Boston; but, being one of that "persecuted" sect called Quakers, he was driven out, with others, and passed over into Providence, Rhode Island, and thence into Windham County, Connecticut, where he became engaged in the Susquehanna Purchase in 1754, and in 1762 he and one hundred and eighteen others removed to Wyoming to possess themselves of the Purchase. In October, 1763, they were driven off by the Indians, and returned again to Connecticut, where they remained until the spring of 1769, at which time they again, with about three hundred others, removed to Wyoming, and took possession of their lands.

John Jenkins took possession of and held all the lands from the township line of Kingston and Exeter to the head of Wyoming Valley, between the river and the foot of the mountain. His residence was fixed just above the northwestern end of the Pittston Ferry Bridge, where he, in connection with others, built what was known as Jenkins's Fort. He was driven thence by the Indians, British, and Tories on the day before the memorable "Wyoming massacre," on the 2d day of July, 1778, and fled into Orange County, New York, where he died in 1785.

He was a surveyor and conveyancer by profession; was elected one of the members of Assembly for Westmoreland in the Connecticut Assembly for its session commencing in May, 1774; also for May, 1775; and the session of May, 1777. He had the honor of presiding at the town meeting on the 1st of August, 1775, when resolutions in favor of liberty were adopted.—See *Miner's History*, p. 165.

His loss by the depredations of the Indians, as stated in the journal of John Jenkins, Jr., was £598 1s. 3d.

Colonel John Jenkins, the younger, was born in Windham County, Connecticut, on the 27th of November, 1751, O. S., and died in Exeter, Luzerne County, on the site of Wintermoot Fort, where he settled immediately after the close of the Indian wars in the Valley, about 1780. He was married on the 23d of June, 1778, in Wyoming, to Bethiah Harris, who was born in Colchester, Connecticut, on the 14th of September, 1752, and died August 12th, 1842, aged about ninety years.

Previous to the Revolution, Mr. Jenkins, with four other men, were surveying in the State of New York, and lived principally in cabins in the woods. On one occasion five Indians came to their camp, and appeared very friendly. The Indians wanted some provisions, and said they were going down the creek hunting, and would return in a few days and give them venison.

That night those five Indians came back and fired upon them as they lay asleep, killing one man and wounding another: Mr. Jenkins jumped up, took his compass-staff, and commenced operation in the way of desperate self-defense. On looking behind him, he saw an Indian with his tomahawk just in the act of striking him in the head, but with one blow knocked the Indian into the large fire that was burning before the cabin door. On turning around again, he saw another Indian in the act of striking him over the head with his gun: he caught the gun and wrung it from the Indian, and drove him through the fire. The Indians then fled, leaving their bloody tracks on the snow as they went. Jenkins and his surviving comrades made a litter, and carried the wounded man to the settlement, leaving the dead one rolled up in his blanket.

A party of men went in pursuit of the five Indians, which were soon found and delivered up as prisoners. They were taken to Newtown, Elmira, where it was determined that Jenkins should decide on the mode of punishment. He found that four of the party had been induced to commit the terrible act by an old savage by the name of Big Hand—having previously been wounded in the hand, making it considerably larger than the other. The four young Indians caught hold of Jenkins's coat and begged for mercy; Jenkins had compassion on them and let them go; but old Big Hand had to be punished, and his death-warrant prescribed that he should be pounded to death with pine knots, which was heartily done, most of those present taking an active part in this terrible infliction of capital punishment.

Mr. Jenkins was taken prisoner by the Indians in November, 1777, and returned to Wyoming on the 2d of June, 1778.

The following is Mr. Miner's account of Mr. Jenkins's captivity and release: "In November, 1777, he was on a scouting party up the river near fifty miles. Mr. York, father of the Rev. Miner York, was one of his companions; Lemuel Fitch was another. They were ambushed not far from Wyalusing captured by a party of Indians, and taken to the British lines. An Indian chief of some celebrity was a prisoner to the Americans in Albany, and Colonel John Butler sent Mr. Jenkins, under an escort of Indians, to be exchanged for the chief. On the way he suffered exceedingly, and, had it not been that a young savage had become warmly attached to him, Mr. Jenkins thought he should have been massacred, and was almost sure he should have been starved. Ardent and constant in his attachments, as implacable and cruel in his resentments, the savage presents a character in which vice and virtue are strangely mingled and strangely contrasted. The young Indian, amid rum and riot, for his sake kept himself sober and calm, fed him, protected him; and Mr. Jenkins was prompt, at all times, to do justice to his faithful friend, though, from the cruelties practiced here, the savages were generally objects of horror and detestation.

"Arrived at Albany, the chief for whom he was to have been exchanged had just died of small-pox. The Indians insisted on taking Mr. Jenkins back with them. From their conduct and character, he felt certain that they would take his life, in revenge for that of their chief, the moment they were beyond reach of pursuit. He was protected, and found his way home to a cordial welcome from his friends."

On the 5th of June, 1778, he commenced keeping a journal of events transpiring in Wyoming and at other points where he was called in the discharge of his duties. He kept no journal during his captivity among the Indians. He was not married previous to his captivity, but three weeks subsequent to his return. He was a surveyor and conveyancer by profession, and he followed this business in early life, and for many years after the Revolution. It is understood that at the time of the massacre he was in command at Forty Fort. Immediately after the massacre, he, with others, went out to meet Spaulding's company, which they found at the Lehigh River. He joined Spaulding's company on the 6th of July, 1778, and was invested with the position of lieutenant in it. He continued in active service in this company until the close of the campaign of 1782, when he resigned his commission, and returned home to take part in the defense of the Wyoming settlement.

In the winter of 1778 and 1779, General Hand, in command of the forces at Minisink, New York, wrote to Colonel Z. Butler at Wyoming for information in regard to the Indian settlements on the head waters of the Susquehanna and in the west of New York, desiring to know their strength and position, and the facilities, if any, for an expedition against them by way of the Susquehanna River. Colonel Butler replied, giving the information desired, and expressed in his letter his obligations to Lieutenant John Jenkins for the information he had been able to communicate. Soon after General Hand had received the letter of Colonel Butler, he ordered Lieutenant Jenkins to appear before General Washington at head-quarters. In pursuance of this order, he set out on the 1st of April, 1779, and on the 6th of April waited on General Washington. From the facts laid before General Washington at this interview, he planned and put in execution the expedition under General Sullivan against the Western Indians. General Sullivan arrived in Wyoming June 22, 1779, and, taking Lieutenant Jenkins for his chief guide, started with his expedition up the river on the 31st of July, 1779. This expedition was entirely successful. The information possessed by Lieutenant Jenkins in reference to the Indians and their country was obtained by him during his captivity among them.

In her efforts to establish her jurisdiction over the disputed territory, Pennsylvania found active and influential opponents in Colonel John Franklin and Colonel John Jenkins. Luzerne County was fully organized in May, 1787, by the agency of Colonel Timothy Pickering, who was appointed for that purpose by act of Assembly. Colonel Pickering was a New England man, but had become a citizen of Philadelphia. Having business in the northern part of Pennsylvania, he passed through Wyoming. Upon his return, he was questioned with regard to his impressions as to the best method of quieting matters in that disturbed district of country. He had conversed with many of the people, and freely imparted the information which he had received, and gave his views of their disposition to have quiet upon reasonable terms. Presuming upon the advantages he would have as a New England man, as well as his capabilities, the appointment was made, and he removed his family to Wyoming. He was a man of fine address, and was a great tactician. He soon raised a strong party among the old Yankees, who preferred to be "quieted in their possessions" under the laws of Pennsylvania to being in endless strife and a state of insufferable vexation.

Colonel Franklin headed a counter movement. While he was organizing his forces and agitating the public mind, he was arrested upon a charge of treason against the state, under a warrant issued by Judge M'Kean, by four officers specially commissioned for the purpose in Philadelphia. He was seized in "the old red tavern" in Wilkesbarre. Colonel Pickering says, "The four gentlemen seized him. Two of their horses were in my stable, which were sent to them; but soon my servant returned on one of them, with a message from the gentlemen that people were assembling in numbers, and requesting me to come with what men were near me to prevent a rescue. I took loaded pistols in my hands, and went with another servant to their aid. Just as I met them, Franklin threw himself off from his horse and renewed his struggle with them. His hair was disheveled and face bloody from preceding efforts. I told the gentlemen they would never carry him off unless his feet were tied under his horse. I sent for a cord. The gentlemen remounted him, and my servant tied his feet. Then, one taking his bridle and another following behind, and the others riding one on each side, they whipped up their horses, and were soon beyond the reach of his friends."

This violent proceeding aroused the indignation of Colonel Franklin's partisans, and Colonel Pickering, anticipating retaliatory measures upon himself, fled to Philadelphia. After it was presumed that the heat of the excitement had passed, Colonel Pickering returned to his family in Wyoming. It was not long before he was taken from his bed at dead of night by a party of men, and carried up the river and secreted in the woods. Colonel Pickering has left a particular narrative of his abduction and detention, which will be found published in Mr. Miner's History. We have a manuscript copy of the narrative, together with the whole course of Colonel Pickering's proceedings under the authority of Pennsylvania, now before us. Colonel Pickering's views of the whole question in difficulty are herein lucidly set forth.

In his narrative of his peregrinations through the wilderness, among the mountains and ravines of the north, in the neighborhood of the Susquehanna, the gallant colonel notes some instances of abuse and some of kindness. He was bound with fetters of iron, and a chain attached to him, because poor Franklin was lying in jail in irons. But they roasted for him a piece of meat occasionally, and once prepared him a dish of "coffee," made of burned "Indian meal." He says this "was an agreeable change for our green tea." The "green tea" was made of wintergreen. He was several times asked if he would "intercede for Colonel Franklin's pardon," to which he uniformly answered, "No, I will not."

The militia had been in pursuit of the party, and some skirmishes occurred, in which men were wounded on both sides, and one of "the ruffians" died of his wound. But, finding Colonel Pickering inflexible, the "rioters" sent him home down the river in a boat, and he made his appearance at his own door, to the great joy of his family. After washing, shaving, and changing his clothes, the dignified functionary was himself again. He had been absent twenty days.

Colonel Pickering speaks of Colonel Jenkins in terms of great severity, and goes so far as to charge him with being the contriver of his abduction, and then meanly deserting his pliant tools. "After encouraging and engaging them in the diabolical outrage upon me," says he, "he had deserted them." This is a most uncharitable and unwarrantable view of the case. In the first place, Colonel Jenkins had nothing to do with the abduction, and, in the next place, he was too honorable and brave a man meanly to desert his friends. The following may be presumed a fair and truthful answer to this unjust and cruel imputation, and is a complete vindication of the character of Colonel Jenkins. It is from the pen of Hon. Steuben Jenkins.

"There is a circumstance mentioned in Miner's History, p. 423, upon which I deem a few words necessary. Soon after the appearance of Stone's History of Wyoming, about 1839, my attention was called to it by seeing it in that history. I asked my grandmother concerning the circumstances connected with the abduction of Pickering, and she gave me the following account. A meeting of the friends of Franklin had been warned on the night of his abduction, for the purpose of taking into consideration some measures by which they might obtain his release. It was thought by all that Pickering had the power to release him at any time merely by writing to the proper authorities for that purpose, and it was therefore proposed by some to make an amicable adjustment of the matters in dispute with Pickering; by others it was proposed to take Pickering, and confine him as a prisoner until he should cause Franklin to be released. John Jenkins, who until this time had taken part with the most zealous friends of Franklin, was opposed to this last proposition, considering that it would tend to exasperate the friends of Pickering, and render the confinement of Franklin more close, and would be productive of no real utility, but, on the other hand, might result in serious injury both to Franklin and his cause. The hot-blooded carried the day, and John Jenkins refused to have any thing farther to do with it, and so declared himself at the time. By those who failed to enlist him in their schemes he was declared to be an obstinate man, and they attributed to his position in this matter the defeat of their plans.

"It was one of Colonel Jenkins's distinguishing traits, that when he once said he would or would not do a thing, that was the end of it. To do as he agreed was worth every effort of his nature, and he usually gave it to that end. During the controversy between the Connecticut and Pennsylvania settlers he declared that he would never yield—that he would never hold an inch of land under a Pennsylvania title. True to his word, he never did own an inch of land with a Pennsylvania title, and by reason of not taking title under Pennsylvania he lost a large amount of valuable property. He owned six miles square of the townships of Blakely, Carbondale, Greenfield, etc., but refused to take title for it under Pennsylvania, and therefore lost it all.

"In September, 1786, he and Colonel John Franklin, as a committee of the Wyoming settlers, went to Philadelphia to fight against the Pennsylvania claimants, and against the Connecticut settlers being compelled to take out Pennsylvania titles, and to ask for some measures of relief. On the 11th of September they had a conference with his excellency B. Franklin, President of Council, laid their affairs before him, and were heard by him with great attention and respect. While in attendance there on council, to wit, on the 25th of September, 1786, Luzerne County was established, and that put an end to their mission by effectually putting the territory under the laws and officers of Pennsylvania. But still the fight with him did not end here.

"He appealed, and went to Congress, where he was in 1801 and 1802, asking relief from that source. Failing in that, he returned to Wyoming, and was, in 1803, elected one of the members—Franklin being the other—from Luzerne County. Here they renewed the fight, but, being defeated, they gave it up, and concluded to let Pennsylvania rule, but still hold to their Connecticut titles, which they did."

Colonel Pickering seems to have imbibed a strong prejudice against Colonel Jenkins. This was natural enough, as they had come into violent collision upon a question which Colonel Pickering had greatly at heart. What is a little strange, however, is the fact that his dislike increased in acrimony with the lapse of time. The conflict raged from 1787 on, and in 1798 Colonel Pickering drew up a statement of the whole case, entitled, "A concise Narration of the Wyoming Dispute," in which he gives a very fair view of the reasonable expectations and just claims of the Connecticut settlers. In 1818, in connection with a history of "the outrage committed on him," in a letter to his son, he reviews the matter of the Connecticut claim, and sets it down as utterly baseless, and characterizes Colonel Franklin and Colonel Jenkins, and those who acted with them, as "rioters" and "traitors" for resisting measures which, according to his well-considered opinions at the time, were oppressive and inhuman.

For a clear understanding of the position of Colonel Jenkins on the question at issue—for this is the point we are laboring to bring out—we need no information excepting that which Colonel Pickering gives us.

*First.* He admits that it is not "surprising that Connecticut should claim that part of Pennsylvania which was comprehended in a charter twenty years older than Mr. Penn's," and that, all circumstances considered, the Legislature of Pennsylvania should be disposed "to view the subject in dispute in the most favorable light for the unfortunate settlers."—*Concise Narrative*, p. 11.

*Secondly.* He admits that, when he took the appointment from the Pennsylvania Legislature, it was with the distinct understanding that the Connecticut people would be quieted in their possessions, and their titles under Connecticut would be confirmed; and that, in his efforts to bring the people to terms, he had assured them that this would be the case.—*Concise Narrative*, p. 9.

*Thirdly.* Upon the presentation of a petition from "near three hundred of the Connecticut claimants, praying for a confirmation of their titles, to the General Assembly," the petition was "substantially" granted.—*Concise Narrative*, p. 9, 10.

*Fourthly.* "Instances of bad faith" on the part of the General Assembly furnished ground of suspicion "that the confirming law itself would be set aside as soon as they should be effectually brought under the government of Pennsylvania."*—*Concise Narrative*, p. 13, 14.

---

* In giving an account of a public meeting, which he held for the purpose of explaining to the people the disposition of the General Assembly of Pennsylvania to do them justice, Colonel Pickering says, "But just as I was closing prosperously, as I thought, my month's labor, a pretty shrewd man, John Jenkins, a major of their militia, arose and said, 'They had too often experienced the bad faith of Pennsylvania to place confidence in any new measures of its Legislature; and that, if they should enact a quieting law, they would repeal it as soon as the Connecticut settlers submitted, and were completely saddled with the laws of the state.' This was

*Fifthly.* "The confirming law" was repealed by the Legislature in 1788. "This," says Colonel Pickering, "always appeared to me unjust and cruel."—*Letter*, p. 36.

*Sixthly.* The efforts to dispossess the Connecticut settlers by law wholly failed. Suits were brought against them, and "after eight years they had partly tried one cause."*—*Concise Narrative*, p. 20.

*Seventhly.* What is called the compromise law was passed in 1799, and this closed all farther legal proceedings against the Connecticut settlers.†

By the terms of this law, "commissioners were to re-survey lots claimed by the Connecticut settlers, whose title—precisely as in the confirming law—originated before the decree of Trenton. A certificate was to be issued to the settler, on presenting which to the land-office, and paying the compensation fixed, he should receive a patent."‡—*Miner's History*, p. 454.

prophetic; but I had then no faith in the prophecy."—*Letter*, p. 15, 16.

\* Colonel Pickering says: "Although one suit was brought by a Pennsylvania claimant against an old Connecticut settler, and judgment in a court of the United States was given in favor of the plaintiff, yet the Connecticut settlers kept possession of their farms. They were too numerous to be removed and driven as vagabonds upon the wide world. The magnitude of the evil became more sensible [evident], and at length the Legislature yielded to expediency what they had denied to equity."—*Letter*, p. 37.

† "They passed a law to secure the Connecticut settlers in their possessions upon their paying some small prices—not a twentieth part of the intrinsic value—for their lands, varied according to their qualities. Thus the controversy was ended, but infinitely to the loss of Pennsylvania."—*Colonel Pickering's Letter*, p. 37.

‡ "Terms of the compromising law of April 4, 1799. Commissioners were to divide the lands into four classes. Pennsylvania claimants who preferred to release their lands to the state, rather than have them appraised by a jury, were to receive, for the first

A portion of the Connecticut settlers, as a matter of principle, refused to pay to Pennsylvania the price for their lands required by the compromise law, and Colonel Jenkins was one of these. He considered it a piece of assumption—an act of injustice—and continued to protest against it to the last.

The facts above presented, mostly from Colonel Pickering, the Pennsylvania functionary, will present the course pursued by Colonel Jenkins in its true light, and will relieve his fair fame from the disparaging imputations cast upon it by the same Colonel Pickering. Had the latter gentleman been free from the prejudices generated by opposition and disappointment, he would probably have viewed the conduct of Franklin and Jenkins with more charity. Both parties were pursuing what they considered the line of duty. Their interests and their opinions came into collision, and they both fought with courage and ability.

How strongly Colonel Jenkins adhered to his position will farther appear by the following anecdote. When the Pennsylvania commissioners were surveying the Wyoming lands, they found that the Connecticut settlers did not like the idea of having their lands surveyed by the Pennamites. It was in the time of buckwheat harvest, and Colonel Jenkins was drawing in his buckwheat with a yoke of oxen and sled, and a wooden fork. The commissioners came up to the line on the flats, and John Jenkins commanded them to stop, and not undertake to cross his land, at their peril. They, seeing that Jenkins meant what he said, retired,

class, $5 00 an acre; second class, $3 00; third class, $1 50; fourth class, 25 cents. Connecticut claimants were to pay, for lands of the first class, $2 00; second, $1 20; third, 50 cents; fourth, 8¼ cents."
—*Miner's History*, p. 454.

and returned to Wilkesbarre. Soon after, they took Jenkins with a warrant and put him in prison. One of the witnesses swore he had an iron fork, but afterward proved that it was only a forked stick, with which he beat back the corps of surveyors. Colonel Jenkins was kept in jail until the commissioners completed their survey, and while he lived he lived under Connecticut laws, and would never succumb to Pennsylvania "aggression." He was never conquered, but went down to his grave protesting against "Pennsylvania usurpation."

A claimant of a still different character obtruded himself upon the attention of Colonel Jenkins, who was summarily disposed of.

One of the descendants of the Wintermoot family, who formerly owned his farm, came to see Jenkins in regard to title, etc. Wintermoot was quite inquisitive, and asked a good many questions about the land and title before he made himself known. As soon as he said that his name was Wintermoot, Jenkins raised a chair, and threw at him with such violence as to break it in pieces; but Wintermoot made good his escape. Jenkins told him to leave, or he would put him in possession of his land in short time.

Colonel Jenkins died March 19, 1827, aged seventy years and almost four months. A large circle of his descendants live in Wyoming and Exeter. The old place at Wintermoot's Fort is still in the family, and the antique residence is still in a good state of preservation. The glorious old *spring*, from which the Wintermoots, and Colonel John Butler, and his Tories and Indians, slaked their thirst on the memorable 3d of July, is there yet, and there will doubtless remain till time shall be no more.

OLD JENKINS HOUSE.

Colonel Jenkins had his share of the sufferings and misfortunes of Wyoming. The great "ice-flood" carried away his house and furniture, he recovering little except "bed and bedding," which were found lodged in the tops of the trees below Toby's Eddy.

In person Colonel Jenkins was of medium height, stout, well-proportioned, framed for strength, endurance, and activity combined; extremely hospitable, remarkably clever, yet grave almost to austerity when in thought. When animated in conversation, there was a pleasing expression on his countenance. His style was brief and sententious. Like Atreus's son,

"He spoke no more than just the thing he ought."

(See Miner, App., p. 29.)

## XXI.

#### ORIGINAL JOURNAL OF CHRISTOPHER HURLBUT.

The following brief record of the events of the wars in Wyoming was kindly furnished us by Samuel Hoyt, Esq., of Kingston, and it is published, not so much for its incidents, as for the confirmation which it affords of the leading facts to which reference has been made in the preceding pages. It is the testimony of a witness and an actor in the scene. Mr. Hurlbut was a man for the times, of more than usual education—a good mathematician, and a practical surveyor. His plots of large tracts of lands surveyed by him in the county of Luzerne are acknowledged data. His field-books, plots, bearings and distances, are all executed with great skill and accuracy.

> "Blood hath been shed, ere now, i' th' olden time,
> Ere human statute purged the gentle weale:
> Aye, and since too, murthers have been performed
> Too terrible for the ear."—SHAKSPEARE—*Macbeth*.

"REMEMBRANCE OF WYOMING WARS.

"*First, of the Indian War.*—In the year 1777, the Indians and Tories up the river went with the British army to besiege Fort Stanwix, and, failing in their object, they returned home in the fall of the year. Late in the fall, Colonel Denison went up the river with a considerable body of men, and took several Tories, and wounded an Indian that attempted to run away from them. The same fall the Indians took York and Kingsley prisoners from Wyallusing, and carried them to Canada.

"Early in the spring, Colonel Denison, with about one hundred and fifty men, went up to Wyalusing to assist a number of families in removing from the place. I was in the company. We made rafts of old houses, and took on the people, with their effects, and went down the river. This spring a company was raised to garrison Forty Fort and to scout. Some time this spring three Indians came to Forty Fort, doubtless as spies. They were put in prison. The last of June I went out to Lackawaxen to meet my father's family, who were moving into the country, and was there until the result of the battle was known.

"On Tuesday, the last day of June, the Indian army was discovered. On Wednesday the settlers collected the men and went up to Sutton's Mills, where they found that the people had been killed and the houses burned.* It appeared that the Indian army had gone into the woods, and proceeded over the mountain to Kingston, and by that means the two armies did not meet there. On the same day the Indian army took Jenkins's and Wintermoot's Forts.† The alarm was given, and the men assembled at Forty Fort.

"The next morning—the 3d of July—and toward night, they joined battle with the Indians, and were

---

\* This was the place where the Hardings were killed, and Gardner made a prisoner.

† According to Mr. Gardner, Jenkins's Fort could not have been taken on that day. He says it was the day after the battle that the fort in which he was—the one opposite Pittston, which was Fort Jenkins—was entered by the Indians. Mr. Hurlbut was not on the ground, and might be mistaken. Mr. Gardner was in the fort, and must know whether it was surrendered before the battle or afterward. The theory which we have adopted elsewhere is, that the agreement to surrender the fort was entered into two days before it was actually entered by the enemy; but this was not on the last day of June, but on the 2d of July.

entirely defeated; only sixty escaped out of the battle. The next day was spent in negotiating a capitulation, and on Sabbath the fort was surrendered, when an indiscriminate plunder took place, and nearly all the buildings in the settlement were burned. The people escaped, none being killed excepting two, Mrs. Leech and St. John.

"The beginning of August, Colonel Butler, with Spaulding's company of the Wyoming soldiers, and a few of the settlers, returned and took possession of the place, and built a fort at Wilkesbarre, driving off what few Indians were there. Shortly after the Indians killed John Abbott, and some others, above Wilkesbarre.

"In September, 1778, Colonel Hartley went, with two or three hundred men, by the West Branch, over to Towanda and to Sheshequin, and collected a considerable number of cattle, and drove them down the river. When he had got below Black Walnut Bottom, he was fired upon by the Indians, and at Tuscarora Creek a considerable action took place: some few were killed on both sides. The next day after they arrived at Wilkesbarre, the Indians killed two or three of his soldiers at the lower end of Kingston Flats.

"In the fall the Indians took Swetland and Blanchard at the Nanticoke mill, and burned the mill. Early in November the Indians killed Jackson, Lester, and Franklin, and wounded Hagaman; they took prisoners Pell and Lester's wife and daughter—a little girl—from Nanticoke, in December. Tripp, Slocum, and Kingsley's son were killed in Wilkesbarre, not far from the fort, and a little girl carried off prisoner in February, 1779. Buck, Williams, and Pettibone were killed, and Follett scalped on Kingston Flats, and an Indian was killed in an attack on the block-house. On the 20th of March Bidlack was taken, the block-house attacked, and all the cattle and horses on that side of the river driven off by a large party of British, Indians, and Tories. On the 22d Wilkesbarre was attacked, as also Stewart's house, and all the cattle that were out on that side driven off; and all the remaining buildings on both sides of the river that were not near the fort, or Stewart's house or block-house, were burned.

"Shortly after the attack on Wilkesbarre, a considerable body of troops—the advance of General Sullivan's army—arrived at Wilkesbarre, and early in April another detachment coming in, two officers and five soldiers, that were in advance of the main body, were killed at or near Laurel Run, in the mountain. Some time that summer, Sherwood, at Huntington, was wounded by the Indians while hunting, but escaped.

"Sullivan's army penetrated the Indian country as far as Genesee River, and in October returned to Wilkesbarre, and so back to join the main army, leaving a garrison in Wilkesbarre.

"After Sullivan's expedition my father's family moved into the country, and went on to his farm in Hanover. The settlers were now getting on to their farms, in expectation of not being farther troubled by the Indians.

"The last of March, Hammond, Bennet, and son went to plow on Kingston Flats, above Forty Fort, and were taken by the Indians. Near the same time, Upson was killed and Jonah Rogers taken prisoner below Nanticoke Falls. Another party of Indians took Van Campen, Pence, and a boy, and killed several on Fishing Creek. On Harvey's Creek they took Pike, but dismissed his wife. The same week Hammond and Bennet rose on the Indians, and escaped and came in. Three or four days after Van Campen and company came in, having killed the Indians who took them prisoners.

"After this no Indians appeared about Wyoming until December, when twenty British soldiers and five Indians came into Plymouth in the evening, and took all the families which were there prisoners. Selecting some men, that they carried off, they dismissed the women and children. The last of March, 1781, a number of families had begun to build houses, intending also to build a fort on Shawnee Flats, where they were attacked in the night by the Indians. Ransom was wounded; one Indian was killed, and the rest fled. In September the Indians took Franklin's boys, with five horses, and burned all the grain—perhaps twelve hundred bushels of wheat and rye—on Nanticoke Flats.

"In 1782 some men began a saw-mill in Hanover. They raised the mill on Saturday, in April. The next morning Franklin's family were taken prisoners, and his house burned. Baldwin, with nine others, went up the river and got ahead of the Indians, and on the Frenchtown Mountain they had a severe engagement of six or seven hours. Bennet was wounded, also Baldwin himself, but none were killed. They retook three of the family, the woman and a small child being killed. In July Jamison and Chapman were killed in the road in Hanover, near where the meeting-house was afterward built. Peace took place the winter following. The next spring, in 1783, Baldwin and Garnsey were carried off by the Indians from near Black Walnut Bottom, but no other mischief was done by the Indians, as they were sent to take a prisoner by whom they might ascertain whether peace was really made, as they had only heard a rumor of it at Niagara. They were dismissed soon after their arrival."

### THE PENNAMITE WAR.

"In December, 1782, the Decree of Trenton was passed, adjudging the right of jurisdiction and preemption to Pennsylvania. The next spring peace took place between England and the United States, and the garrison was removed from Wilkesbarre, and a company of Pennsylvania state troops took possession of the fort. What pretense there was for continuing the garrison after peace, I know not. All was peace that summer, and numbers of people moved in from Pennsylvania and New Jersey, mostly persons of no property or respectability. Toward fall it appeared that a number of Pennsylvanians met secretly in the settlement and proceeded to elect justices of the peace; and in September the Assembly of Pennsylvania passed a law authorizing the President and Council to commission those persons so unlawfully elected; and they soon began to execute the laws by suing every Yankee that they could by any means bring a charge against, and very soon the most violent proceedings took place. Men were imprisoned by the aid of the military, and sundry persons whipped with gun-rods, and otherwise most shamefully abused. A number of respectable men were confined in an old house without a floor, and mud shoe deep. In cold weather in the winter they were obliged to lie down in the mud on pain of being shot. If three Yankees were seen together, they were sure to be imprisoned and otherwise abused.

"At last, as our situation was no longer to be borne, a number of us determined to draw up a petition to the Legislature, then in session, stating our usage, and begging for protection. As not more than two of us dare be seen together, the difficulty was to confer together. Our object was effected by going around and notifying a meeting in the evening; and, in order to prevent suspicion, the meeting was appointed within forty rods of the fort, where a number got together and darkened the windows, and then drew and signed a petition, and engaged a man to carry it to Philadelphia. Upon the receipt of this petition, the Assembly appointed a committee to repair to Wyoming and inquire into the cause of the complaint. The committee came to Wilkesbarre, and by testimony we established all that we set forth in our petition, and much more. The committee returned and reported, but nothing was done to afford us redress.

"In March was 'the great ice-flood,' which nearly ruined the people, drowning their cattle and horses, and sweeping away their houses, as they were nearly all built on the flats for safety against the Indians. Most of their breadstuffs was also destroyed. In May, after the ice had melted away, and the people begun to put up their fences, the Pennamites, with the soldiers, went through the settlement in considerable bodies, and took all the good guns, and the locks from others, from every Yankee who had one, and directly after this they turned all Yankee families into the street, taking them under guard. A few only were able to flee up or down the river; all the rest were forced to go out east by the Lackawaxen. Thus the Pennamites got full possession of the country. Shortly after this the soldiers were discharged, but many of them continued in the country, and the Pennamites kept up a garrison in the fort.

"The last of June the Yankees began to assemble in the woods, in order, if possible, to regain their possessions. It should be remembered that all along, from the first beginning of the outrages, applications had been made to the legislative, executive, and judicial authorities of the state for protection and redress, but none was obtained. Also let it be understood that those pretended justices before referred to as having been unlawfully appointed, headed by Alexander Patterson, a man of considerable abilities, but bold, daring, and completely unprincipled; aided by D—— M——, insinuating, plausible, and flattering, covering his enmity by pretended friendship—a most designing enemy to the Yankees; and J—— S——, with just information enough to act out the villain without disguise, had no idea of doing justice to the Yankees, but their object was to compel them to leave the country.

"About the 15th of July, a party of Pennamites and another of Yankees, both armed, met in a piece of woods in Plymouth unexpectedly to both parties. They fired on each other; two were killed, and several wounded; the Pennamites fled, and were pursued to the fort; the fort was immediately invested, and hostilities were continued for several days. When information was received that a party of men was coming in to relieve the besieged Pennamites, twenty-seven Yankees went out and met the party at Locust Hill. They fired upon them, and they retreated to a house, and, as they appeared sufficiently frightened, the Yankees left them and returned. The party then left the house and fled back. They had one killed and several wounded. Of the Yankees, only one slightly wounded.

"In the mean time, several justices and the sheriff of Northumberland County came to Wilkesbarre to try to put a stop to the fighting. After considerable negotiation, both parties agreed to stop. The Pennamites remained in the fort, and the Yankees returned to their deserted homes. In two or three days a body of two or three hundred men came in, headed by the famous John Armstrong and a Mr. Boyd, two members of the Senate of Pennsylvania. The Pennamites, in part, pretended to surrender, when they called on the Yankees to surrender, as they said they were determined to disarm both parties, so that there should be no farther resort to violence, but an acknowledgment of the supremacy of the laws. When the Yankees laid down their arms they were made close prisoners, and Pennamite sentinels set to guard them. Those who were at Locust Hill were sent, under a strong guard, being first ironed, to Easton jail, the others to Sunbury; those who went to Sunbury were speedily admitted to bail, and returned home; those at Easton were kept close prisoners five or six weeks, when they broke jail, and about half of them escaped; the remainder were kept until October, when the Supreme Court was held at Easton; then the grand jury found no bill against them for murder, and they were discharged, after paying jail fees and other expenses to the amount of twenty-five dollars each.

"In the mean time, those who had escaped, with a few others—about twenty—headed by John Franklin, had obtained arms, and kept together until about the 18th of October, when a body of men came into the settlement and proceeded to make prisoners of such as they chose. They had taken seventeen and confined them in a corn-house, which they kept well guarded:

but they failed to take Franklin and his party, who continually gained in numbers until after the company returned home. After this the Yankees attacked the fort in the night, and killed two officers. Shortly after the fort was evacuated, and all the Pennamites who had been fighting the Yankees were obliged to leave the settlement.

"When they got out into the country they made a loud outcry about the cruelty of the Yankees, and as to how they were plundered of all they possessed, and by this means prevailed with a number of the inhabitants of Northumberland County to petition the Legislature in their behalf. The Legislature then appointed three of their number to go to Wyoming and endeavor to put a stop to farther disorders. In the beginning of May they came in, and, after conferring with the Yankees, returned. Nothing was done effectually until the fall of 1786, when a law was passed erecting the disputed territory into a county, which was called Luzerne. A time was appointed for holding an election for county officers, with justices of the peace. The election was held in July, 1787, and from that time law reigned and peace was fully restored."

THE NEW YORK
PUBLIC LIBRARY

ASTOR, LENOX AND
TILDEN FOUNDATIONS.

THE UMBRELLA-TREE.

## XXII.

### MISCELLANEOUS ARTICLES.

#### THE UMBRELLA-TREE.*

The umbrella, round-top, or signal-tree, is situated on the mountain west of the Valley, about four miles from its head. It is of the variety *Pinus rigida*, or pitch pine; is about ninety feet high, and two and a half feet in diameter at the base. It is apparently, at a distance, on the summit of the mountain, and surrounded by woods; but it is about forty rods from the apex, and stands in the centre of a ten-acre field, on the estate formerly owned by Mr. Pierce Smith, now by the Kingston Coal Company.

My imagination had pictured the tree to be something immense, and, from the misconception, I was somewhat disappointed, as it is not as large as one would be led naturally to suppose, judging of its appearance at a distance, its longevity, etc.; but it is more remarkable for conspicuity of position than for size or height.

Many are the traditions in regard to this old stand-by, and perhaps nothing in our early history is more vague and unsatisfactory than the reports in circulation concerning it. Its conspicuity from the east and northeast made it a landmark through the unbroken wilderness to this land of promise, and we can hardly imagine the joy that its prospect lent, when at its sight the weary traveler considered himself almost home. It is said that its lower branches were clipped or hewn off, to render it more observable at a greater distance; and one tradition, or rather a more late fiction, says that they were cut off as a signal of battle, and ominous of the dire fall of our little army.

* Here is a group of interesting objects. "Tuttle's Creek" passes through the culvert which appears on the right of the foreground. The house partly concealed by the shade of the trees is the veritable house erected and long occupied by Colonel Denison, now occupied by his grandson, Hiram Denison, Esq. Last season—1857—it exchanged its original red covering for a new white one, and, but for its antique form and large chimney, would now exhibit quite a modern appearance. The house on the left was the residence of the late Mrs. Tuttle, only sister of Mrs. Myers. This is the spot where stood the four block-houses from which "the Yankee Boys" fired the last shot at the Pennamites and killed Captain Bolen. The road which crosses the Creek here is the old road on which the little army marched to attack the Tories and Indians. The umbrella-tree is seen in the distance, upon the mountain's height.

We think that any other view than that it is just as God made it would rob him of some of his due glory, and detract from it much real beauty, as being remarkable from nature rather than art. This view is substantiated by almost every physical sign, and the fact that, upon close inspection, it bears no appearance of having had its branches cut off. It has some dead limbs, which show no sudden fracture, as would be the case if they had been hewn off, but, on the contrary, extend several feet from the shaft; and, besides, it has several large limbs, unperceivable at a distance, about half way up. Immediately under the top there is a space of ten or fifteen feet looking quite smooth, showing no abrasion of knife or hack of hatchet. Its top is rather small for the shaft to be compared to an umbrella, and looks more like a delicate parasol put on a large umbrella handle. It is the only tree in a large field, and, although the woodman has cut down all around it, he has paused with a praiseworthy veneration to humble its proud crest in the dust. There it stands nearly as it was a hundred years ago; there it stands erect as God made it; there let it stand till He, in his wisdom, sees fit to fell it. We reluctantly turned our back upon this old pine, and left it "alone in its glory." * * *

## PROSPECT ROCK

is situated on the eastern mountain, directly back of Wilkesbarre, and about midway between the two extremes of the valley. From its prominent position may be distinctly seen both sections of the valley, above and below. It is a steep ledge of light conglomerate, composed of strata four or five feet thick, resting at about an angle of forty-five degrees in position. Its eastern verge is quite precipitous, showing an abrupt fracture from the plane of the strata below, which was caused in its upheaving to its present position. The western surface is convex, and more continuous with the slope of the mountain. A few small pines stand upon it here and there, and dip their roots into its crevices, deriving their nourishment from an almost imperceptible and inconceivable source. The upper section of the valley of Wyoming appears to be an extended plain; the lower a series of hills, undulating up higher and higher until they reach the Nanticoke Mountains. Above, it seems continuous with the Lackawanna Valley, and the gray front of Crag Campbell marks the entrance of the Susquehanna; below the mountains curve gracefully as the bow in the clouds for the egress of the river.

To get a proper appreciation of the view from this rock, you should spend a night at one of the hotels a short distance below, arise with the sun, with the mental energies fresh and unimpaired with the toils of ascent. It was in the month of July that I made my visit, and all nature was dressed in her most varied and pleasing garb. Spread out beneath were the fields of every shade of green and of gold. There were the shock-dotted fields, where the farmer had been gathering together into convenient heaps his means of subsistence and profit; fields of still waving grain, interspersed with meads of fresh-springing grass from newly-mown hay-fields. Black lines mark the course of fences dividing possessions and fields, showing a beautiful simile to the checkered scenes of life, where every man is moving for his own advantage. Immediately beneath is the borough of Wilkesbarre, with its small houses and tiny spires, as though contrived for the habitation of Liliputians. Directly across from it is the village of Kingston, below which are the scattered houses of Plymouth, and above, toward the head of the valley, is the village of Wyoming, still more diminutive in the distance. Here and there are scattered throughout the country habitations and public works, showing the insignificance of puny art in such a vast area of beauteous nature. "Oh, pigmy man, how small thy workings are! Thy boasted rule has not the power to even mock at heaven, for who could mountains make, or paint a scene like this?" These are naturally the feelings of an observer and student of nature when impressed with the power of the magnificent and sublime; he pauses in a reverie of inexpressible delight, and is forced to admit the inability of language to convey his thoughts to others. This rock has the advantages of position in presenting to the view nearly all parts of the valley, neither rendering it dim by too great distance, nor unpicturesque by being too near. A large area is here placed before the vision, concentrated into one grand conception, subject to one contemplation. In the west are the horizon, scalloping hills, giving glimpses here and there between them of the country beyond. The Susquehanna is occasionally visible, and the three islands here seen seem like "Arks of nature's make floating on to join the sea."

There is another view from what is called the White Rocks, but a short distance ascending to the right from the Spring House, which has advantages in rendering some parts of the valley still more perspicuous than Prospect Rock does, on account of their more jutting position.

Time had been "winging us away" faster than we were aware or wished. The sun had already dipped his lower verge below the western mountains, giving their tree-clad summits an appearance as

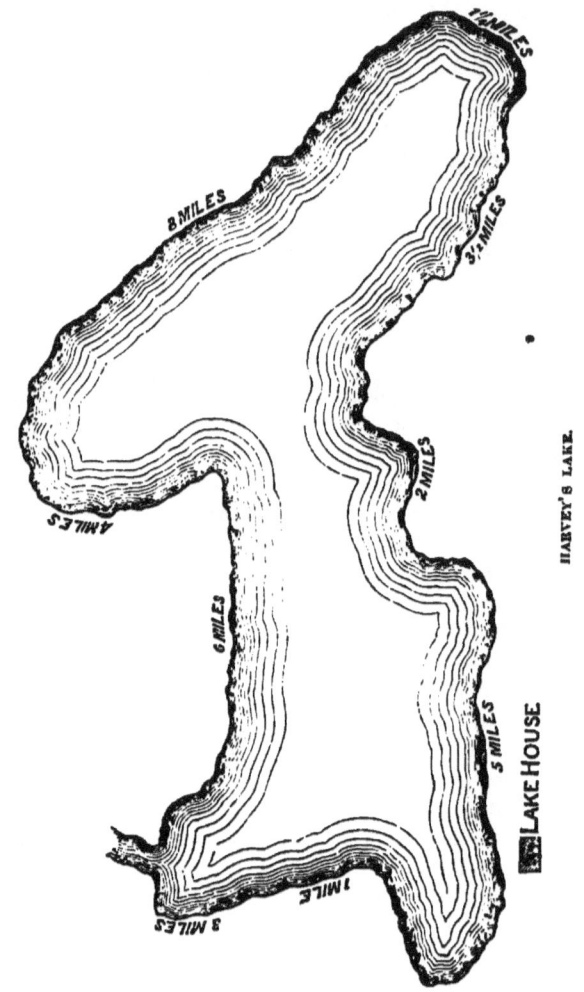

if fringed with fire. As our little giddy world wheeled eastward, leaving the king of day gradually sinking from the horizon, he seemed to kiss the western hills with his ruddy lips, and, bidding us good-night, sank in a sea of glory.     * * *

---

### HARVEY'S LAKE.

THE following sketch of a trip to Harvey's Lake is contributed by Miss Miranda Myers, of Kingston:

Bright and early, long before the purple hill-tops environing Wyoming were illuminated by the rising sun, we presented ourselves at the gateway, ready for a drive to this romantic summer retreat some twelve miles distant.

Passing the wild scenery of the Narrows, and through a beautiful rural district, we inquired, for perhaps the dozenth time during our ride, How far off is Harvey's Lake? An honest-faced Hibernian answered, "Shure and you are right on it; and you have only to drive a bit ahead and turn into the lane, and you'll get there." Thanking him, we prepared to follow the direction, if it only brought us to our destination. We soon had the extreme satisfaction of seeing the Lake House, with its fair proportions, loom up before us. As we drove up, the accommodating proprietor, Mr. Clayton, met us at the door, ready to attend to all our wants.

The house is built upon a slight elevation on the eastern shore, a few rods from the water's edge. It is large and commodious, handsomely furnished, and capable of accommodating a large number of guests. From the verandas, which extend around two sides of the house, a magnificent prospect feasts the eye—a scene of unrivaled and quiet beauty—the calm and unruffled surface of the lake sparkling in the sunshine, begirt with beautiful hilly woodlands. These afford covert for herds of deer and other wild game, while the lake furnishes an abundance of the finest fish. Harvey's Lake has been resorted to for hunting and fishing ever since the first settlement of the country, long before there was a road cut through the mountains, the old hunters tracing their way through the dense forests by means of marked trees. It is said that the lake was discovered by one of the early settlers of the Valley noticing that the wild ducks flew very high, and in a northerly direction, from which fact he concluded that there must be quite a large body of water not far distant.*

---

* The lake derived its name from Benjamin Harvey, who settled upon the outlet below Plymouth, and it is supposed by his descendants that he was the first white man who discovered it. The descendants of Thomas Bennet suppose that

Below us, in front of the house, a wagon-road winds along the shore, and is soon lost from sight among the trees. Looking across the lake toward the west, we observe a small clearing with several dwelling-houses; one is pointed out to us as the property of Hon. Warren J. Woodward. Casting our eyes down along the shore in the direction of the outlet, through a gap in the hills we behold the faint outlines of distant mountains against the sky, in fine contrast with those nearer by.

At our left is the inlet, though, properly speaking, the lake has none, being fed by springs at the bottom. A rude, unfinished bridge crosses the inlet. This can be used only by foot-passengers, as it is sunken considerably near the centre.

Having finished our observations from the house, we betake ourselves to the boat, a number being always in readiness. The white, pebbly bottom of the lake is distinctly visible for quite a distance from the shore; but as we near the centre it gradually disappears, the water becoming very deep, and assuming a look of inky blackness. We were told that a line ninety feet in length had been sunk here without reaching bottom.

We were recalled from our aquatic expedition to the house by the sounding of the gong. Here we found an elegant dinner awaiting us—fish, flesh, and fowl, served up in every possible style, with vegetables, tarts, puddings, pastry, etc., in profusion, calculated to please even the most epicurean palate. Dinner over, we again sallied forth in quest of enjoyment.

Noticing upon one of the pillars of the lower veranda a diagram of the lake, with the distances along the margins given, we made inquiries of Mr. Clayton, and learned that some scientific gentleman,

he is entitled to the honor of the discovery of this lake, and that he was led to the search for it by the flight of flocks of wild ducks. It is quite probable that these hardy pioneers each made the discovery in the same way, one reaching it from the lower extremity of the Valley, and the other from Forty Fort. It is certain that Mr. Bennet cut through the first bridle-path from Kingston to the lake, as that path is noted on the field-books of the earliest surveyors, and is called "Bennet's Path." Andrew Bennet, son of Thomas Bennet, launched the first canoe upon the placid waters of this lake in the year 1800. John Bennet, Esq., son of Andrew Bennet, says that the canoe was made in the Valley, and shod with hickory saplings, and drawn over the mountain by two horses attached to it tandem, and that he, then a lad, rode the leader, and that his father led the way on foot, and that another man followed and kept the "dug-out" right side up. They arrived sufficiently early in the day to launch their craft, and steal upon a fine buck standing in the edge of the lake, and shoot him down. The canoe was kept concealed at the head of the lake in a thicket of laurels. The lady traveler who contributed this article is the great-granddaughter of Thomas Bennet.

TOBY'S EDDY.

TOBY'S CAVE.

whose name we have forgotten, made an actual survey for the benefit of visitors. We give it as it appears there.

Lovely as the lake is in the rich glow of the morning sunlight, its romantic beauty is by no means diminished when bathed in the glorious coloring of the afternoon sun. The rippling current flashes and sparkles, the wild duck skims gayly over its surface, regardless of the lurking sportsman, and the splashing oars of the pleasure-boat keep time to the harmony of nature; every tree growing upon the margin of the lake has its counterpart slumbering motionless beneath the water. But we must turn our backs upon this scene of bewitching loveliness, for the lengthening shadows warn us that the sun is sinking in the heavens, and we have yet twelve miles between us and our valley-home.

Persons visiting Wyoming should not fail to take a drive to the lake; we are certain they would be amply rewarded. Indeed, we see no reason why Harvey's Lake may not become as fashionable a resort during the summer as the more crowded watering-places, accessible as it is from our cities, within twelve miles by railroad, and affording every facility for enjoyment.

## TOBY'S EDDY.

This famous locality is situated at the mouth of Toby's Creek, near Kingston village. The beautiful scenery copied in the opposite engraving lies between Ross Hill and the river, and is one of those lovely, secluded spots where one delights to spend an hour or two in retirement from the busy world. Here the students of the seminary hard by often meet to shake off the blues and recruit their exhausted energies. Here they bathe, walk, swing, and exchange pleasant greetings. Here many a pleasant picnic has been held, and glances have been exchanged full of meaning, and ominous of happy days at new homes.

But, alas! progress and civilization have made sad ravages upon this sweet and beautiful spot. The railroad has utterly ruined its beautiful unity. Its jagged, rocky embankment, running through the centre of the little natural paradise, has broken its ancient enchantments, and dispelled the bewitching associations which clustered around it. So goes this world of ours. What God made is perpetually changed, if not improved, by the inroads of art and the spirit of the age.

### TOBY'S CAVE.

WHAT is called Toby's Cave is found in the hill-side west of the Eddy. It is not deep or large, but might once have constituted a place of retreat for old Toby the Indian, whose haunts were once along the creek to which his name has been given, and who planted corn upon the flats above. It is said by some of the old talkers that this cave once extended quite to the opposite side of Ross Hill, the distance of three fourths of a mile. Curious legends of strange supernatural appearances in this cave are told by an old gossip still living, all of which may be doubted without just exposure to the charge of unwarrantable skepticism. Stories of strange sights and superhuman noises, which used to be told about Toby's Cave by superannuated nurses, and believed without a doubt by children, are not worth repeating; still, they have left their impression, and they continue to cling to the locality with which they were originally associated. Legends, however incredible, often constitute classic ground, and give a sort of importance to objects and localities which otherwise have little about them to render them noticeable. There are in the world many such objects, and among them is Toby's Cave.

### SEMINARIES.

THE great changes which have taken place in Wyoming are remarked in nothing more clearly than in the means and appliances of education which constitute both its power and its pride. We give brief sketches of the origin, progress, and present condition of the three leading institutions of the Valley, arranging them in chronological order.

### THE WYOMING CONFERENCE SEMINARY.

This is a school for both sexes, and was opened September 24, 1844. The opening address was delivered by the Rev. J. P. Durbin, D.D. The first seminary building was of brick, thirty-seven feet by seventy feet, and three stories high. The cost of the building and fixtures, $6089, of which about one fourth was contributed by Thomas Myers, Esq., of Kingston. The building for the accommodation of the ladies and for a boarding-hall was erected by Mr. Myers, and subsequently sold to the trustees.

The school opened with thirty scholars, and the whole number in attendance the first term was forty-seven.

There were three teachers: Rev. R. Nelson, A.M., Miss Ruth Ingalls, and Mr. E. F. Ferris. The patronage continued to increase for every succeeding term until there arose a pressing necessity for an additional building. In the winter of 1850-51, while the trustees, without funds, were deliberating upon the subject, and vainly endeavoring to devise a plan for enlarging the buildings, they were happily relieved from their embarrassment by the noble and generous proposition of one of their number, William Swetland, Esq., to defray himself all the expense of the erection of such a building as the trustees should deem necessary to meet the wants of the school. Accordingly, a building was erected and finished in the fall of 1851, at a cost of between three and four thousand dollars, and named "Swetland Hall."

At the same time, Hon. Ziba Bennet, of Wilkesbarre, donated to the institution $1000, to be expended in the purchase of a library, which was appropriately named by the trustees "Bennet Library."

Within six months from the completion of "Swetland Hall," all the rooms in the whole establishment were occupied, and the trustees began to arrange for putting up an additional building. They had contracted for its erection, and excavating for the foundation had already been commenced, when, on the 15th of March, 1853, the buildings were entirely destroyed by fire, supposed to have originated from a stove in the third story.

While the ruins were yet smoking, the trustees were stimulated to an immediate effort to rebuild by the remarkable liberality of William Swetland, Esq., already referred to, who, together with his son, Mr. George Swetland, and his son-in-law, Payne Pettibone, Esq., donated to the institution in all something over $8000. They were also greatly aided by the liberal donations of $1000 by Isaac C. Shoemaker, Esq., of Wyoming, $500 by Hon. Urbane Burrows, of Gibson, and $500 by Amos Y. Smith, of Wyoming. The above, with other contributions, enabled the trustees to erect four buildings, three of them being of brick.

The entire value of the whole establishment now can not be estimated at less than $30,000.

The institution has an experienced and efficient board of teachers, a superior philosophical and chemical apparatus, an extensive library, and a valuable cabinet. .The Rev. R. Nelson still presides over the institution with great ability and success.

The catalogue just issued shows an attendance of 676 students during the year. The success of this institution is without a parallel in the state.

### LUZERNE PRESBYTERIAL INSTITUTE.

This institution is located in one of the pleasantest portions of the Valley, in the village of Wyoming. Rev. Thomas P. Hunt, so widely known for his able advocacy of the cause of temperance and religion, first suggested and labored for the establishment of a literary institution at this place, and has ever been most earnestly devoted to its interests with time and means. Not less indispensable have been, from the first and always, the abundant services and liberal benefactions of Mr. Thomas R. Atherton, or the efforts and counsels in its behalf of Rev. J. D. Mitchell, its first principal and always firm friend and supporter, as well as those of others, its early and constant, or more recent friends, among whom are the entire board of trustees as at present constituted, consisting of Rev. T. P. Hunt, Rev. N. G. Parke, H. Hice, T. F. Atherton, Hon. C. D. Shoemaker, Rev. H. H. Welles, Rev. C. R. Lane, W. S. Shoemaker, Hon. Steuben Jenkins, Theodore Strong, E. A. Lawrence, and Joseph P. Atherton, with Rev. J. Dorrance and James Jenkins, former members.

The great aim of the institution is to furnish facilities for a sound Christian education of youth. It is not sectarian in its teachings, but Christian, and invites to the enjoyment of its privileges youth from all denominations alike. Instruction is given in all the English branches, sciences, mathematics, languages, and ornamental branches common to our higher seminaries, preparatory for college, for teaching, or for the active duties of business and social life. It has a male and a female department, a normal department at some seasons of the year, also philosophical and chemical apparatus, and geographical, astronomical, and anatomical maps and charts. The institute building is out of debt, and will be enlarged as soon as the state of the times will permit. There is a good boarding-house; students also board in private families, while lads and others, as desired by parents, board with the principal.

Classes were first formed in 1849. An act of incorporation was obtained the following year.

Rev. Reuben Lowrie, now a missionary in China, Rev. C. R. Lane, now of Tunkhannock, and Rev. P. E. Stevenson, acted as principals of the institution in succession. E. A. Lawrence, A.M., extensively known and approved as a highly accomplished teacher, is now principal, and, although the pressure of the times has unfavorably affected the attendance, as in many other institutions, the condition of the institute is encouraging and promising. Several of its students are preparing for the ministry, while others of them are already proclaiming the Gospel to a dying world.

### THE WILKESBARRE FEMALE INSTITUTE.

A number of gentlemen, citizens of the borough of Wilkesbarre, deeply sensible of the importance of a thorough and Christian education for their daughters, and believing that the female character requires a system of instruction and discipline differing somewhat from that adopted in reference to the other sex, after consultation, determined upon the establishment of a female seminary of a high order—one which should preclude the necessity of seeking beyond their own borough the facilities for a finished education.

Accordingly, a subscription for the erection of a suitable building was opened, and some ten or twelve thousand dollars raised. The subscriptions, several of which are very liberal, were principally from members of the Presbyterian congregation. Of the whole sum, nearly one half (including recent donations) is the contribution of George M. Hollenback.

A charter for the contemplated institution was obtained in the summer of 1854, during which year the seminary edifice was completed. This is a neat and commodious building, three stories in height, with suitable school and recitation rooms, lofty and well ventilated. There is also good accommodation in furnished rooms for some forty or fifty boarders under the same roof with the family of the principal; the grounds are ample; and the site, fronting the Susquehanna, with an open common intervening, is one of unusual beauty.

The school was opened in October, 1854, with some fifty young ladies, under the charge of Rev. Joseph Eastburn Nassau, since which time, though subject to temporary fluctuation, it has made encouraging progress. Quite a number of young ladies have completed the prescribed course of study, which is equally extensive and thorough with that of our best seminaries, with honor to themselves and the institution.

The average number of pupils in actual attendance is now about seventy, and is steadily increasing. The principal, R. S. Howes, A.M., who has had a successful experience of sixteen years at the head of select and high schools, proves to be well fitted for his position, and gives to the trustees and patrons of the institution entire satisfaction.

The institute is, by its charter, under the supervision of the presbytery of Luzerne, by which body the trustees are appointed.

The object of this supervision is not the inculcating of sectarian tenets, nor to render the institution an organ of proselytism, but to secure an enlightened, homogeneous, and salutary religious influence, with the hope that our daughters, while subjected to thorough mental discipline, will also be adorned with those Christian graces which are the highest and loveliest accomplishment of the female character.

# INDEX.

Alexander, Mrs., her account of her father's death and mother's escape, 111; character of her mother, 120; account of Mrs. Gardner, 353.
Armstrong, Colonel, comes on under authority of Pennsylvania—gross treachery, 64, 217, 413.
Bedford, Mrs., character and parentage of, 201; her account of the Indians, *ib.*; of a mission to Queen Esther, 202; a war demonstration, 203; the battle, 204; of the flight to Middletown, 209; return, 210; Franklin family, 212; keeps house at Forty Fort, 218.
Bennet, Thomas, captivity and escape of, 201.
" Rufus, wonderful escape of, 302.
" Solomon, escape of, 160.
Bolin, Captain, killed, 184.
Bones of the patriots, 377.
Brant, history of, 71; at Unadilla, 73; at Oriskany, 74; ravages on the Mohawk, 78, 84; not in the battle of Wyoming, 87; cruelty of, 94.
Brockway's, Widow, a fight there, 183.
Butler, Colonel Zebulon, commands at the battle, 38; report of, 40.
" Colonel John, invades Wyoming, 38; faithless conduct, 45; report of the battle, 52; character of, 96.
Butler, Walter N., destroys Cherry Valley, 80; Colonel Stone's apology for, 86; cruelties of, 82; death, 85.
Campbell's Ledge, 10, 344.
Cherry Valley destroyed, 81.
Connecticut people, object of, 26.
Corey, young, tortured, 214.
Decree of Trenton, 63.
Delaware Indians, war, 11, 12.
Denison, Colonel, came from Hartford, 147; in the battle, 39; remonstrates with J. Butler, 162; robbed of his shirt and hat, 163.
Dick, Captain, defeated, 146.
Esther, Queen, 152; prisoners escape from, 285; Colonel Stone's apology for, 287.
Follett stabbed and scalped, 213.
Fortifications, ancient, 13.
Forts, situation of, 56.
Forty Fort erected, 136; strengthened, 30; capitulation of, 43.
Franklin, Colonel John, opposes Colonel Pickering, 190.
" Roswell, family of, carried off by the Indians, 212.
Gardner, Richard, 351.
Gustin, Dr., carries a flag of truce, 162; assistant surgeon, 201, 206; settles in Carlisle, 200.
Hammond escapes from Bloody Rock, 285.
Hartley, Colonel, marches against the Indians, 60.
Hollenback, Colonel, comes to Wyoming, 100; enters the army, 102; escapes from the battle, 106; engages in grubbing, 109; returns to Wyoming, 110; trades in Canada—trip with John Jacob Astor, 116; followed by robbers, 118; is a magistrate and judge, 119; character, 121; residence, 123; anecdote of, 124; resolutions of the court—character by Judge Scott, 127; votes for Jackson, 131.
Hopkins, Noah, life saved by a spider, 369.
Hurlbut, Christopher, journal of, 405.
Ice-flood, 173.
Indians make preparations for war, 154; plunder the people in the fort, 162.
Jenkins, Colonel, 388; capture by the Indians, 391; opposes Colonel Pickering, 394; employed by General Washington as a guide to General Sullivan, 393; fights the Pennsylvania claim, 402.
Johnson, Sir William, 31.
" Guy, 32.
Lackawanna, events at, after the battle, 221; flag of truce, 222; a singular triumph at, 225.

Luzerne County organized, 398, 414.
Manning, Captain, his house defended by hot water, 141; removes to Lackawanna Island, 142.
Marcy, Mrs., history of her troubles, 220; flees across the mountain, 227; a child in the woods, 228; reaches her father's, 229; account of the Pennamites, 230.
Massacre at Wyoming, erroneous accounts of, 56.
Monument, Wyoming, 376.
Myers, Mrs., character by authors, 133; her account of her father's leaving Rhode Island, 135; coming to the Delaware, ib.; visiting Wyoming, 136; removing his family, 137; his imprisonment, 143; hard toiling, 148; affecting incident, 151; the battle, 156; separation of the family, 161; goes to Sunbury, 167; crosses the mountain, ib.; spends two years in the east, 171; returns to Wyoming, 172; usefulness, 173; account of the death of Satterlee, 183; married, 191; subsequent history, 159.
M'Allum, captivity of Daniel, 235.
Nanticoke Indians, 11.
Northern border wars, 31.
Ogden, Captain Amos, heads the Pennamites, 139; repulsed, 145.
" Nathan, killed, 140.
" David, attempts the life of T. Bennet, 144; drowns Satterlee, 183.
Pencil shot by his brother, 371.
Pennamite and Yankee wars, 20, 26, 180, 184, 215, 410.
Pennsylvania, policy of the proprietors of, 19; lease Wyoming, 25.
Pickering, Colonel, 190, 304, 895, 399.
Pike, Abram, 304.
Plunket, Colonel, expedition of, 140, 215.
Plymouth Company, 21.
Prospect Rock, 418.
Ransom, Colonel George P., captivity, 317; whipped, 320; taken to Prisoners' Island, 321; escapes, 322; great sufferings of, 324; marries and settles, 326; an assault and battery, 327.
Rogers, Jonah, captivity and escape of, 304.
Schuyler, Fort, invested, 33; siege of, raised, 36.
Seminaries, 426.
Seybolt, Mrs., her story of the battle, 221.
Shawanese Indians, 11.
Slocum, Frances, captivity, 239; her father killed, 243; family seek for her, 244; is discovered, 248; visited by her brothers, 255; second visit, 264; portrait, 267; her story, 274; act of Congress, 281; last days of, 282.
Smith, Dr. W. Hooker, 181, 201, 206, 219.
Speedy, William, released from prison, 147.
Sullivan, General, expedition of, 61; leaves a garrison in Wilkesbarre, 173.
Susquehanna Company, 22; purchase of the Indians, 23; send on forty pioneers, 25.
Sutton, Esquire, settled in Wyoming, 101; visits Queen Esther, 202; flees down the river, 207; builds a mill, 210.
Toby's Eddy and Cave, 425, 426.
Tories, cruelties of, 46.
Umbrella-tree, 417.
Van Campen, Moses, 304.
Westmoreland, town of, 27; town meeting of, 28; erected into a county, 29; companies of, organized, 29.
Wyoming, name, 9; visited by New England people, 14; first settlement, 24; lives lost in, 26.
Zinzendorf, Count, 14.


THE END.

www.ingramcontent.com/pod-product-compliance
Lightning Source LLC
Chambersburg PA
CBHW032141010526
44111CB00035B/757